The
LOBLOLLY BOOK
II

The LOBLOLLY BOOK II

Moonshining,
Basket Making,
Hog Killing,
Catfishing,

and Other
Affairs of Plain
Texas Living

Edited by Thad Sitton and Lincoln King

★

TexasMonthlyPress

Copyright © 1986 by Thad Sitton and Lincoln King. All rights including reproduction by photographic or electronic process and translation
into other languages are fully reserved under the International Copyright Union, the Universal Copyright Convention, and the Pan-
American Copyright Convention. Reproduction or use of this book in
whole or in part in any manner without written permission of the
publisher is strictly prohibited.

Texas Monthly Press, Inc.
P.O. Box 1569
Austin, Texas 78767

A   B   C   D   E   F   G   H

Library of Congress Cataloging-in-Publicaton Data

The Loblolly book II.

    A collection of articles by various students which originally appeared
in the Loblolly.
    1. Texas—Social life and customs. 2. Country life—Texas.
3. Folklore—Texas. 4. Handicraft—Texas. 5. Texas—Biography.
I. Sitton, Thad, 1941-   . II. King, Lincoln.   III. Loblolly.
IV. Title: Loblolly book 2.   V. Title: Loblolly book two.
F391.L822   1986   306'.09764   86-5935
ISBN 0-87719-017-8

Contents

Preface

In 1980 I returned to Texas with the idea of editing a "Texas Foxfire Book" from the several high school journals of folklore and oral history published in the state. I approached Texas Monthly Press about this project and suggested we call the book *Texas Folk*. Properly encouraged, I set out on the formidable task of reading through scores and scores of back issues of the student magazines *Loblolly* (the first of the Texas cultural journalism projects), *Chinquapin*, *Old Timer*, *The Plum Creek Express*, and *Black Gold*.

Every one of those student journals represented a noble effort against long odds, deserving every encouragement. To do justice to all, I hoped for a fairly even distribution of articles between the various magazines, but that was not to be. As I applied the cold eye of the editor to the journals, the pile of articles chosen from *Loblolly* grew to embarrassing proportions. The *Loblolly* material was similar to that from the other magazines, but it had something special about it; Lincoln King and his *Loblolly* staffers had a feel for the true vein. The *Loblolly* articles focused on such important and largely untouched topics of social history as mule agriculture, sacred harp singing, faith healing, the ranging of razorback hogs on the river bottoms, and the customs and practices associated with death and burial. What *Loblolly* collected in its homeland of Panola County had meaning all across Anglo Texas. This was the all-but-forgotten cultural heritage of many of us, drawn from the fragile memories of older men and women who still recollected a world that often seemed as remote from the present as the Middle Ages.

Another factor that favored *Loblolly* was the depth of material for many of the topics it covered. The *Loblolly* staffers had persistence and perseverance—and the hunter's instinct. They would begin with some research topic and then doggedly hang on, scouring the countryside for additional sources and recording every one they found. That approach had resulted in a two-hundred-page edition on Panola County economic history, special issues on mule agriculture and the outlaws Bonnie and Clyde, and (over the years) extensive life history collections from such colorful local personalities as Monroe Brannon and Sheriff Corbett Akins. When the editor had done his work and some of *Loblolly* lay on the cutting room floor, there was usually a lot left!

In the end, it was only simple justice that *Texas Folk* became *The Loblolly Book*.

Late in 1983, following the publication of the first anthology, Lincoln King's students were challenged to produce a sequel. The first *Loblolly* was in a sense an editor's book, drawn from more than thirty back issues of the Panola County journal with important contributions from *Old Timer*, *Chinquapin*, and *The Plum Creek Press*. The second book would be very different. At a late summer meeting at Lincoln King's home in Carthage, we presented his current generation of *Loblolly* students with the opportunity and the challenge. Could they conceive, research, transcribe, and edit a *Loblolly II* in little more than a year and a half? The answer lies before you in such chapters as wild game cookery, outhouses, hangings, hog killings, box suppers, basket making, and the many uses of the black wash pot. In East Texas the springs of folk tradition still run deep and strong, and once again *Loblolly* has shown that it knows how to find the true vein.

Thad Sitton

Introduction
The Origins of Loblolly

In December of 1972 my wife, Mary Nell King, received as a Christmas present from her Uncle Wayne a copy of *The Foxfire Book* (Doubleday, 1972). We discovered it to be an anthology of Appalachian oral history and folklore collected at a high school in Rabun Gap, Georgia. The articles gathered together in *The Foxfire Book* had previously appeared in quarterly issues of a student magazine published since 1966. Topics in the book were wide-ranging—from building a log cabin to planting by the signs—and all were entirely fascinating.

I read *The Foxfire Book* cover to cover during that Christmas vacation and was profoundly impressed that high school students had produced a product of such quality. But what really got my attention was the introduction written by Eliot Wigginton in which he told how *Foxfire* got started and why he thought it was important. For me, the heart of Wigginton's message lay in these words:

> Looking beyond Rabun Gap and Foxfire, I can't get over the feeling that many similar projects could be duplicated successfully in many other areas of the country, and to the genuine benefit of almost everyone involved.
>
> Daily our grandparents are moving out of our lives, taking with them, irreparably, the kind of information contained in this book. They are taking it, not because they want to, but because they think we don't care.
>
> The big problem, of course, is that since these grandparents were primarily an oral civilization, information being passed down through the generations by word of mouth and demonstration, little of it is

1

written down. When they're gone, the magnificent hunting tales, the ghost stories that kept a thousand children sleepless, the intricate tricks of self-sufficiency acquired through the years of trial and error, the eloquent and haunting stories of suffering and sharing and building and healing and planting and harvesting—all these go with them, and what a loss.

If this information is to be saved at all, for whatever reason, it must be saved now; and the logical researchers are the grandchildren, not university researchers from the outside. In the process, these grandchildren (and we) gain an invaluable unique knowledge about their own roots, heritage, and culture.

To me those words came as a challenge; if they could do this in North Georgia, why couldn't we do it here in Panola County, Texas? When I returned to school in January 1973, I discussed the idea with the school administrators and received a tentative approval. I had a sharp group of freshmen who had survived half a year of world geography with me. They were ready to try something else and gave an enthusiastic assent to the idea of producing a magazine.

East Texas has a rich cultural heritage and many fascinating people to talk with. I discussed with the students how together we would choose topics to investigate, find people to provide the data, and perform the tasks to produce the stories in magazine form. It was an ambitious idea, and we were all pretty naive at that stage. I had no background in journalism and thus was ignorant about such things as magazine production. Also, there was no money available in the school budget for such a project. But the students and I were willing to accept the challenges involved.

The immediate problem was how to find enough money to start the magazine. One of the students suggested selling stock to raise the necessary funds, so we offered stock for sale to the public at two dollars a share. In the beginning, the investors really didn't know what they were buying and we didn't know what we were selling! For two dollars a person would receive a copy of the first magazine, and for ten dollars he would get five shares plus a year's subscription. It was quite a challenge for the students, for they were only selling an idea at that stage. To raise additional funds we sold ads in the magazine to local businesses. Between our two strategies, money was raised to pay for printing the first issue, to purchase a tape recorder, and to make a down payment on an IBM typewriter.

Another early challenge was how to sell the idea that learning could take place outside the classroom. This was at the core of the *Foxfire* concept but a revolutionary idea to tradition-minded school administrators, teachers, and parents. Moreover, the thought of leaving school during the day to go out and interview old people didn't fit in with the school experience students had come to expect and even to depend on in Gary. What I was asking them to do was unfamiliar and a little frightening. As I told someone in an early interview, "At first I almost had to shake the kids. They are conditioned like the rest of us. They sit in school waiting for someone to tell them what to do. All of a sudden someone comes along and says, 'What do you think about this?' They had to learn to make decisions."

Small groups of students began going out daily, tape recorders and cameras under their arms, to work on the interviews. Because they did not have driver's licenses, I frequently accompanied them, and I quickly found that if I could get a student to break the ice in a single interview, all was usually well. Student Emma Blair described her first interview in these terms: "We were scared to death. Mr. King had to push us through the door. We had made out a list of questions to ask her. She had told us a few things about herself. We were scared and worried that she would hush and then we wouldn't know what to say, but it didn't work out that way. She just talked for hours. Every once in a while we would try to get her back on the subject. She took us out and told us the names of her chickens and things like that."

We were fortunate enough to have some good help in the local area. The publisher of the county newspaper advised us on journalistic skills we would need. Instructors at Panola Junior College were valuable sources of information on folklore and interviewing techniques. Others in the community, and the students themselves, provided us with good leads for our first interviews.

We were also fortunate in finding excellent interviewees right from the beginning. One of them was Tressie Cozart, who was a skilled soap maker. Students spent the day with her, learning to make lye soap while recording her words on the tape recorder and taking photos with a camera borrowed from the yearbook staff. Another person interviewed was Carolyn Malone, a well-known character in Carthage, who had raised four children on the proceeds of a paper route she had operated for more than twenty years. But the best storyteller of all was found right across the road from the school in the person of 86-year-old Monroe Brannon, who had detailed memories of his life back to age two and a half. Brannon had been a pioneer druggist in Gary, first coming to Panola County with his parents in 1895. Because he had lived in Gary almost all his life and because his memory was so complete and detailed, students would use Brannon as a source on almost every major story. As student Lauri Gauntt observed, "It was fantastic the way he could remember dates—the exact day and year that something happened. And it seems like he's done everything. He's been a pharmacist, he's been a detective, a farmer. And also you can tell by talking to him that he had a lot of fun when he was our age. He's still got a mischievous air about him." In fact, Panola County would turn out to be full of such colorful characters. One of them was Corbett Akins, county sheriff for many years and, according to his own account, the only man who had been shot between the eyes and lived to tell about it.

The students went out in teams of two or three to record the words and capture on film those they interviewed as they learned outside the classroom. After their initial nervousness they discovered that older people were glad to share their stories with them and that the generation gap was just a myth. During class time students worked on the tedious task of transcribing the tapes. Working from handwritten transcriptions, the students selected the best portions to be included in their articles. In the *Foxfire* style they wrote brief introductions to the articles, which were primarily verbatim texts of the interviewees' comments on selected subjects. The edited portions of the interviews were typed on the staff's new typewriter and laid out in a six-by-nine-inch magazine format. At one staff meeting, the students and I chose a name for their magazine—*Loblolly*, after the hardy scrub pine native to this section of East Texas.

Our first issue came out in April of 1973, and community response surpassed all our expectations, as the first printing of five hundred copies sold out almost immediately. We were ecstatic, and the kids were bouncing off the walls as I ordered a second printing. It was the first time they had ever done anything in school that really mattered to someone besides themselves and their teacher. Now something they had produced had been published and distributed for everyone to see.

Motivated by their success, the students continued to gather information for a second issue of *Loblolly*. For the next year the project was given permanence at Gary as an elective course. In October 1973 the second issue of *Loblolly* was published, and with increased confidence I mailed a copy to Eliot Wigginton at *Foxfire*. Wigginton replied with a most complimentary letter, saying that he was at the present time working with a Washington-based group (IDEAS, Inc.) in an attempt to replicate the *Foxfire* success all across the country. IDEAS and *Foxfire* had a large Ford Foundation grant to help accomplish that, but they were surprised and delighted to find an independent project like *Loblolly* making a go of things entirely on its own resources. As Wigginton later described his response to *Loblolly*: "Watching Lincoln's project evolve has been one of the most humbling experiences of my career precisely because he did exactly what I had hoped hundreds of teachers would do: take an idea, adapt it to their own particular student clientele, and run with it, without lots of hand-holding."

More encouragement was forthcoming. At the same time I wrote Wigginton, I also sent a copy to Max Haddick, who was director of journalism for the University Interscholastic League, which coordinates high school extracurricular activities in Texas. Max Haddick wrote back to *Loblolly* on the same day he received the sample magazine, and his response was a turning point in our growth. "*Loblolly* is the finest magazine published by a school that I have ever seen. I don't know how you inspired this fine staff to do this outstanding work, but I wish I did. If I could isolate whatever technique you used to motivate them to do this, I would immediately write it up and send it to every journalism, English, and history teacher in the state." With the kind words, Dr. Haddick sent certificates of accomplishment for each student staff member. His was the first real outside recognition of what we were doing. It gave us all a boost and deeply impressed the students that someone outside the community could be so moved by what they had accomplished. It made them realize they were producing something of worth.

In the next two and a half years, the *Loblolly* staff continued to produce an issue every three months as their special class project. This original group, the seniors of 1976, conducted many follow-up interviews with Monroe Brannon, who had proven to be such a rich source of information on a variety of topics. They also talked several times with former sheriff Corbett Akin, who told of shoot-outs on the Carthage Square and captures of stills and moonshiners. Students also visited with quilters, barn builders, shingle makers, and syrup makers to record and photograph them at work. In the end, they often joined in the activity to actually learn how to do it. Thus the old traditions of the community were being preserved and passed from one generation to the next.

In 1976 the remarkable first staff of *Loblolly* produced its final effort, a two-hundred-page bicentennial issue focused on the economic history of Panola County. As Thomas Gjelten observed in his article on *Loblolly* in Paul M. Nachtigal's anthology *Rural Education* (Westview Press, 1982):

> The group of indifferent ninth graders who produced the first issue only under the threat of having to return to geography class had in their next three high school years followed with twelve more issues, each a higher quality product than the last. It had in that time become an accepted fact of Gary High School life. Children along the elementary wing of the school regarded the high school journalists with the same reverence they felt for the local basketball heroes. They looked forward to the years when they, too, could go out on interviews and see their own names appear in print in those magazines stacked on the counters of groceries and drug stores in downtown Carthage.

The twenty-member class of 1976, all of whom had been active on *Loblolly* throughout their high school career, asked their loyal patron Max Haddick to be their commencement speaker. In their final year as *Loblolly* staffers, the class had trained fourteen juniors to continue the magazine after they graduated. Within a month after the seniors left the school, a summer issue prepared completely by the juniors was published. In the following fall, the *Loblolly*-yearbook journalism class was formalized as an elective activity open to juniors and seniors, an arrangement that continues to the present.

By 1978 the community followers of *Loblolly* were almost fiercely loyal to this celebration of community history and tradition. As Gjelten concluded:

> Few school activities anywhere in the nation could hope to exceed the popularity of the magazine in Panola County. "People love them," re-

ports Mrs. Sistrunk. "They like to keep the old-timey ways alive. Every one of their issues was sold out. People get one, read it, talk about it, and start looking forward to the next one." When Sheriff Corbett Akins was asked what he thought students got out of their interview with him, he responded, "I don't know what they got writing it, but I sure as hell got a kick out of reading it."

In the fall of 1978, the twenty-second issue of *Loblolly* reached the news-stands. It was a special issue on the escapades of Bonnie Parker and Clyde Barrow in East Texas, as recollected by relatives, acquaintances, and people whose paths the famous outlaws had momentarily crossed. It sold out within two weeks. Seven years later, *Loblolly* students are still out in the community with tape recorder and camera recording the vanishing folk traditions of East Texas. We feel as if we've only just begun.

Lincoln King

Syrup Making

One of the editors has faint childhood memories of syrup-making operations at his grandmother's farm—the patient mule going round and round the cane mill, the fragrant stream of the juice as it cooked off and the festive atmosphere of the occasion among syrup makers and onlookers alike. Syrup making is one of those country crafts that are still practiced on isolated farms down the back lanes of rural East Texas. In earlier times syrup makers were common, but now only a few keep the tradition alive. One of those enduring craftsmen is Mr. Luther Guinn, who told *Loblolly* how he does it.

Luther Guinn

Now, for your seed cane, you cut your cane down and you windrow it. You stack it on an angle so it doesn't lay right on the ground. And you lay the leaves on top of it. Then you cover it with soil. That protects it through the winter where it won't freeze. Now, that's your seed cane. I'm going to use this to plant for next year. In the spring you uncover it and take it and start your planting.

You drop the cane lengthwise in the furrow and cover it up with a turning plow. Give it about three weeks, and then you'll see it sprouting through. The sprouts come from the eyes in the cane. And then you start to cultivate it. You need to plant it in February; that's best, whatever the weather permits.

Once you get it to grow, you strip the stalk and cut it off, and it's ready to go to the mill. It might get five or six feet high. I've known it to get nine feet high. That's back when we were raising cane right. You strip it, then you're ready to haul it to the mill.

You need plenty of water by the mill to keep it washed off. You use the posts for stalking the cane. The man who is feeding the mill can just reach down and grab it. Your truck or wagon you use to bring the cane to the mill is off aways some, so you just unload the cane where it's handy to the man working the mill, that is, feeding the cane into the mill.

You can put in four or five stalks at a time, whatever you want. Then the juice runs down into the barrel. Then it runs out the hole at the bottom of the barrel to the hose that runs down to the evaporator where you cook it. Now, on top of the barrel you lay a piece of burlap, and on top of the burlap or in the barrel itself you put some hay. So between the burlap and the hay, they strain the juice before it gets out of the barrel. You catch the dregs. It works like a filter on an automobile. It helps you. The backing, the pulp, you can feed to the cattle.

The evaporator, or pan, is what you cook the syrup in. The juice comes from the mill to the evaporator, and you fill it full with the juice. You build your fire in the furnace underneath, and the juice begins to boil. Now, it's going to boil in the middle first. So from one end of the pan to the other you have raw juice. You want to get the syrup to the front end where you can draw it off when ready.

What you got to do is pull the stopper and draw the raw juice off. Then you pour it in the back end with the other raw juice, and that forces the syrup down to the front end of the pan. You let the syrup get done and to the right color.

You got three bars to divide the pan. You got two skimmers and a dipper. You use the dipper to get your half-done juice up the next bar to keep it the same color. The skimmer you use at the front you don't use on the back. Use the other one at the back end. You use them to get the skimmings or dregs off the top. The skimmer at the back has more dregs to get. You get the dregs out to keep the syrup clear. I use a pot to keep the skimmings in, otherwise you have a sticky mess all over the ground.

You can tell when the syrup is done by the color. It's kind of a red color. Different land can mean difference in the color. If you raise the cane in dark soil, it will be darker. To double-check if it's done, you can lift some up and let it drop off of your skimmer. If it drops long drops it's almost done. But when the drop begins to get lazy, why, your syrup is done and you can open your stopper and draw it off. If it just runs off of the skimmer, it's not done yet and will sour in the can.

You have to keep the syrup skimmed good. Your pan is sitting about six inches over your furnace and it's going to boil in the middle and the skimmings are going to roll to the side. So keep it skimmed off good and you'll have better syrup.

The fine skimmer is used by the cooker, and the other man uses the one with the larger holes. He uses that where the juice goes in at the back end. He also feeds wood to the furnace.

When you're finishing up, you push the last of the juice to the front end for cooking. Then block it off behind so it's two inches or so. You finish that and then start to wash out the pan with water.

Now, if you have another man come along with his cane, you can use his juice to come behind the first one's last syrup. It acts the same way to get the finishing syrup to the front end. Your last syrup won't be as clear as the rest because of the last of the dregs, but it can still be good enough.

The syrup when you draw it out of the pan goes into another barrel. Then you put the syrup into cans, and it's ready to use at the table.

Now that's about all there is to it, but you can't cook syrup and stand around and gossip; you got to watch it. Two people can do the cooking, one man skimming and feeding the wood and the other at the front end where it's getting done. You also need someone running the mill and keeping an eye on the juice.

The main thing is to have you some good wood for the furnace. The best wood is what we call cord wood. Pine works good if you cut and split it in the summer and let it dry. It can take a couple of cords to do your syrup.

I've been making syrup a long time. I grew up with it. The mill here belonged to my daddy. My uncle taught me how to cook syrup. I'm seventy-seven now, so it must have been over fifty years ago. Then I kept on cooking myself. I'm going to try to plant some sorghum cane this year if I can get the seed. What I've used and have stored in the field is ribbon cane. Some like one or the other best, but they both make good syrup.

I ran about fifty gallons of syrup last year and sold it for seven dollars a gallon. You can't make any money on it, but I'm old-timey and love to do these things. I've lived right here all my life. I don't have a regular helper but have relatives to work with me to get it done. People are still interested in doing things the old way.

Now, if you've got plenty of juice and good you can cook up to seventy-five to a hundred gallons of syrup a day. That takes a lot of cane. I'm not sure how many gallons of juice it takes to make one gallon of syrup. It's got to be over ten, but I'm not sure. I couldn't give you a definite answer.

Tractors can do a good job plowing, but I can do better in the garden with my horse. Don't get me wrong; tractors are good, but for fine work you can't use a horse or mule.

I'm going to keep busy. You quit and you die. I can farm, carpenter, or do mechanic work. I've had to slow down, but I still do pretty good.

1. Stacked wood for use in cooking syrup. Tires on the far left are used to start the fire.

2. The cane in place as things are readied to grind at the mill.

3. Billy Guinn pushing cane into the mill.

4. Feeding the mill while Welton Guinn works the tractor.

5. Crushed cane coming out of the mill.

6. Luther and Billy Guinn watching the juice barrel next to the mill. The juice is strained through the burlap on top of the barrel.

7. Juice running into barrel.

8. The fire box, or furnace, under the cooking pan. Luther Guinn watching juice in the pan.

9. Drawing juice from the pan.

10. Ophelia Guinn uses bucket to move raw juice from front of pan (near smoke-stack) to rear of pan (foreground) to let it cook. Marzella Tatum skims the juice in the background while Luther supervises.

11. Lost in a cloud of steam, the juice is being cooked.

12. Marzella Tatum dumps pan skimmings in waste barrel.

13. Luther skims off pan as Robert L. Jones watches.

14. The syrup is nearly ready to "come off."

15. The final stages of the syrup are watched closely.

16. Implements of syrup making. Left to right, the mop used to push juice and syrup in pan, small-hole skimmer used with syrup, large-hole or "bug" skimmer used with dirtier skimmings, dipper used to move syrup around within the pan.

17. Debe Grissom of the *Panola Watchman* tasting raw juice. Most of these photos were taken by *Watchman* staff.

Moonshiners and Bootleggers

The basic know-how for home distilling of whiskey came over with the first settlers to this country, but the practice did not really become widespread until the beginning of National Prohibition in 1929. Professional distillers were put out of business, and the stage was set for local folks to fill the gap, plying their trade by the light of the moon. In the twenties, thirties, and forties the East Texas economy was hard hit, and many persons who had never dreamed of making whiskey went into the moonshine business. Bootleggers served as the middlemen between the moonshiner and the thirsty customers who awaited his product. For a variety of reasons, Northeast Texas (including Panola County) became a special hotbed of moonshining and bootlegging activity. Many persons entered the trade, and law enforcement officials were both overwhelmed by the numbers of transgressors and somewhat reluctant to enforce an unpopular law. Also, if we can believe the moonshiners, at least some of the agents of law and order were on the take.

Moonshine recipes were varied and the techniques of production equally diverse. But in East Texas, as elsewhere during Prohibition, traditional tried-and-true methods were forsaken for such speed-up innovations as the use of large quantities of sugar in the mash, the installation of "thump kegs" or "doublers" to get passable whiskey in a single run, the recycling of old automobile radiators as replacements for the traditional copper coils, and the addition of such dubious substances to the mix as lye and battery acid. Small wonder many customers reported cases of "jake leg" and "pop skull"!

But jobs were scarce, and if you could find one the pay was little or nothing. So many turned to moonshining and bootlegging, where the money was good, the labor was easy, and the risks were generally acceptable. Included below are the personal accounts of a few of the persons who braved the law to provide a service and product for their customers and an income for themselves. *Loblolly* offers its special thanks to Bill O'Neal and his students at Panola Junior College in Carthage, who did most of the interviews of these unrepentant (and in some cases still practicing) "shiners" and "leggers."

A Friend

I got into making homebrew beer and whiskey a long time ago. Me and my husband worked in a turpentine mill about fifty years ago in Louisiana. Our boss brought us a one-hundred-seventy-five-dollar copper still and told us we could have it if we gave him the whiskey free.

After we moved to Texas we kept the still and continued to make the homebrew. We never had to advertise our selling it because it just sells itself. I would just sit in the yard and people would come by and buy it.

After I made the homebrew I would give the leftover corn to the hogs and they would get so drunk. But it sure was a good way to fatten them up. Near the end of my career I would get hauled in every Friday night and be charged between one hundred fifty and three hundred dollars. And I ended up losing money.

Booker Johnson

I got into making whiskey because times were hard. We were so poor, and I had a wife and eleven children. All I had was what other folks gave me. They would give me cottonseed to plant and grow, but by the time the crop was in I owed everything back to them. The winters were real hard, and that is when I would make whiskey. I just made enough to make it through the winter.

My still was located way back in the woods, not anywhere near my house. If there was a path or a trail leading from your place to a still, the federal men said it was yours even if it wasn't. And if you tried to lie about it, they would nearly beat you to death. I was only caught three or four times, and I had to spend a little time in jail. But the folks around me knew I was a good worker and all, and usually all I had to do was meet a fine and they would let me out.

I've been out of moonshining for many years, ever since I was able to support my family without it. But as I look back over it, I will have to say those days hold some fond memories for me.

Cleo Alton Wise

I was born in 1904, the youngest of eight children. My father was Jerry Wise, and mother, Laura Wise. They were farmers, poor and very religious. My brothers and I were allowed very little freedom and were not allowed to drink at all even if they could have afforded it. The state and county were dry at this time.

When I was about twenty-one years old I married and went out on my own. I made my living as a logger in the woods. About 1925 my brother Zebb, who was also married at this time, taught me how to make whiskey. This was done not only to bring in more income but for our own use as well, because we loved to drink and could not afford to buy it.

The stills were located back in the baygalls, always near a stream, between Hillister, Spurger, and Fred on Beach Creek. The stills had to be moved from time to time in order to not get caught by the revenuers.

To make the whiskey, fifty to seventy-five pounds of sugar would be mixed with fifty pounds of rye or chops [corn that is not full kernel but is chopped up smaller], depending on whether you wanted rye whiskey or corn whiskey. In cold weather a cake or two of yeast would also be used. This mixture would be placed in a barrel with five or six gallons of water and left to ferment for four or five days, depending on the weather. When the mixture stopped fermenting, it was placed in a large cooking barrel. Twenty-two-foot copper tube was connected to the top of the cooking barrel. The tube was curved from the cooking barrel and went into a barrel filled with water. The tube was coiled in the water and came out at the bottom in the form of a spigot, which was used to fill the bottles.

The mixture went from the cooking barrel through the copper tube to the coiled tube in the water in the form of steam. As the steam cooled down in the water barrel, it became whiskey. It tested at about one hundred proof.

To age the whiskey, it was placed in a charred white oak keg. The keg, with its bunghole open, was placed in a barrel of cold water. The water in the barrel was heated to the boiling point, but care had to be taken not to boil the whiskey. When the whiskey was hot, the keg was taken out of the water barrel, resealed, and left to cool down. After about twenty-four hours, the whiskey would taste as if it had been aged five years and greatly improved the taste of the whiskey. The chops and rye were very inexpensive. The sugar cost about five dollars per hundred pounds. This was the only cost in making the whiskey except for the barrels and copper tubes. The kegs used to age the whiskey were picked up from stores, as most everything was packed in kegs at this time.

I sold some of the whiskey around home, but most of the sales were made on the courthouse square in Woodville. I would have the whiskey in the back seat of the car. When my friends and customers would see me parked on the square, they would get in the back seat to talk and visit. When they got out of the car, they had their whiskey.

Hoyet Walker

I was raised in a town called Whitecity, which was in San Augustine County. We made rye whiskey in this area.

The ingredients called for fifty pounds steel-cut chops, fifty pounds rye, and fifty pounds of sugar. This would turn out five to six gallons. After this, you would use same steel-cut chops and rye for five or six runs. The last few runs for the steel-cut chops and rye is the best whiskey. The first run was so weak you would work it into the rest of the runs, usually a gallon at a time.

You have a jug under the coil barrel, which catches the whiskey. The coil would come out of the cooker into the barrel with as many curls as possible. You had to keep the fire at the right temperature or it would belch your coil and it would ruin your whiskey. You could turn out more whiskey if you had good spring water.

In the nineteen thirties it cost fifty cents to make a gallon of whiskey. It was sold for about two dollars a gallon. This was some of the best pure whiskey you could get. To age the whiskey you would use a triple-x chartered keg. You could also take white oak chips, put them in the oven, and bake them until almost burnt. Then take them, put in pan with whiskey, and bring until almost a boil.

To color the whiskey you would add some caramel coloring. This was pure rye whiskey. You could drink this until you were drunk and never get a hangover.

This was during the Depression, so the sheriff didn't run us in or tear up the stills, because this was the only way for the people to make a living.

There were no feuds or gun battles between moonshiners in those days. If one person was making more money than the other they would just call the federal people in. These federal people would try to settle things down by tearing up some stills and so on. The moonshiners just kept on making it.

There was only one place, one of the two grocery stores, that didn't sell moonshine. Everyone that was asked sold moonshine; I'm not saying everyone sold it though. Moonshine was this town's main source of income. Now if you go to Freestone County, that's the place for moonshine. Freestone is up near Fairfield. But at one time things got a turn for the worst up there. The government sent some people there to get inside with the county people. Four miles northeast of Fairfield the sheriff started at midnight one night and at daylight one man was left in the community. I don't know if it was the preacher or not. Every male that was old enough to know what moonshine was was either selling, buying, or making moonshine.

Mr. Nero

You get a big barrel. It holds fifty or sixty gallons; then buy a good bit of copper pipe with a mouth about the size of a nickel. You put the barrel into the ground except for six or seven inches, then put a top on it very tight and cover it with leaves and pine straw to keep the dogs, armadillo, and other animals from gettin' in it. Then you had to get a pit, similar to our barbecue pit, and the ashes and the heat of the pit would make the water in the barrel start to heat. The other ingredients are fifty pounds of sugar, fifty pounds of chops for cattle, and two square yeast cakes.

How did you know if it was good? Well, first if no animals got in it, then it would be good. Secondly you could get a little lead cotton, about the size of a dime, and drop it in the barrel. If the cotton went straight to the bottom, it was one hundred proof, and if it did not, then you would guess what proof it was just by where it stopped.

The way you made sour whiskey was to put it in a big crock and put it in the creek where it would cool and leave it there for several weeks.

Oftentimes the law would not shoot up or axe up a still if the bootleggers would make a deal with them. The only way that this would happen would be if the bootleggers were really good and their whiskey was usually one hundred proof.

The whiskey was sold for eight to twelve dollars back then, depending on the proof. The first time that you are caught with bootleg, you are probably going to be given a suspended sentence. But the second time, they send you to the pen to stay for a while.

Mrs. Nero

Once when Mr. Nero was locked up, I had to go and get him out. Well, I was in the courthouse in Marshall, and I opened a door and, oh, there was a room full of copper pipes and those real good barrels! If there was one in there, there was fifty. Once I was also going to town and the revenuers had found a man's still. It was one of the most nice stills I had ever seen. But they did not bust it up. There was an ax laying beside the truck where the revenuers were going to load the still up. Well, this man, while the revenuers were not looking, took the ax and bust the still up himself because he did not want them to have it and keep it.

We had many parties at our house while he was making this whiskey. Every Sunday, for about two or three months, there was a party at the house. It was not my idea to have those parties, but it was Mr. Nero's house just as it was mine. Twice the revenuers drove by but never stopped. One time, I got real upset and told all of the people that there would only be two more parties at the house because if the revenuers came they would take me even though I was not drinking. I decided that I would have a little fun, so I took a gallon jug of whiskey one afternoon and took it down to the creek and dug out a place in the side of the creek just under the water level and packed mud around it. Well, two weeks later at their last party I slipped off to the creek and got the jug. It was nice and cold. I took it back to the house where many had already passed out and began to pour the whiskey. If you did this to the whiskey then it was real good, sour, cold, and thick. It would knock you out. One lady who knew her whiskey saw this and asked if she could buy a pint for her own. I got the biggest kick out of watching all of those people get so drunk that they could hardly stand up. This day was about the funniest day of my life.

Joe Adams

In making moonshine one would use a fifty-five-gallon barrel. They were wooden back then. One would fill the barrel with one-third corn, three yeast cakes, twenty pounds of sugar, and the rest water, and let it sit for five days. The contents would then be poured into a kettle with a copper tube running out the top with a lid clamped tightly on the kettle. Since alcohol is lighter than water, the fire would cause the alcohol to evaporate through the tube in the top. Many times the tube would run through a stream of cold water, thus causing the alcohol to condense more quickly. At the beginning, the alcohol would be about two hundred proof, but the moonshiner would cook the kettle until the later contents would be more water and about fifty proof.

I know of one man who used shorts in his brew and it clogged the tube, causing the kettle to build pressure and explode, nearly killing the moonshiner. He didn't use shorts anymore.

Moonshiners were nearly put out of business when some people started making jake moonshine in their bathtubs, using ginger. This style of homebrew was abandoned when people started getting jake leg.

Jake leg was paralysis which set in the legs of those who drank jake. Victims of jake leg never recovered. I didn't know exactly why it caused paralysis, but I believe that people mixed their homebrew with rubbing alcohol.

There were not only people who bootlegged moonshine, but there were those who made their income by manufacturing and bootlegging stills.

My personal adventure in bootlegging was with government bond alcohol. My job was to pick up in a wet county and bring it to Shelby County for a local bootlegger. The biggest problem for a bootlegger was having someone to deliver it who wouldn't get caught. At the time, I taught Sunday school and worked as an insurance man, so I was not the type the law would suspect. I'd throw my insurance collection book in the front seat of my '41 Dodge and head out for Longview once a week. I could haul eight cases in my trunk, and there were twelve pints in a case. The bootlegger would buy it at two dollars per pint and sell it at five dollars per pint. I as the delivery man got paid for each trip. The bootlegger, Harry Owens, along with all the other known bootleggers, paid the sheriff to leave them alone. Since the sheriff made no salary, this was how he made money. Everybody made money, including the cab driver who took the consumer to the place of purchase for a dollar. The alcohol was concealed in a place called the Big Ditch.

One other way people could get their thirst quenched was to go to the local doctor. He would write a prescription for a half pint at the local drugstore for fifty cents. It seems that almost everyone was involved in bootlegging.

Wyatt A. Moore

Around '21 or '22 people in this area [Harrison County] got the recipe for making alcoholic beverages. I was twenty years old and a lot of us turned toward that as a sideline, and sometimes it was a complete line. The method of operation here was usually kind of small outfits, comparatively small. Over in Mississippi, they would dig a hole in the side of a hill and put a still there that would hold several thousand gallons, and make it in a big way and haul it off with trucks. But here, our method was mostly to put a platform out over the water in Caddo Lake, in thickets where only a small canoelike boat could go into it and would carry five or six barrels of mash.

I had a wintertime spot and a summertime spot. I'd move in a little paddle boat at night and haul a little at a time. I'd move as I was making a run. As the barrel would get empty, I would put it over into my little paddle boat and move the whole outfit over a half mile or so to another platform and set it up on the platform, and then when I drained the cooker I'd drain some of that hot fluid out in the boat and just use it for a tanker, and paddle over to this other place and pour it in. So when the next run come off, I was moved. I moved sort of while under operation.

You put water and hops and yeast cake together, and then you cook it in a container, preferably a copper still. But most everybody used oil drums—cleaned 'em out good. There was one-hundred-ten gallon drum could be had from an oil company in Shreveport. I had several of them, and some of them rusted out during the eight or ten or fifteen years of operation. I maintained an outfit on a platform that I could set up on some sort of carpenter-type workhorses and then lay the decking down and wouldn't make any noise establishing a location like hammering and building a platform.

We usually used wood to burn and put this drum into a brick furnace and fixed it up with this old chimney mud that you can get around here. There is a white-looking post oak clay—they mix grass with it and build mud chimneys. Anyway, we brick it up, make a furnace, put a smokestack around the end of the drum, and it was a pretty efficient burner. Usually the best whiskey to be made is to boil it once and run your fluid out through a copper tubing in the lake to let the lake cool it and back on the platform and run up a bunch of it. Then you put all that you've got back in your drum and run it again to get it real strong. You could get up to one hundred seventy or eighty proof, almost pure alcohol. Then you cut it down with, preferably, rainwater to where it's about one hundred proof.

Then you could buy a proof gauge, a little hydrometer-type thing, and put it in charred oak kegs that you could buy anywhere and age it awhile, and it was pretty good material. In fact, I expect it was as safe to drink as any they've got now.

Then it got to be that the price of the product was so low that we got to making it with a thumper. A thumper is a smaller tank that sits between your copper boiler and the coil that goes in the lake to cool it that acts as sort of a settling bulb. That way, at one run, you can make pretty strong liquor. It's not as good as the complete double run, but it is pretty fair if you'll fire it slow.

Alcohol leaves fluid at one hundred eighty degrees. You seen the old-time car gauge where the heat indicator was painted red at one hundred eighty degrees? Well, at one hundred eighty degrees, the old-time alcohol antifreeze would boil out of your radiator. Well, water don't make steam till it reaches two hundred twelve degrees; therefore, the secret of making good liquor was to keep your temperature between one eighty and two twelve. Then only the alcohol would come out and you wouldn't get boil-over of mash or nonalcohol. Some of them didn't know that, but I had a doctor friend and he liked the material we was making, and he showed me how to put a temperature gauge on it to hold it in the proper perspective, or what they call now the proper quality control. Lot of people have told me that my product was as good or better than most.

I never was arrested. I was nipped at a few times. I always managed to dodge them. It was just pure luck. If you operated truthfully, they got what they called for and sampled it. I gave them a swig out of mine. I never did sell around the house or have any drunks around. In fact, we lived on the lake and operated a fish camp and built boats. I used this operation as a sideline, but at times it was just about the mainstay.

Once, it brought eight dollars a gallon. Finally people got to selling it for as low as two dollars a gallon, but I never did sell it for less than three. I figured it cost me a dollar a gallon to make it and if I sold it for three, and sold half as much as those who sold it for two, I'd still make just as much clear money and do just half as much work.

At one time I had a still so close to the house that I could see the smoke from the house and the thumper would make a *bump, bump, bump* noise when you fired it up on a cold morning. I had an irrigation pump on the bank of the lake, and I irrigated a little truck farm. When I had people around the house, I'd fire up the little water pump to drown out the noise of the thumper down there. And anyway, I never did have any trouble.

The smell never did go anywhere other than right close by. I could smell pretty good 'cause I never did smoke—haven't yet—and I never did notice a smell to amount to anything. Sometimes I guess I smelled like whiskey and duck and money and fish all at the same time.

If you operated right, you could sell it to doctors, lawyers, bankers, and people who really didn't want other people to know they were getting it. You could make a kind of pest out of yourself by not using it carefully and making poor stuff and getting in the wrong kind of company with it. But the sheriff liked good whiskey, you know. However, I don't know anybody in this county who actually had a deal with any of the law enforcement officers, whatever, in order to get by. It might have been that they was nice to them or took them a mess of fish or something, but as far as any actual payoff, I don't believe there ever was. The federal revenuers was the only ones the people in this area was ever afraid of. But this is a large area of Caddo Lake with lots of swamps, shallow water, and big trees where you could go back and build you a platform whereby an airplane couldn't even see it down in the thick cypress trees.

I went down to Huntsville once and tried to spring my uncle who had moved to town and went to selling in town and they got him. If he'd stayed on the lake where things was wild like he was, he would never have got caught. I didn't spring him, but he got out later. A lot of my neighbors went to the Federal Correctional Institute of Texarkana and Tyler, but somehow I managed to squirm by, myself. I guess you might say I'm really the only uncaught one in the area. I don't attribute it to anything uncanny except that maybe they didn't as many people know about me as I thought knew. And people wanted to know, wasn't I scared? And I told them, "Yes sir, I'm scared. I stay scared." Maybe that's the reason I didn't have any trouble. I never did have a trial; I had a grand jury vote to bill me once and I got kind of underground wind of it and I pulled a few strings that night and the next day they voted that maybe they didn't have enough evidence for conviction and believed they'd throw it out.

People would get their stills tore up—I never had one tore up. People would get brazen and put it out in an open spot and let it get found, and of course they had to tear them up. They didn't refuse to tear them up. To satisfy the Christian Temperance Union and the bootleggers, too, they had to have both sides make a showing. It still goes on that way everywhere now—you scratch my back and I'll scratch yours, though I never did scratch many backs. I figured if it got to where I had to oblige myself, I'd just do something else, but there wasn't anything much else to do then.

Perry Martindale—Moon Boy

I was making my own whiskey by the time I was twenty-three, and that was young because of the great risks involved. My folks were dead, and I lived with my aunt until I was twenty-eight.

I did most of my shining during the night. My still was only about five miles from town, and you had to burn wood under the main boiler in your still. So, to keep anyone from seeing the smoke, I ran it at night. People who knew me called me Moon Boy. If you came up to me and said, "Hi, Moon Boy, everything sweet?" I knew you was wanting some of my whiskey.

There were five other boys who knew where my still was. Ben was the only one of us that had a truck. We used Sammy's dad's cafe as the main place of distribution. We had to give Duke forty percent of what we made. So then the five of us—me, Ben, Sammy, Billy, and George had to split the sixty percent left. Ben and I got more because we had more difficult jobs. Duke helped a lot. He knew a lot about bootlegging.

We used quart jars to pack the stuff around for three reasons. One is because you could get jars easier than anything else. Second, if you were in trouble you could break the jars and you wouldn't have no shine on you. Last, you could slip a quart jar right into the top of your boot, put your overalls over the tops, and no one could see a thing.

I had to quit when I had been leggin' about ten years. It was the fall of 1939. I was thirty-four and was running a sawmill in town. I sold my whole makings to Sammy and Duke. They paid me one hundred and twenty dollars. But people still called me Moon Boy.

I never was caught. I don't even believe I ever had a close call.

I did it because it was quick money. I could spend lots of money but save some too. So, I saved a good chunk and started me a sawmill.

Clarence Fountain

I started making moonshine when I was eight years old. Since then, I was never convicted, but I have been in every jail from here to Beaumont on suspicion of moonshining. At one time I had five stills operating. They were well spread out, and when the law would be watching one still I would just go to another. I would hide the moonshine by putting it in stumpholes. I would hide up to five hundred cases at one time.

Once me and my buddy were going to make a hundred gallons. We were making it ten gallons at a time. We both got drunk by just standing over it and stirring it. My buddy passed out, and I myself hit the ground. While I was on the ground, I was laying over a hole. Then I felt something bite me on the rear. I jumped up and yelled and woke up my buddy because I thought I was snake bit. Me and my buddy poured two gallons of moonshine into the hole, and out came the biggest crawfish I had ever seen.

W. R.

First you need a copper-lined boiler and copper-lined hoses. This prevents you and your customers from getting poisoned. Next, mix up some corn and sugar and let it sour. Then pour it in your boiler and start cooking it. Keep it right at a boiling point; this lets steam go up through the coils, which condenses back to whiskey and runs to the end, and that's where you catch it and put it in your jugs. Then drink it or sell it. Charter moonshine is the best. The way you make it is to mix it with the same as regular moonshine but let it set days in charcoaled oak barrels and it absorbs the charcoal color. It looks and tastes like bonded whiskey, but most people say it's better than bonded whiskey. If you wanted to make some fast money though, you just got a car radiator, poured your mixed ingredients in it, then poured battery acid in it and sell it and then relocate. One drawback from this method, though, was the lead contents from the acid caused jake leg or lead poisoning.

Corbett Akins

While I was sheriff of Panola County we located a still in Brushy Creek bottom. I found three barrels of mash and a fifty-five-gallon cooker. After looking at the mash I decided it would be two days before it would be ready to run. I knew from the color of the mash because it turned sky blue, and all the grain and chops settle to the bottom. So we decided to watch the still and waited for the owner to come back.

It was in deep winter. I stayed with the still for three nights. The third night there was ice and frost everywhere. About four or five o'clock that morning I heard a man coming. It was a large black man. He checked the mash and got a bottle of whiskey from behind a bush and took a drink. We told him to hold it, but he tucked the whiskey under his arm and hit out running, and I took out after him. He ran up a hilltop, and when I got there, he ran into a shack and into the kitchen and took the cap off the stove. He threw the whiskey in the stove and it exploded. I saw the stove and part of it went through the roof of the house. The explosion knocked the wall down and the black man down. I put the cuffs on him. I went in the kitchen, and there wasn't a stove anymore, but there was some clothes hanging on a ceiling joint above where it had been. There were three little kids, and they had gotten scared and ran out the door and jumped in the barrel, tipped it over, and began to roll down a hill. The barrel hit a tree and out came the little kids. I guess they didn't have any clothes to sleep in because they were buck naked. They ran back to the house and began screaming for their mama. The woman came crawling out from under the bed. The explosion must have blown her skirt off because she didn't have any clothes on from the waist down. I arrested the man, and I think he was glad to go with me because his wife acted like she wanted to kill him.

George Tiller

Fifty years ago, River Hill and Dead Wood were thriving moonshining and bootlegging country. They made it with corn and sugar. After distilling, it could be as potent as one hundred proof, or they would dilute it with water. Occasionally, red oak chips were added to obtain the natural whiskey color, or red soda pop was sometimes used. Some of the distillers would add lye to speed up fermentation. When consumed, this lye would cause the lips to swell tremendously. They bottled it in empty liquor bottles.

Those that owned stills would take string and run it around the area of the still. If the string was broke they could tell if anyone had been around. If they found it disrupted they would usually send their wives down with some excuse, like picking berries, to see if the law was waiting for them to return.

One man who had a still near the river sold his in a very unique way. A person would go to a certain spot on the river and honk their car horn three times. Then he would put the money in a stump and leave for thirty or forty-five minutes. Upon returning, the liquor would be in the stump and the money gone. In this way a person never knew who was making and selling the brew.

One man had a still near Debarry. The man left his crippled son at home one day and told him to take no one down to the still unless he knew them. A man arrived and asked him to sell him some liquor. Before arriving the man had taken soap and put it around his mouth, and he was shaking as if he was in dire need of a drink. The young boy, not knowing what to do, asked the man to push him in his wheelchair to the still and he would sell him some. The next day the sheriff arrived with the man and went directly to the still. The distiller was tried and sentenced to two years in prison. But the story has a happy ending, because in six months he was out and brewing again.

Elzie Pilot

I got out of the moonshine business in 1968. I never actually made it, I just delivered and drank the stuff. I delivered it for a man named Buckwheat because he was my supplier. I usually made my deliveries early on Sunday mornings. I would start my run about four-thirty, because it was dark and I still had time to make it back before church.

One particular morning I was making a run to Timpson, and I started hitting the jug along the way there. And my stomach started feeling like it was going to explode and I began to get the hots and I finally passed out.

I knew I was in trouble when I woke up and the Timpson constable was standing over me. I thought the end was near. I felt like I had been kicked in the gut by a mule. They carried me to the hospital, and I spent ten days there for blood poisoning. After I got home my wife got after me with a iron skillet, and I had to go back for three stitches in the head and a slight concussion.

Needless to say that was my last run and I've been out of the business since then. I'm sixty-three years old, but I still hit the bottle every once in a while.

Mrs. McClelland

During the county history of a dry time, bootlegging was a big profit-making business. Mr. McClelland would sell it for much more than he paid for it in neighboring wet counties. The price for their big business was the risk of being caught by lawmen.

There was one day that was pretty frightening then but kind of funny now. I hadn't been up for very long that day. We had an icebox full of whiskey, wine, and beer to sell. A car pulled up. It was about time for my bath, and I was in my duster with the water running in the tub. I went to look and see who drove up, and to my surprise it was the sheriff nearing the door. I got all the beer and liquor and ran and put in in my bath water. I added

Ivory dishwashing soap to the water. I told him I was so long in coming to the door because I was enjoying a bubble bath when he knocked.

He had a warrant to search the house. He searched, finding nothing. I really enjoyed bootlegging; it's fun remembering.

W. R.

Now, I used to make runs for this old lady. What I would do would be to go to Marshall and load my trunk full of cases of beer and then load my back seat—just as much as it could hold—with whiskey and wine. Then I'd easy back to Carthage, slowly, so I would not get caught. You see, this lady had a bunch of runners, but the police had spotted them all and picked them up. But they didn't know I was a runner, so they left me alone. But that lady would pay me what it cost for all the booze I had gotten plus eighty dollars—not bad if you ask me. Now you can go to Longview and after hours you can call a cab and most likely he can tell you where to get some whiskey or sell it to you himself.

Rosa Bell Pass

Well, in 1937 Copeland, my husband, started making homebrew because times were hard. I was eight months pregnant and he needed extra money. Somebody reported him, they turned him in for making it, so one day the law came down. I was sitting on the bed reading the paper, and you could see right through the wall of the little old house. It was a shotgun house, you know, and you could see right through it.

So I jumped up and there was four bottles of beer sitting on the counter in the kitchen and I went in there and put them in a can of meal. Well, before they got in, I decided that wasn't a good hiding place. So I took them and went out the back door and went to the chicken house. Behind the chicken house was a pile of lumber, and I put them under this pile of lumber. I was afraid they'd move the lumber, so I sat down on it. Well, this cop come around and picked up the end of the board I was sitting on and said he had to look under there. I just got up and there was an iron cookstove settin' there at the end of the pile and I went to pick that beer up. I was putting it in my arms like stove wood. One of the bottles was empty, but I didn't know which one it was. One of the bottles of beer broke, and it cut this cop's face. Well, that one breaking gave me an idea. So I broke the other bottles on the little stove. The neck of the bottle was all that was left in my hand. So after I broke the bottles I went back in the house and went into the kitchen. We had a wood stove, and there was a pile of stove wood laying there. The cop came up to the door and wanted to know if I had anything he could put on his face. I told him, "Yeah, a stick of this wood." So, he went on. I guess they were worried because I was so big, pregnant, you know. They hung around and watched me, I guess to see what was going to happen. Finally, they left. They couldn't really do anything anyway because they looked in the woods and they found the crock he made the beer in but they didn't find any of the beer. He had about thirty bottles of it hidden in the woods and didn't find any of it.

Joe Doe

I was born in Carthage, Texas. I've lived here all my life. I've been a bootlegger for about fifteen years. I began selling liquor because there wasn't nothing else I could do. I've been paralyzed for twenty years. A tree fell on me and paralyzed me from the waist down. I get good business, mainly because people want to help me. I'm real careful, and I only keep one case of liquor on hand. I go to Marshall or Longview to pick up my liquor. My sister keeps about three cases. She is a nice old lady. The cops would never be suspicious of her.

I make about two hundred fifty dollars a week. I sell short cans of liquor for seventy-five cents and tall ones for a dollar. I don't have a gambling shack; I just sell liquor. I ain't never been caught. I've got people watching out for the cops. I have to know someone before I'll sell them liquor. If a stranger comes to my house, I tell them I don't sell liquor.

I don't drink myself, but I enjoy selling liquor. I meet people and talk to them. I get lots of visitors. That's mainly why I do it. I don't need the money all that bad.

Mr. Blackjack

My stills are located in the Sabine River bottom, although I won't reveal the exact location. I've been in the business for about fifteen years and I ain't about to stop, because the money is too good. I make just about all my money from the whiskey. I make enough money to hire two helpers to help me carry the corn meal and the sugar to the stills. We do all our work at night. I try to do this on nights when the moon is full and bright because I am very nervous about using lanterns because the light might attract too much attention.

The type of whiskey I make is corn mash. I make it out of corn, sugar, and water. Sometimes if I run out of fresh water, which is the best kind to use, I just draw a few buckets of water out of the river. But I guess it don't matter—the customers never seem to know the difference.

Weighing the risk and profits, I think I will be in moonshining for many years to come, as long as the risk don't become too great.

Hot Rick

I've been in the business since I was about fourteen years old. I've made good money over the past thirty years. In fact, I've made enough to give my family pretty much the best of a lot of things.

During all this time of moonshining I was only caught once and had to spend about forty-five minutes in jail.

After that I was pretty damn careful about who I told that I made it and where.

I make two kinds of whiskey, a corn whiskey and a rye whiskey. The people I sell to mostly prefer corn whiskey, but there is some people that I have as customers that like rye. In making whiskey I like to use soft water because the hard water makes the whiskey harsh. Unlike the hard water, it is smooth and easy to drink.

After being in moonshining so long I don't think I could quit. It's not because of the money but just because I enjoy it.

Mr. Sam

I think moonshining and bootlegging is some of the easiest money in the world. It is very unlikely you will get caught unless you're just awfully careless. I have two stills about two hundred fifty yards behind my house in a dense thicket, and that's where I do most of my brewing.

There is only one way to make good whiskey, and that is knowing what you're doing. I make two kinds of whiskey, corn and rye, although I've tried a few different substitutes.

They way I make my whiskey is to mix up some corn or rye, whatever be the case, with water and sugar.

Then I let it sit for a few days in large barrels until it sours and turns to mash.

Then I boil it down in my cooker. I have a tube on top of my cooker which runs to the jugs. When the mash boils in the cooker, it turns to steam and goes through the tube and condenses and runs into the jugs.

This has been my recipe for thirty years, and it must be pretty good because my customers keep coming back.

Big Ops, Blues, and Little Fiddlers

"While Brother John was workeing with the steers I concluded to catch som fish, I had som large cat hooks with me such as I had been fishing with in the Irish Buyo and I set som of them out one night and next morning all my hooks was broken and Thorn soon told me that the store baught hooks would not stand the fish in that river. I went to the shop and had me a hook mad and baited it with a whole rabbit, set it out, and next morning I went to my hook, and it had caught what I turmed a large fish and another larger one had come along and swallowed it above its side fins and hung, and I could not take them out of the watter. I went back to the house and got Mr. Thorn and a negro man, both large stout men, and they taken them out of the watter, tied a rope in ones mouth, put a pole in the loop and shouldered it up and at least a foot of the large one draged the ground.

The large one weighed 107 pounds, the small one 49 pounds, so I caught 156 pounds of fish at one time and on one hook. Thorn said he had caught one larger than that since he lived thare, and now dear reader, if you are inclined to dout this wolf story about the big fish, I cant help it for I believe the witnesses are all dead and the papers destroyed except my memorandon book."

From *Now You Hear My Horn: The Journal of James Wilson Nichols, 1820–1887,* Catherine W. McDowell (ed.). The University of Texas Press (1967).

As James Nichols's account from the 1820's attests, big catfish tales go far back in the history of East Texas. And that is true whether they are told as "wolf stories" or as the soberest of recollected fact.

Eighteenth-century French explorers observed that the native Caddo Indians used a kind of bank-to-bank setline with dangling hooks on it, possibly the earliest form of trotline. Pioneer Anglo settlers adopted the Caddo trotline or perhaps carried their own version with them when they came. Over the years, other methods evolved for taking the native oppelousas, blue, and blue-channel catfish, as well as the freshwater drum, the buffalo, and other species of river fish. Legal and extralegal, they included, besides the familiar trotline and cane pole, throw lines, bank hooks, limb lines, draglines, snag lines, jug hooks, hoop nets, trammel nets, gill nets, wire traps, and such ultimate measures as dynamite and the deadly telephone or microwave " 'lectro rig."

The intrepid "grappler," "grabbler," or "cooner" was in a class by himself. He went after big catfish with his bare hands, feeling ever so gingerly under submerged logs and in holes in the riverbank, hoping not to chance upon snake or snapping turtle.

Many men set out trotlines, but most, as Gibson Waits told me, "just don't know how ." At a time when the majority of fishermen seek the man-made lakes, the master catfishermen of East Texas rivers are a declining breed. But some are still in business, setting trotlines and throw lines with old-time skill and cunning, not so much simple fishers as canny huntsmen of the big ops and blues that are still down there, just as they were in James Nichols's time. In the pages that follow, three master catfish hunters tell us about their craft. (Note: "Big Ops, Blues, and Little Fiddlers was researched and edited by Thad Sitton, who—forgive me, Eliot Wigginton!—could not bear to let *Loblolly*'s students have *all* the fun.)

George Tull

When we was kids, about twelve or fifteen, we got started to fishing in this backwater on the Neches River. The river overflowed, and we fished in the creeks where the river come through in the backwater. We got started to fishing that way, and first thing you know, after we learned the woods good, we was fishing in the river.

We used trotlines in the backwater, and you don't need water over four feet deep. In warm weather water that deep's deep enough to fish in.

And I'll tell you, if you gonna go fishing and fish for big fish you gonna come up fish hungry! You need to fish for these channel cat, you know, two or three pounds. You just want a light sinker, such as a spark plug; you don't want a heavy sinker. If the water's a little swift I'll put a railroad spike on it. I usually use two-ought hooks, but a one-ought is all right for these little ol' channel cats. They'll hold. I caught lots of fish on hooks like that that weighed over fifteen pounds. Tie your line on something limber.

You just have to guess at where to put your line where the water's all over. You pick a place that looks pretty good for a trotline. Sometimes I'd get in a thicket and put one, and sometime I'll set in open water. But always fish 'cross the water, don't fish with the water.

We'd put out our lines in the backwater close to the top. Them fish gets out in that water, they mostly feed on the top. And you want to use a lighter sinker—sometime I just use one spark plug on a line. If you're using a heavy sinker on your line and you get a channel cat on that weighs three or four pounds, if there's a heavy sinker he can just keep jerking till he pulls the hook out. If he's got a light sinker he can pull around he won't get aloose.

They's a lot of fish back in them days when we was kids. We caught a lot of fish. If fish wasn't biting—what we called wasn't biting—we'd catch fifty pounds a night. We don't got that kind of fishing now. But kids them days didn't have nothing to do, you know, and we'd make a lot of good money a-fishing. Them days, Diboll down here didn't have nothing but "Diboll checks," company scrip. We'd take out fish and peddle 'em in the quarter and come out with a paper sack full of them checks! Ten cents a pound, and then you couldn't hardly sell 'em. That was the Hoover days!

Back in them days we caught lots of fish, maybe they'd weigh fifteen or twenty pounds, but we didn't catch no big fish. But we caught one big fish down there in the backwater that we didn't get. I believe he'd have weighed a hundred pounds. Had him on a six-ought hook, and oh, I'd say his head was a foot wide, it look like. I was trying to get his head there at the front end of the boat, and my brother was sitting in the middle. That fish come up out of the water, and he run his hand around his tail, thought he was gonna help me bring it in. But boy, when he did, that fish made a roll and straightened that hook. That was a big fish, but that was the only big fish I ever hung like that. That was in the backwater, where the creeks makes out of the river.

That big fish, he don't bite but about once a month. He'll eat him a fish weigh about a pound or so and fill up. Me and my brother was fishing in the backwater one other time—I guess we was almost grown—and I caught a mud cat I guess would weigh a couple of pounds. Big old yellow mud cat, you've seen them old yellow creek cats? They are good to catch an op on. I says, "Buddy, I'm gonna put this one on this hook." I had a big hook there in the boat. I said, "I'm gonna put him out." He says, "You know there ain't no fish in here big enough to eat that fish!" I says, "Well, if he don't we'll take him off in the morning." So I run that hook through his mouth, tied a knot in it, and stretched the hook back around and hung it in his tail. Next morning I had a fourteen-pound op on it—a fourteen-pound op trying to eat that two-pound fish.

When the river got down 'bout half banks and we fished the river, I'd pick my places. I'd like to fish above a log, a tree top, or something—put me out a line and kind of let it drift back to that place. The main thing in fishing with a trotline, leave plenty of slack in your line. That'll help hold your fish. You got a tight line, the fish'll get off. Sometimes, if the river was low, we'd pick a pretty swift place on account of when it's low fish will get in that kind of water.

I keep a few big hooks in my boat, and when I get ahold of a pretty good bait I'll put that big hook on there in a good place where I think I might catch a big fish. We done that last year and caught about a fifteen-pound cat. And I used to keep a regular trotline with all of 'em six-ought hooks, big hooks. I'd be after the oppelousas. He's a fish that won't eat nothing but live bait. But I'll tell you, you'll hang a big fish where you ain't expecting to lots of times, in shallow water. I've caught a many a good op where I didn't think about one being in that place.

We used soap altogether mostly here fishing. I got thirty or forty years old and we started using soap. I bought a million bar of soap! I got bars of soap older than you are. I wouldn't catch a fish and I'd say, "I ain't gonna use it no more, no more," but first thing you know, I'd get to using a piece or two and catch a fish on it. P&G soap is about as good a bait as you can use. Now, we use this here Ivory. When the river first gets down I like to seine me some bait out of them sloughs. Seined bait out of the river is the best you can get, but you gonna have to run those lines—turtles, gars, and grinnels will tear 'em up. That's what I like about soap—won't nothing bother it but a channel cat and a drum. Them gars and grinnels and turtles won't bite that soap.

My grandson-in-law, he set out trotlines that are what you call draglines. Don't put no bait on the hooks. He come in here one night and he had a twenty-six-pound high-fin blue, and he had a twenty-three-pound op, then he had one weighed seventy-two pounds. He caught 'em on a dragline. Catch 'em in the side or tail or side the head—that's how he caught 'em. He tried to show me. It's the way you put your hook on, and it's about a five- or six-ought hook, and it's got to be real sharp. The way you tie the hook on this line, if you drag that line over your hand like that, when that hooks gets there it'll whup over and catch your hand. That's the way it's rigged up. If a fish swims by that line, that hook will get him.

And I've grabbled fish, but I ain't done that for thirty years. I done learned better, too many snakes and turtles. Them days, back in the Hoover days, you take a place wasn't over waist deep and 'bout dried up in the fall of the year and get them muddied real good. They'd be a few logs in there, and every time we went down there, three or four old boys, we had a gallon of white lightening in them days. You get up aside of them logs, put your hands in the water and bring 'em together, and boy! Sometimes them fish would jump all over you! I got twenty-seven mud cat out from under one log one time, them old yellow cat.

But if you done know where them fish are settled you didn't have to do that; you'd just ease under and ease your hand on 'em. They'll stay if you'll ease. I remember one time I carried some boys down there with me. They were afraid to do that for a while, but after I got to doing it they did too. I got ahold of a big grinnel—I know he was three foot long. I got my hand on him and I kept easing that grinnel down in that deep mud so I could hold him. I told one old boy, says, "Come on, I got one I want you to get out for me. I know I can't hold him." That boy got him, got his hand around in his gills, and brought him up holding him. He was trying to flounce and directly he said, "He 'bout to get away!" Boy, that grinnel did make a round, and he did get away! I put my hand on a big snake one day, and I got away from that place. But I'll tell you what, I brought a big turtle up one time. I got ahold of him and threw him out on the bank.

But them big old loggerhead turtles is the reason I quit. They'll get to weighing two hundred pounds. They caught one down here in Ryan's Lake. Fellow caught it on a trotline and couldn't get it out. He shot it two or three times with a twenty-two, and so the next day this turtle climbed out on the bank and died. I went down and looked at him. I taken my rule and measured, and from the end of his nose to the end of his tail was four foot long. And across his back I believe was twenty-three inches, and he was about fifteen inches high. I asked a lot of fellows what they thought that turtle would weigh, and they said they thought he would weigh two hundred fifty pounds. He was a big 'un. His feet was bigger than my hands. Them big old loggerheads is the reason I quit grabblin'.

I just like my trotlining. I sure do. I laughed at old man Purdy; he used to be a Diboll printer long years ago. Just a year or two before he died, me, him, and another fellow went to B-Dam fishing. And he's talking about how people used to catch these fish on these throw lines and set hooks—these bank hooks. He says, "You don't do that no more, do you?" I says, "No, Mr. Purdy, I don't do that. I use trotlines." He says, "Why don't you use them throw lines and bank hooks like we used to?" I says, "Mr. Purdy, I like to set on my —— and fish, that's the reason." He says, the old fellow's funny, says, "Uh-huh, that's what I thought."

I caught a duck on my trotline once. He just got on there. There's a boy come up here a-fishing. He worked down with Gibson in Houston when Gibson used to drive a truck. He used soap for bait, you know, and he caught a coon on his trotline. You can do that—this coon might have got caught on his first hook, maybe. But he went back down there to Houston telling them boys about it, and they didn't believe it. They laughed at him and hoorahed him about it. In a little while one of them Houston boys went a-fishing, and this first old boy asked him what did he catch? Says, "Two coons, a possum, and a mink!"

But I'll tell you a lie. Here a while back there's a fellow telling another fellow 'bout how he caught a fish weighed 500 pounds. This other fellow told him, says, "Well, I caught one that had swallowed a coal oil lantern that was still burning." This fellow that had caught the big fish says, "I don't believe that." Second fellow says, "Well, you cut off part of your fish and I'll blow that lantern out."

Gibson Waits

I was running with three-quarter Cherokee Indians. Three-quarter Cherokee was what they were. Indians. They would take me with 'em and they wouldn't let me paddle a boat, and they wouldn't let me get out in the water. If we'd come along and the water was shallow, why they'd get out and pull, but they wouldn't let me get out in the water. But they'd carry me along with 'em—drive three miles to my house to get me. Say, "Come on, you go with us. You bring us good luck." And they'd carry me around, and I'd watch them and learn how to trotline fish.

Those two Indians is the best fishermen in the country right there. What they say is, "Fish gotta eat too," and every so many days they'll tell you when the fish is biting. But they don't go fishin' when the moon is bright. They just don't do it. They'll wait till a dark night, and they'll just go down and find a big hole of water and put a trotline right across the upper end of it, where the river's running down, you know? And then maybe at a bend in the river, just above the upper end of it there. And I'm telling you, them boys could catch 'em. Lot of people go and put out trotlines, but they just don't know how.

Once, I told the Indian where to put a line and he caught a big one, and he said, "How'd you know that?" I says, "Well, I figured if I was a fish and gonna feed I'd go right over there and do it." I says, "If I was a fish I'd go right over there and feed," right around that drift. They looked at each other and then they looked at me, and he says, "I got a trotline down here right in the bend of this river." And I says, "Yeah, and there's a fish on it, too." And sure enough, we went down there and there was about a five- or six-pounder on it. Anyway, he looked at me and says, "You goin' with us from now on."

They was good; boy, they could catch 'em. I went with 'em one time. They told me, says, "We're going up here to a place called Wiley Bend." I says, "Okay." I was done grown, then. That was just right after I married. We all went up there, and I got sleepy and just lay down and went to sleep, and him and the other one, they run the trotline. He woke me up one time, says, "Gib, you know what we done tonight?" I says, "No." He says, "We done caught fourteen of oppelousas off of that line up yonder on that bend, and every one of 'em weighed about eight pounds. They're all the same." We caught 'em bitin' that night, and man, we come out of there with a boatload of fish! And in the morning we like to sunk it when we run over a log in the river. He run over it and the front end went under the water, but it come back up quick, and you ought to have seen him grab the bucket and go to dipping water out of that boat! He was afraid it was goin' under—coming down that swift river!

I like to fish right up next to the bank, about two foot off the bank. I like to put my trotline all the way across or up and down, either one, just according to where you're at. Up and down, put it out about two foot off the bank and let it lay on the bottom. I've done it with barrel swivels on it, and you could stand up on the bank and look down and see them brass barrel swivels in there. You see, that fish he come up there and he works that bank feeding. The first one I put out like that I went back and had a five-pound blue and a five-pound op on that line. I had one down there running up and down the bank. I took thirteen off one morning—sixty-five pounds.

That's where them good uns are. Reason why I run it up and down that away, I was always catching on my lines right next to the bank. I say, "Well, heck fire! That's where I'm gonna start fishing." And that's where I went to catchin' 'em. Other people will fish up and down, but they'll get out about six or eight foot. I practically put it right on the bank! Them ol' Indian boys, they'll do it too. They sure will.

I can go out anytime and catch some fish. What we used was number thirty-six cord for trotline and number twenty-four cord for the staging line that goes on the hook. Put it about a foot and a half below the trotline and tie your hooks on the line about five foot apart. We'd always make a loop in that number thirty-six cord so the hook lines wouldn't slip up and down, and then we'd run the trotline across. Then we'd come back and bait it out and put about three or four sinkers on it with about a two-foot string on them and let it go to the bottom. But now, if you got a big ol' perch or something like that you want to lay him right on the bottom of the river—let him go on down to the bottom. You shortened up on your sinker lines and layed your trotline on the bottom of the river if you wanted to catch a big fish. Then, be sure to tie it to a good limber limb on each side of the river, so if you do hang a big one you'd have some spring there.

Once we set a line like that on a grapevine. We had got our lines broke three or four times there before we put a big line in there. Before, we'd have a big perch or pollywog on it, and he'd just carry it on up in them willow bushes and break it. He'd hang it, and then he'd just go ahead and pull hisself loose.

So, we tied this big line onto a two-inch willow bush on one side of the bank and run it out in the river down the river and give it a lot of slack. We let it go to the bottom and then put our sinkers on it and went on across and baited it out. Then we come back and pulled it out in the river, 'cause we knew where there was a bluff bank down there, and we just hung it off of that bluff bank there, and boy, we caught ninety pounds of catfish off of that one line in one week!

We could feel that jump-off. I says, "Well, that jump-off's right there, but I don't want to get down in there." But my brother says, "Let's drop it off in there; that's where the big uns is." And so we put a line there, had six hooks on it. Tied one end of it on a grapevine and the other end on that little ol' willow. When we came back a big one was on there, and he had that grapevine stretched out so tight and he was shaking that other one! My brother thought it was hung. He says, "This thing is hung as tight as it can be. Let's go to the other end." Then he says, "Lookee yonder, look at that limb there!" And he grabbed ahold of the line and went to hollerin' for me,

says, "You gonna have to come up here and get it." I says, "You can get it good as I can!" And we started to pulling up on the line and he got him up pretty close to the boat and that thing just took off toward the center of the river. I felt the wind in my face! He got out there far as he could go and just turned around and made one big slosh and pulled that hook out. He didn't break the hook, 'cause that hook was a special kind of hook, but he tore off. I looked right at him when he come up on top of the water and made that big slosh. And heck fire! That thing look like it was two foot wide! I know he was five foot long.

They's some like that right down there in Lake Dam B. Once, there was some scuba divers goin' down there working, and they come out and says that they wasn't going back. Says there was some catfish in there that was longer than they was. That would've been a two-hundred- or two-fifty- or three-hundred pound oppelousas. They says they wasn't goin' back in there no more. Says them ol' ops would come up there and look at 'em! Says, "No! They're big enough to swallow us!"

Them big ops come up the river from the lake in the spring to lay eggs. That op, he travels a lot slower than the blue cat does. All he got to do is lay on the bottom and open his mouth down there, and he can get all the feed he wants. That's the trouble of it. They don't run around and look to scavenge. Blue cat, you know, he goes everywhere—right up next to the bank, all around—oppelousas lies right on the bottom. That's the reason for that big ol' soft belly, you know. They slide right on the bottom and go slow, just creep around. Most of the time, them big uns, they'll lay down and open their mouths, and if something get in there they'll just close their mouth and swallow it and open their mouth again. That's the reason you don't hardly ever hang a big one.

And you have to set special lines to catch one that big. This time I told you about, we hung that big one on a big goggle-eye perch. It was a big goggle-eye on one side of that sinker and this pollywog, an ol' black cat-fish, on the other side. It was laying right on the bottom. And we caught this other one on the other side that was thirty-two pounds. What it was, it was a male and a female, you see. He's a big ol' male, and the one we caught was a female. They travel together.

Course them things, a lot of time they'll get off. They'll start raising cain. I saved out one time a thirty-pounder. He was about to go over the front end of the boat, and I grabbed the boat paddle and hit him right on the nose and knocked him back in. And once me and my nephew caught a thirty-five-pounder, and he grabbed that line from that fish's mouth and tied it around his leg. Says, "If he goes over I'll be going up and down with him!"

The ops won't bite nothing but live bait. Blue channel cats, you can catch them on beef heart and liver, but they love chicken liver. They'll take your line away from you on chicken liver! I lost my whole rig down there at Lake Houston, right behind the dam. I says, "Well, I'm gonna try this

chicken liver," and I let that thing down, and something grabbed it and just took my line with it. I held on to my rod, says, "You ain't gonna get this rod! Heck fire, no way! I ain't gonna let you get this rod and reel!" And he just kept going until he got to the end of the line and just popped it and kept going.

If I was going after that big un down there, I would get me about a number thirty cord staging—we call it staging going from the trotline to the hook. That's what I would do. Put it on there and then get me some big perch or pollywogs and get about ten-ought hooks, steel hooks, and tie it on something limber so he won't tear loose and so it'll give him some play and wear hisself down. If you put it on something solid, anything like that, it won't work.

Well, heck fire! There's a creek comes in up there, and that's where I'd love to go and put a big trotline. Yes I would. We'll go up there and just sink it right down on the bottom and just let her lay there. Put some big perch on it and I bet you we'll come out of there with some good uns too! We'll do it!

Dudley Denmon

I'll tell you what—you fool around on these rivers and you'll locate fish just by fooling around. When I was doing commercial fishing I could open that boat wide open and go down one part of that river, and I could tell you there's no scale fish there. Then you'll hit another section of the river, and I'll tell you, "Yes sir! There's buffaloes in this river." I smell them ——, you see! I smell for 'em.

I'll tell you my whole amount of experience in trotline fishing. Around in the month of October, clean on into about December or January, is good months to fish. I been catfishing since I was a little bitty boy, and I have learned that if you use live bait on your hook deep down in the water, just off of the bottom, in the fall of the year and in the summertime, you'll more likely catch fish.

I'm the first man that ever started baiting with soap. I started baiting with soap when I wasn't over seven years old, and I'll be seventy years old right away. I started baiting with P&G soap. My mother loved to wash in an ol' tub, and we'd have soap for the water, and I asked her could I have a piece of soap. Took it out there to put it on my trotline, 'cause I couldn't get no other kind of bait, and the next morning I had two ten-pound blue cat on it! Well, man, I been fishing with soap ever since. P&G wrote me a letter and told me, says, "Mr. Denmon, we're fixing to close out on the P&G, and if you want a case or two, you had better go right now to the store to get what soap you want to get, 'cause we're gonna close out on it." So, when they closed out on P&G, I went to Ivory soap, and I been using little bitty blocks of Ivory soap ever since.

Now, for little ol' fiddlers, three-pounders on down to pound-and-a-half channel cats, these little ol' fiddlers, you can catch hell out of 'em on soap. If it's springtime and the water's up high, you get back out in the backwoods in the water and set you a tightline, what they call a tightline, in the water. Look like a clothesline out there. I have fished 'em with fourteen or fifteen hooks on 'em, thirty-six inches apart. Adjust your hooks about two inches in the water. That's the law; that's legal. Now, if you gonna fish a tightline in the river, you gotta get somewhere out of the boats roads. You cannot fish a tightline across the river or anything like that; you gotta get up against the bank with it and hang your hooks about two inches deep in the water. Anyway, pull that line just as tight as a fiddle string, and then put your hooks on your line and let 'em hang about two inches deep in the water, and you'll catch them fiddlers or the little blue cat up to about three- or four-pounders.

Now, for bigger fish than that, you gonna have to use sinker lines. You can use sinker lines and just use one sinker on that line, a short line. You never use nothing but short lines in this river here. If you try to use a long line, you gonna get a hogwater—got a lotta trash—and it's gonna break your line all to hell and gone. I usually always fish with from three to five hooks on a line, right up against the bank from a treetop back to the bank or from an ol' snag back to the bank, right along beside the bank. Fish are funny things; they feed along aside the bank, but they got regular runs. Just 'cause you set a trotline out there and you didn't catch nothing, that don't mean there ain't no fish. You just missed 'em; that's all there is to it!

I used to be a commercial fisherman, and I done a lots of net fishing when net fishing was open—hoop nets, trammel nets, and gill nets—all kind of net stuff. The most fish I ever caught in one day is one thousand seven hundred eighty-six pounds, but hell, I had thirty-seven hoop nets and a thousand foot of gill net and about six hundred fifty foot of trammel net. So that's why I was really catching some fish. That was back out in the ol' lake places and out in the backwoods. You don't do that in the river. Trinity River is the only place I know of that you can really catch them buffalo and blue and drum—some people call 'em drum, some of 'em call 'em ghoul—out in the river. On Neches River, you gotta net or trotline fish against the bank. In Trinity River, you gotta fish right in the middle of the river to catch 'em. Over here in the Sabine River, you can fish a net against the bank, a hoop net, just like you do in Neches River. But now, you get on down in Trinity River and you put a net alongside the bank, you won't catch a fish a month!

What you do, to set your hoop net, you start from one side of the river with a drag, a line with a weight on it, and go towards the other side. You'll find a drop-off out there somewhere. Somewhere in that river there's a channel with a little ol' drop-off, what they call a second bank. Now, when you find that second bank, fill you a tow sack 'bout half full of sand and drop it down there and tie your tail line of your net to it. Any kind of weight that'll hold that net is all right. Then let the net stretch out good and tight. I always tie a piece of trotline onto my rope lead line. You gotta have a rope on there that you can start pulling on whenever you go to lift up on your net. You tie a piece of trotline on the end of that lead line and tie you a chip on it where it will float, then pull that string out straight in the river. And about two to four feet from the end of that line you put a sinker on it, any kind of a little old sinker to hold the end of it down. You gotta have a bush spotted over there on the bank when you go to pick it up. You pick up that trotline thing that you got tied on the end of your lead line. You pull up on it until you reach your rope, then you take the rope and pull the front of your net on up. And sometimes, over there in Trinity River you'll have as much as two hundred to two hundred fifty pounds of fish in one net. Well, I want to tell you something; you get about two hundred pounds of them —— in a net and them trying to get out, and they're something to pull in a boat! There's an art to raising that thing just like there is to everything else.

Now, about trotline fishing, I'm gonna tell you something. Out of all my experience, I wouldn't give a three- to five-hook line for no trotline that is in the river, because I find that what you gotta do, you gotta find where the fish run. You gotta find the run wherever they're feeding at or running to. And if you don't find that, you can put a long line, short line, any kind of line you want to out there, and it ain't gonna help very much. Put you three to five hooks on a little bitty line and just use one sinker in the middle, or you can use two sinkers, one at each end, and pull it down kind of straight across. You go from a stob to the bank or from a treetop to the bank. You don't go straight out, you go angling.

In this river here, it like to run me nuts when I first come here because at all the other streams I've ever fished in in my life you fish across the current. Whichever way the current's running, you want to go straight across it. But not in this river here! My friend, you'll starve to death fishing that way. You've got to fish right up close to the bank and you've gotta stay out of the way of that trash. This river's got the most trash in it of any place I've ever fished. Ever time it rains, why, man, it'll tear your tackle all to pieces if you go from bank to bank.

You'll have to use live bait, because oppelousas fish is mostly what you'll catch in deep waters. When the water gets hot up on top, you have to go to deep water—deepest hole you can find. These people that use these telephones and microwaves, they done found them deep holes, too, and they tear 'em up. I knew the first boy that ever raised a fish out of the water with a telephone. I told him then and there, "Boy, if this thing is widely spread, there won't be no fish." They say it don't hurt a scaled fish—it does. It hits him in the gills and it goes out his poopsie, or else it'll hit him in the poopsie and go out his gills. And it'll turn them eggs just as black as smut, when them eggs are in a certain stage in a scaled fish. And a telephone kills every crawfish that gets in the range of it, and a microwave does the same thing. But this old boy that I was telling you about that come up with that hookup, the first one I ever seen, I went to raising hell with 'em in Austin right then. Said, "Get a law passed on electrical devices." But those people in Austin laughed at me, said, "Oh, hell, you'd have to have a REA Caterpillar and pull a generator up beside the river to kill them fish." And I said,

"You're ―― wrong, my friend." I said, "By God, you send me six game wardens over here, 'cause I want to show them ―― something, and then they'll sure have you all's minds convinced." Well, they sent me six game wardens. I hooked up one of them phones and took 'em out there and showed 'em what they'd do. They went back and they passed a law against electrical devices being used in the water with a fine of twenty-five dollars or something. ――! You just as well forget that twenty-five dollars! Fellow, they'll make twenty-five dollars in twenty-five minutes! What in the hell does a twenty-five dollar fine mean? Finally they got it up there when they put a two-hundred dollar fine and six months in jail.

Now they don't use the old-timey crank phone, but they do still do it. I called the game warden up here a while back and he picked up two highway patrol and a deputy sheriff to get one of 'em, and they took him out of town and turned him loose! Now they're using them microwaves. Man, a microwave ain't bigger than a penny matchbox! And hell, it knocks out everything. People don't realize it, but it destroys the catfish's food, the food for all kind of fish. When it kills a minnow, he goes to the bottom, he don't come to the top. Listen, fellow! Use to, you could set out any kind of a little ol' shrimp trap for freshwater shrimp in any of the holes around about, and you could catch all the freshwater shrimp you wanted to bait your lines with. But you can't catch a shrimp anymore, for the simple reason that them 'lectros, they killed 'em! When I was about seven years old we taken a tub of water and put some crawfish in it and give that thing one little crank, and it killed every crawfish in that tub. It killed 'em dead, and they do not rise. So, I been hell on these 'lectros, on any kind of electrical device. I've always wanted to see a time when you or me or anybody could go and set 'em out some hooks and catch 'em a big mess of fish. If people would adhere to the legal laws, they're for the protection of these things.

These boys that's got 'em an ol' telephone or microwave that just goes out there every once in a year and catches a mess of fish, that don't hurt the fish population real bad. But what does hurt is some of these ―― skunks that do commercial fishing. They're so lazy they ain't gonna bait no hooks. They'll run down that river and they'll set out three or four lines, as a cover, and they'll tie out can after can of dog food. They'll put a sinker on it and jab it full of holes and tie it to a snag. Bait them fish up and then they hit 'em with a telephone or microwave. That's bad business.

An oppelousas is not very bad about biting nothing when he first sees it. That son-of-a-gun will just lay around there and he'll watch it and he'll watch it and he'll lay around, and it may be three or four days before he decides to bite it. And if he's gonna bite it, he's gonna swallow it from the head. He'll take on anything from the head. Once, I caught one weighed thirty-seven pounds on a three-pound ghoul. That ghoul come along and got caught on a shiner that I had on a little ol' hook on my line, and I hooked that ghoul through his eyeballs and him hanging there. I just left the ―― there 'cause I don't like 'em no way. I left him there for bait, and about four days later there was a thirty-seven-pound oppelousas had swallowed that son-of-a-gun, and there wasn't no hook in that oppelousas at all. He swallowed that ghoul from his head, and the old ghoul raised up his fins—every time you pulled on that ol' ghoul them fins would stick in that ol' oppelousas' gut on the inside, and you could lead him just like leading a horse.

But you've almost got to have some kind of live bait for an oppelousas fish. If you're going after a big op you got to have some live bait and 'bout a number six hook. I'll tell you exactly how that come about. It was the strangest thing you ever seen. It was when I was about fourteen years old. I drove my old rig as close to the river as I could get going over an old logging road. I didn't have no boat, so I went off down the rivers and sloughs around there looking for something or another I could build a raft of. I found a little dugout boat that had a hole burned in the bottom of it. I taken a old bunch of rags and stuffed 'em in that hole and put that little ol' dugout boat in the river and set me out some trotlines out there. I caught me some sun perch, big ol' sun perch big as your hand, and I found a deep hole over against the left bank straight across from a sandbar. I put some of them sun perch on the line. It had, I think, ten or twelve hooks on it, something like that. I sunk it down way deep—I'd say them hooks was hanging about four or five inches from the bottom of the river. I hooked them sun perch most of 'em through the back, where they could swim. Then I went out there and discovered I had caught me a big fish out there. What I did, I went to the sandbar side and I took the hooks off it back down to where I would disturb the ol' fish. then I eased on around to the other end where I had it tied and untied the branch of a snag I had it tied to. Then I taken both ends of that trotline and I headed for that sandbar just paddling like hell, 'cause there wasn't no way in the world I could put that fish in no dugout canoe!

I was leading that fish, leading him just like leading a horse, and when I got over there where the water was little more than knee-deep and stepped out of that little ol' dugout, I shoved the thing real hard to make it go to the bank. Then I got that ol' fish coming and I was carrying him so fast I done skidded him ten feet up on the sandbar 'fore he knowed what in hell was going on! He dressed eighty-seven pounds. He was a big fish. I sold that fish to a church that wanted a big fish for a fish fry. They gave me twenty-five cents a pound. Back in them days dressed fish sold for twenty-five cents a pound. Hell, I've sold fish for three cents a pound—blue cat.

Later, I caught another one over here in Sabine River big as that. He weighed ninety-six pounds. I caught him on a goggle-eye perch. I set a little ol' line there, didn't have but around half a dozen hooks on it. I sunk it down to about four inches off the bottom.

Now, that's one thing about your trotline fishing, if you're fishing in the summertime and trying to catch a big fish and you use live bait, you want to adjust your sinker string long enough that when the sinker is laying on the bottom your hook will be about four inches off the bottom. You know, catfish got eyes in the top of his head; they ain't in the bottom. They looking out to the side or they looking out ahead or they're looking above, but that's about it. They can't very well see something flat on the bottom. I never had any luck catching any kind of big fish without the bait kind of swinging, you know. Them things feed on the bottom, sure, and what they'll do they'll move into them leaves around them sandbars and places and run them shrimp out, and they feed off them shrimp and them shiners, off them little fish.

That ol' loggerhead turtle, that's something! The old lady caught one not too long ago. That son-of-a-gun, his old hull is mossy-colored, you know, mossy-looking, old loggerhead, and he'll open his mouth, he turns his bottom-side upward, and when he opens that mouth he's like a steel trap. He buries that head down in the mud or leaves, and he's got a long black tongue that he sticks way out and makes it wiggle like a worm. A little ol' fish come up there and grabs him by his tongue, and he stuffs that tongue in and snaps that fish and eats him. He don't ever prowl around and hunt fish. Whenever his eating gets scarce he just moves over to a new location and sets up housekeeping again. See, he can't run nothing down to eat it, so he got to make a way of catching his food, and that's the way it is. His ol' mouth can bite a broomstick in two or a hoe handle. Hell, I've caught one that weighed eighty pounds. I brought him from down here on the hill to Mr. J. W. Primrose when he was living. He had some cotton scales. I took him out there and weighed him and he weighed eighty pounds. Well, about a week from then I caught another one on the same line that weighed forty pounds. They both looked just alike, but one of 'em was a male and the other one of 'em was a female.

I did one time in my life catch a turtle in a hoop net. And that —— was so big he couldn't go in the back of that net at all! He went into the front pocket of the net, but that son-of-a-gun couldn't get out of there and he couldn't go through the back. I just guessed at his weight—I'd say he weighed somewhere around ninety or a hundred pounds. He was a hard hull. My oldest daughter was with me when I raised the net, and I seen what it was—that ol' turtle was blowing water everywhere—and I let the net back down and went home and got the shotgun and carried it back there and shot him, 'cause that's the only way you can handle them things. You gotta shoot 'em, 'cause, hell, they'll bite your arm plumb off.

I've got a gar's picture here at the house, a picture of a gar that measured eleven feet eight inches long. I had an ol' '54 Chevrolet car, and it could not pull that fish on dry land in high gear. I was fishing gill nets in Hardin County at that time, in the backwater. I went to one of these gill nets one morning there, my wife was with me, and there was an alligator about six or eight feet long with his nose tangled up in my net. I pulled on the net and got him up there and kept flipping them strings off of this teeth and turned the son-of-a-gun aloose. Then I said, "Now, if you get back in there you gonna mess around here and make me mad. I'll go to the house and get the gun and shoot hell out of you!" The very next morning we went to this same net in the same location and there was something hung in the tail of the net, and man, it would run out with the tail of that net and throw water ten feet high! Well, I got hold the lead line and kept easing up there to where I could see what it was, and it was what you call an alligator gar. I just let the net back down and started the motor and went back down to where my brother-in-law lived on the bank of the lake down there. And I borrowed his gun, thirty-thirty rifle, and got two boys in another aluminum boat. I was in a little ol' aluminum boat, me and the wife was, fourteen-foot Arkansas Traveler boat, and we got two boys, our oldest sons, to go with us. And I taken a forty-foot rope, and I threwed that rope over a limb in a tree and tied around that lead line. I told them boys, I said, "Now, you'll put that rope when I tell you, pull up on that rope and keep that son-of-a-gun still long enough so I can shoot him." So them old boys pulled up on that rope on the lead line and got his head up far enough so I could get a shot in him, and I shot him three times right through the head and killed him. Then the wife got over on the boat with the boys. Me and her couldn't stay on the boat and put the gar on there! I drew up that gar's tail, and them boys and I pulled his head up onto the aluminum boat I was on, and the boys pulled his tail up and put it on the boat they was on, and then we laid that ol' gar down on the top of my boat and I didn't have but about two inches of my boat sticking out. Just nobody but me and that gar and that little ol' motor on there. We got to the landing and took that ol' car that I had there and tied the rope around that gar's bill and drug him up the dang bank with that ol' car. Then my wife, my sister-in-law, my oldest son, his first cousin, and another boy and me all got ahold of the rope and were a-heaving and pulling and a-pulling and a-heaving! Finally we decided to tie the rope onto that car and got him up to where we hung him in a tree—we put the rope over a limb. I still got his picture, eleven feet and eight inches long! I'd say he weighed in the neighborhood of three hundred pounds. He could have swallowed a seven-year-old kid and it hardly wouldn't have tick-led his tonsils! That was a big rascal.

When me and the wife first come here, I didn't have no boat, didn't have no motor, didn't have nothing. Had our bed in this old panel-body truck, and we camped right here. I taken a throw line and tied one end of that line to a bush on the bank and put seven hooks on it. I put me a piece of iron on the end of it and put some bait on them hooks and then I throwed that line back out in the river. Well, me and her caught all the fish we wanted to eat for a long time with that seven hooks on that throw line. Well, one day she said, "I'm gonna throw that sinker out there." And she throwed that sinker out there, and she hit this big old fish right in the top of the head! He was out there five or six inches under the water, she hit him in the head with that sinker, and that son-of-a-gun, he really boiled the water! We watched him, and he went nearly half a bend from there.

I hung him one time on the point of a sandbar over here, and he broke my hook. He's a bullheaded blue. That blue cat, no telling how many hundred hooks he's got in his mouth. The rows of teeth he's got in the upper part of his jaws would be about two inches wide. The fins that goes down his back is six, eight inches wide, and its old head is a big old chuckle-headed rascal. Now, he's what they call a bullheaded blue cat, not a hump-back blue, and he takes these ol' little bitty hooks and eats them every morning for breakfast. That son-of-a-gun got more of them little hooks in his mouth than you remember what to do with, but he don't pay 'em no mind. It's not nothing to him. It's just like a little thorn or something. But he can straighten them eight-ought hooks just as straight as your finger, and nobody ever was able to hold that fish.

He moved from up here where I hung him and went down about four bends from here. I located him down there. I was with my kids on a sand-bar with some minnow jars catching some minnows to bait up with, and I kept seeing him churning around in the water. I used to see him about every thirty days. I could recognize him, 'cause when he comes up you can see that big high fin on his back. So, I recognized that old friend of mine, and we set out a line for him and baited that line with sun perch. And we hung him. He decided he wanted one of them, I guess, and come along and we hung him. I got the hook hanging right here on the wall. He straightened them eight-ought hook just straight as your finger. There ain't nobody been able to pick that fish up. There's been lots of people that's hung him. I caught him one time, I led him right up besides the boat one time, and he is one hell of a monstrous fish! I'd say that fish would go from ninety to one hundred ten pounds.

But now listen, I want to tell you something. I haven't seen that fish this whole year. Course, I ain't been on the river very much anymore, but I have not seen that fish. See, he ranges around, he roams around. He'll stay up here at this bend awhile, then he'll go back down about three or four bends from here. But I've not seen that fish in two years. So, somebody could have paralyzed him. Them big fish they stay in a deep hole until it rains.

He's strong enough that an electro or a microwave wouldn't get him there. The times that he's out of that hole, out in the open, that's the only time they'd get to him. They could have caught him out in the open and knocked all the oxygen out of his wind, his oxygen bags. That's all the hell them electros do anyway, them telephones and microwaves. That's why all the little fish, they'll get right up using their tail and go just like hell. They'll jump, or get out on the bank or anywhere—lay their head up on a stick or on the bank or just anyway. Them ——! I'm glad when they get caught.

I'm gonna tell you something. Anything that's an interest and a benefit to the children of this earth, the ones that's here, the ones that's growing up— it's a dirty shame for people to disregard and disrespect the creation of all these beautiful things that have been made, that people have privilege and opportunity to use, during their trip on this planet. They should think about them little fellows that is coming up and allow them the same privilege. If we don't respect this stuff and protect and defend it, they won't never know. They'll just say, "Well, that was something that old John Doe told us about a hundred years ago." They'd say, "There ain't no more of that. That's just an old story told by some of the old generation." I say that everything that the Great Master created is entitled to a certain amount of respect—that's what I tell 'em. I'm not a Christian, I'm just a hardhead, but I think everything is entitled to a certain amount of respect.

I've raised seven children in this world and we've got fifty-one in our family now and me and my wife been together nearly forty-nine years. I'm a-hoping that the things that people love in this world is gonna provide food for all the growing generations so that they can have a little fun and squirrel hunt and stuff. That's for the coming-up generations, not for me. I've got my face pushed up against the door of time.

Airborne Before Wright: The Flight of the Ezekial Airship

15 Now as I beheld the living creatures, behold one wheel upon the earth by the living creatures, with his four faces.

16 The appearance of the wheels and their work as like unto the color of a beryl: and they four had one likeness: and their appearance and their work was as it were a wheel in the middle of a wheel.

19 And when the living creatures went, the wheels went by them: and when the living creatures were lifted up from the earth, the wheels were lifted up.

20 Whithersoever the spirit was to go, they went, thither was their spirit to go; and the wheels were lifted up over against them: for spirit of the living creature was in the wheels.

22 And the likeness of the firmament upon the heads of the living creature was as the colour of the terrible crystal, stretched forth over their heads above.

Ezekiel 1

We first heard of the Ezekiel Airship from Susan Leitner of the *Longview Morning Journal*. She in turn directed us to Mrs. Harry McMinn who lives in Pittsburg, Texas. We visited her there and had an opportunity to talk with her and Roy Roundtree about the Reverend Burrell Cannon and his airship. They took us to the machine shop where Rev. Cannon's airship was built and to the field nearby where it was flown in 1902, a year before the Wright brothers' flight. And they provided us with related pictures and materials, including the report by Lacy L. Davis on the Ezekiel Airship, prepared for the Camp County Historical Committee. The report, in part, follows.

Being a native of this area of East Texas, I have heard of the Ezekiel Airship since my early childhood. I heard my parents tell of this Airship, heard it during my school years and have heard of it in more recent years. The story, of course, varied each time I heard it. Naturally, I have wondered just what is the true story. Perhaps we will never know the true details. Time has a way of erasing these things unless they are recorded. It is now "later than we think," but maybe not too late to get a few notes on what we know and what we have heard about this Airship and to record them before they are lost. You see, most of those close to this project are gone now and the only witnesses left are second-hand witnesses—those who have heard from eyewitnesses. The Camp County Historical Committee decided early in 1975 to secure, if possible, an Historical Marker to commemorate this event and to locate it as near as possible to the original site where the Airship was built. Someone then had to do some research and prove to the Texas Historical Committee in Austin that such an event actually took place. There never has been much doubt that the Airship was actually constructed, but there has been much doubt that it actually flew in a test flight. Here now are the results of my research on this event.

I suppose I should say this Airship had its beginnings in our Holy Bible. Rev. Burrell Cannon studies his Bible and found something very interesting in the first and tenth chapters of the book of Ezekiel. The Prophet Ezekiel described a "vehicle," a sort of "wheel within a wheel," which flew through the air. Also being an inventor and machinist, Rev. Cannon was intrigued with these strange things, and the pages of Ezekiel in his Bible became worn and ragged as he pored over these verses. He drew plans and made models for some twenty years before finally deciding his plans were perfected and he arranged to start construction.

Rev. Cannon was born April 16, 1848, in Coffeeville, Mississippi. He attended Mississippi College at Clinton, Mississippi. He was trained as a blacksmith and a machinist. He was ordained as a Baptist preacher before reaching the age of twenty. He could speak several foreign languages and served for some time as a missionary. He was a member of the Masonic Lodge, became a 33rd-degree Mason, and was chaplain of his lodge at the time of his death. We do not know when he first came to Texas but we do have a copy of a letter, headed at Gladewater, Texas, and dated in 1886. We believe that he came to this area shortly thereafter because there was a Cannon Switch or Station on the Cotton Belt Railroad shortly thereafter, supposedly named for him. I have an old newspaper, *The Lafayette Iron Record*, published at Lafayette, Texas, on November 3, 1893, and it contains the Cotton Belt passenger schedule. It gives the stop at Pine, Texas, and Cannon Station as being the same time. His family tells that he usually purchased a tract of standing timber, cut enough to build a house for his family, then cut and sold the rest. Unless he bought additional timber in the same area, he then moved to another area. You see, he did not make his livelihood by preaching, but rather by sawmilling. Old-time residents of

Reverend Burrell Cannon.

the area say the timber purchased at that time was located south of the present Pine community and just west of the present farm of Carl Pilgrim, also west of the old Bates place, on what later became known as the "Son" Wallace place. This would be just over into Upshire County, south of Pine. Rev. Cannon and his family lived in Pine at that time near where the lone store of that community now stands. We were told that this man preached in this area many times. The Baptist Church at Pine was not organized until 1905 according to the present pastor, Rev. E. P. Wooten. Old-timers say he preached on Sundays in a one-room school house in this community at this time. He was also seen experimenting with "some strange contraption" in a local pasture during his stay there. Mr. W. W. Fowler, now of Gilmer, tells of visiting this man's home and seeing "some strange contraption" on his back porch. They believe these strange contraptions were models of his airship. He was supposed to have built several different ones. Stories now differ as to whether his family moved to Pittsburg later. I have heard all my years in Pittsburg that they lived at what was later 227 Lafayette Street. Mrs. Nina Berry, a retired school teacher of this city, said that this was their home while working on the Airship here. I might add that Mrs. Berry has been interested in this Airship story for many years and has told it many times in her history classes.

After the Airship was destroyed near Texarkana, the family moved to that area and Rev. Cannon once again worked at the sawmilling trade. Later, he moved to the Longview area and lived with his children until his death on August 9, 1923. His body was buried in Grace Hill Cemetery in Longview. His step-daughter, Mrs. C. F. Gordon, resided in Longview until her death a few years ago. Mrs. Gordon was interviewed a number of times by newspaper reporters and I have a copy of several of these interviews. She has children and grandchildren still residing in the East Texas area.

Being a sawmiller, it would seem natural that he would occasionally need the services of a machine shop. Pittsburg had one, the Pittsburg Foundry and Machine Shop, owned and operated by Mr. P. W. Thorsell. Rev. Cannon began to try to interest others in his airship project and in the summer of 1901 he met with Mr. Thorsell and others in the Court House in Pittsburg. They decided to form a corporation to build this Airship. A few days later, this group met at the Carnegie Library and elected officers for the new corporation. The officers first elected were: J. J. Tapp, President; P. W. Thorsell, Vice-President; W. C. Hargrove, Secretary; A. J. Askew, Treasurer; and R. W. Heath, P. W. Tapp, B. Cannon, J. C. Bailey, R. G. Lewis, S. D. Snodgrass, and C. A. Dickson as Directors. This group incorporated the EZEKIEL AIRSHIP MFG. CO. in August of 1901, for the amount of $20,000, and agreed to sell shares for $25.00 each as needed to finance the project. As interest grew, those having the shares were offered as much as ten times their original value for them. I might add that Mr. Charles Winkle, who has had one of these original stock certificates for a number of years, recently gave it to the Camp County Historical Committee.

Work was started soon on the Airship on the upper floor of the new brick building of the Pittsburg Foundry and Machine Shop. This is the same building still standing at 131 W. Fulton Street on the Cotton Belt Railroad, which many refer to as the foundry building. Not so, as the shell of the foundry still stands west of the building. According to local historians, Mr. Rowe Lockett, a machinist at the Pittsburg Foundry and Machine Shop, was assigned to work full time on this project for Rev. Cannon. Mr. Morris Thorsell later verified this for me in an interview with him.

While doing my research on this project, I visited this old building and talked to the present owner, Mr. Haskell Smith. "Hank" took me upstairs and showed me the area where the Airship was built. He took me to a room, one of several now partitioned off upstairs, and showed me three cardboard boxes of old papers. The building leaks and a recent rain had these boxes and papers soaking wet. He showed me some of the papers and gave me permission to take them, look them over, and return them to the shop. I took them home and dried them out as best I could. Among other things, I found about thirty old "work-sheets" filled out by machine shop employees during the year 1902, and having at least one entry of "Airship" on them. It seems that each day each machine shop employee entered on

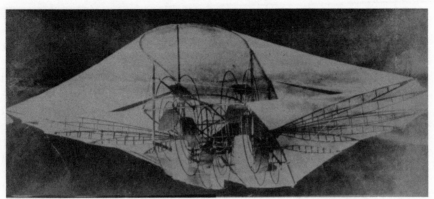

This picture of the Ezekiel Airship, dated 1898, is the only original picture in existence.

one of these sheets the various machines worked on during that day, the owner, time on each machine, and material used, if any, on each job. This I suppose, was the way the front office had in knowing how much to charge each customer. Evidently, Rev. Cannon, or Ezekiel Airship Co., was charged for all work done by machine shop employees. Names of employees having worked on the Airship (as shown on the bottom of the worksheets) were; Bill Roark, J. B. Stamps, Gus Stamps, D. E. Allread, and F. B. Abbott. The dates on these sheets with entries "Airship" were from March, 1902, to October, 1902. After photographing several of these, I returned them to the same location from which I took them. Several weeks later, upon the insistence of Cannon family descendants, I asked Hank for these thirty some odd sheets for the family. He gave them to the family and I picked them up for them—sopping wet from another rain. Mr. Smith was very courteous and helpful to me and was willing to do anything to help in our research. The same was true of his employee, Mr. Gober. Mr. Smith would not, however, say that he would promise to keep the building in good repair—a requirement of the Texas Historical Committee if a marker is to be placed on a building. He said present business conditions would not justify the expense in putting the building in first class condition.

In one of her interviews, Mrs. Gordon tells this story. It seems that after the Airship was finished, it was not possible to move it by way of the stairway and the doors present in the building. Another door was cut in the south wall near the upper floor level through which to remove the vehicle. I found an entry on a worksheet dated November, 1902, marked "door." Could this be that door? Mr. Morris Thorsell, during an interview with him, said he doubted this story. If it is true, then a brick mason did a good job in rebuilding around this door. It looks just like the other doorways.

Other than the dates on the worksheets, no other date has been found to indicate when the Airship was finished. Local stories say it was finished in the winter of 1902–1903. The same sources say the Airship was loaded shortly afterward onto a railway flat-car for transportation to St. Louis for exhibition. I have a copy of a newspaper article stating, "July 4—Rev. Cannon returned today from Washington, where he made application for patents in America and most foreign countries on his Airship which is nearing completion . . ." Enroute to St. Louis, the Airship was destroyed when a storm blew it off the railway flat-car near Texarkana. A granddaughter of Rev. Cannon, Mrs. Lenita Tacea, has furnished me with much of the material used in this research. Among other things, she furnished me with a copy made from newspaper items published in the *Dallas News* of 1923 and other papers as early as 1901. In a recent telephone conversation with her, she told of the Airship being destroyed on the flat-car and that her mother had told of her grandfather's remarks at the time: "God never willed that this Airship should fly—I want no more to do with it," and with that he left the Airship where it lay.

Mrs. Gordon, in another of her interviews, said that Rev. Cannon later became interested once more in his Airship and again sold stock in the Longview area from 1908 to 1913. Another Airship was then built in Chicago and was flown by a Mr. Wilder who went only a short distance before hitting a telephone pole, tearing a hole in the bottom of the ship. Rev. Cannon again abandoned his Airship project and began working on other inventions. Mrs. Tacea does not recall hearing of the second Airship when I asked her about it.

An article published in the *Dallas News* of November 25, 1923, has much to say about the Ezekiel story. It contains articles first printed in the same newspaper in an issue in 1900 or 1901. Rev. Cannon wrote to them of his plans to build an Airship and gave them much data about the Airship itself. He said he had started a model measuring 21 × 26 feet in size. I believe this was the final Airship rather than a model. (The article says the date was 1900, yet in the same article it mentions the company being formed and incorporated. I believe this should be 1901 as the company was formed in 1901. The article also mentioned a "prospectus" being offered by the company.) The "prospectus" offers the stock for sale, saying it will make the owners millionaires. A 8 × 10 photo of the Airship could be purchased for fifty cents and for a two-cent stamp, an explanation of the first and tenth chapters of Ezekiel could be had. The photo now owned by Mr. John Bland possibly is one of these offered for sale in 1901. This same paper said Rev. Cannon wrote, "The machine, as constructed, has four wheels, driven by a gas engine with sprocket chain transmission. Inside each wheel was an inner wheel, a bit smaller than the other wheel, and on each one of these inner wheels was a fan with four blades. The wheels were so hooked up with the engine that when the outer wheels turned one revolution forward, the inner wheels went half a revolution backwards. Propulsive force was given to the machine by the fans striking the air under the control of the inner wheels. The fans moved at the rate of the rim of the inner wheel, and could act on the air at any speed up to three miles a minute. . . . Once in the air, its direction was controlled by the angle of the fan blades. In short, the fans were supposed not only to give propulsive force to the machine but also act as rudders and, in as much as they could be shifted in a moment, turning on the inner wheel so as to strike the air at any desired angle, the theory was that the ship could move in any direction, depending on the angle of the whirling blades without the rotary motion of the wheels being stopped." The company also planned on making ship propellers using this same principle. The propelling force could be changed from forward to backward by changing the pitch and angle of the blades without stopping the propeller. Rev. Cannon was supposed to have obtained a patent on this feature, although the date and patent number is unknown at this time. Rev. Cannon defied any engineer to look over his plans and to prove him wrong in his calculations.

Perhaps by now you have wondered why no mention has been made so far as to the Airship having been flown here in Pittsburg. Since this is the part over which much controversy has arisen, maybe we should first define our terms; such as what constitutes flight. My definition for *Flight* (under these circumstances, at least) would be: it should lift off the ground, travel for some distance, and land—being under the control of some person or persons all the time. Now, if you agree with me, let's see what happened.

Interview with Mr. Morris Thorsell (son of P. W. Thorsell and later owner of the machine shop before selling to Mr. Smith): During the early 1900's, a Mr. Stamps of Gilmer visited the machine shop and talked to him about the Ezekiel Airship. He worked at the machine shop when the Airship was being built and did some work on it himself. Mr. Thorsell could not recall which of the men named Stamps it was. (Two men by that name had signed worksheets as having worked on the Airship.) He also said he was present when the test flight was made and was the pilot. He said the Airship was taken to Mr. P. W. Thorsell's pasture for the flight. This was diagonally across the street and railroad from the machine shop. He got in the machine and the engine was started. He said the ship lurched forward for a short distance before rising vertically into the air. He indicated that it went up only a few feet and began to "drift" for some distance. He noticed that it vibrated considerably and became alarmed and shut off the engine, after which the ship came back down. When questioned about the vibration by Mr. Thorsell, he explained: "The ship was designed to have power from the engine transmitted to the wheels by a chain-link drive." (Bicycles have chain-link drives.) By this time, the backers were discouraged, the company was broke and no more funds could be raised. No money was available to purchase a chain-link drive, so a substitute was used—a poor one at that. The only available substitute was a dust chain, a cheap chain used at sawmills to remove the accumulation of sawdust from under the saw out to one side and out of the way, certainly never designed for power transmission. Mr. Thorsell told of talking to Mr. Rowe Lockett about the Airship. He said all of the Airship, including the engine, was built locally at the machine shop. The engine was heavy, in his opinion too heavy for the Airship, and was designed to operate on kerosene.

Interview with Mrs. Carl Tacea of New Orleans: (Mrs. Tacea is the daughter of Rev. Cannon's eldest daughter, Margie Burrellina Prothro.) Mrs. Tacea has done much research on the life of her grandfather and has furnished me with much of the information I have on his life. She has told me she has heard her mother tell many times that the Airship did fly here in Pittsburg. She said it flew over one hundred and sixty feet, but rose only about ten-twelve feet above the ground during this flight. She said it flew over a fence and hit the fence as it went over. She recalls that the fence was a plank fence and seemed to recall it was built zig-zag fashion, though not a rail fence.

Letter from H. Ray Coley: As a result of publicity recently about this Airship, we received a letter from this man. He says his mother, who grew up in Pittsburg, has often told him of this Airship. Her story told of another man being lifted off the ground as the Airship lifted into the air. It seems he became entangled with a rope attached to it. Mrs. Coley was a young girl, nine years of age, when the test flight was made and is still living at this time. Mr. Coley is under the impression that his mother actually saw this test flight. We are still trying to get more information from this lady.

Shortly after beginning research on this project, I met Mrs. Ann Stroud of Tyler, who is a great-granddaughter of Rev. Cannon. She told me the same story that Mrs. Tacea had told me: Many times they, as well as their children, had mentioned that their ancestors built an airplane (airship) before the Wright Brothers and it flew. No one seemed to want to believe them. Mrs. Stroud was pleased that an attempt was being made to get the Historical Marker and agreed to help in rounding up much of the material held by Rev. Cannon's descendants. This she did and has helped in many ways in making contact with members of her family.

Did the Airship really fly? I believe, after reviewing my information, that it actually lifted off the ground. I believe it traveled some distance through the air and then landed. But—was it under control during its flight? That is the big question. None of those interviewed seemed to indicate that any attempt was made to control its flight. Perhaps, due to the limited space in the pasture, it was impossible.

The Ezekiel Airship

Baptist minister and inventor Burrell Cannon (1848–1922) led some Pittsburg inventors to establish the Ezekiel Airship Company and build a craft described in the biblical book of Ezekiel. The ship had large, fabric-covered wings powered by an engine that turned four sets of paddles. It was built in a nearby machine shop and was briefly airborne at this site late in 1902, a year before the Wright brothers first flew. Enroute to the St. Louis World's Fair in 1904, the airship was destroyed by a storm. In 1913 a second model crashed, and the Rev. Cannon gave up the project.

Texas Historical Commission Marker,
Fulton Street, Pittsburg, Texas

The Hanging of Joe Shields

No matter what a great stir they make at the time, most of the events of a community's history pass away into the oblivion of forgotten documents. Some events, however, are very different and take on a life of their own in oral tradition. The tragic Shelby County hanging of Joe Shields in 1892 is one of these.

Loblolly found many persons who remembered the controversies surrounding the murder of Joe Shields and still had opinions about what really happened on that fateful night. Some of them preferred that we did not use their names in association with the stories they told us, even though almost a century has passed since the events described. Eyewitnesses to the events surrounding the hanging were all dead, so the testimony we collected was not oral history but oral traditional history or oral hearsay—stories told to the children and grandchildren of the eyewitnesses and repeated to us. Because of the general fascination with the tragedy of Joe Shields, these stories have been passed down within families and within the community at large. As they were repeated, they often took on details of folklore and traditional belief. For example, one person told us how someone heard a hen crow on that dark night—a well-known harbinger of death.

We began collecting from the living traditions of community folk history about the hanging of Joe Shields and went on to examine contemporary newspaper accounts and appellate court records. Joe Shields must have been a handsome man and popular with the ladies, and the traditional account attributes his death to the jealousy that evoked in other local young men. As readers will find, however, the full story may have been somewhat different. But as in the case of our account of Bonnie Parker and Clyde Barrow in *The Loblolly Book*, persons must be left to draw their own conclusions.

The Ballad of Joe Shields

In eighteen hundred and ninety-two, to Texas Joe did come.
In the piney woods 'round Timpson town, Grandma and he made
    home.
In the days he worked in the fields and plowed,
But at night his heart grew light
So he went to the parties and he met all the girls
Who' swooned when he came in sight.

Chorus
Joe Shields was his name and he was quite handsome.
He lived good but he died young
At the end of a rope underneath an old oak tree.

A Friend

It was before my time. It happened in 1892. The night of this hanging, my mother was spending the night with a girlfriend. It was about two miles from where she lived. Back then the only social life they had was to spend time with close friends.

She was summoned to the trial of one or two of the men involved in the hanging. She went in a wagon, pulled by two mules, twenty-five miles to San Augustine. And among other things, Momma told us one of the clues in tracing down who was involved in it. The gang who did the act rode horses and mules. Among them was a crooked-footed mule or horse, I forget which. They traced that one to the house where my mother spent the night. They asked her if she heard anyone come in the night with horses, and she told them she did. So, we got what little we knew from Momma. She was like a lot of the rest of them, afraid to talk.

In about 1890, Grandpa and Grandma Pinson moved from Georgia to East Texas. There they cleared out a little spot of ground and built a small house on land my brother now owns. It was a log house. I well remember the log house. We used to go upstairs in cold weather and pick off peanuts with the wind whistling around the house. It's a fond memory to us, that part. We didn't know the bad part.

So after about two years, Mr. Pinson took pneumonia. And of course they didn't have penicillin and other drugs at that time, and he died. So Grandma Pinson wrote back to one of her daughters in Georgia. Mrs. Pinson asked her if she would let Joe Shields come and spend a while with her. Her daughter agreed to let him come, and in about two weeks he showed up.

Joe was a real attractive individual. He was about six foot two and weighed two hundred pounds or a little better. He was just the picture of an outstanding athlete. He had coal-black hair, deep blue eyes, ruddy complexion, and square shoulders. He was much of a man.

Because of the lack of any social life, if you had a neighbor within two miles you were fortunate. And that was the case of Mrs. Pinson. So the sparsely settled community had snap parties for the young people on Saturday night. So out of his loneliness and hunger for associations, Joe got to going to these parties. He'd saddle his horse and ride the three, four, or five miles to a party. So it wasn't long before the girls became attracted to him, at least some of them. And the boys noticed it. They didn't like it and decided to do something about it.

So they selected what they thought was their best fighter to whip Joe. Joe didn't want a fight. It was planned for one night at one of those parties. So this big old boy went to the door. They were in there playing snap. The boy invited Joe Shields outside. One of them challenged for a rassle or a boxing match or whatever, the one who challenged would just throw his hat out in the yard. Back then they wore hats in the house as well as outside. So as they went out on the porch and this old boy threw his hat in the yard, well, Joe knew what this meant. If the challenged one accepted, he just threw his hat out too. This old boy's hat had no more hit the ground until Joe's hat was right behind it. The story goes they went at it like two mad bulldogs. It wasn't long before Joe had pinned him down. And this boy saw that he couldn't cope with this good athlete. He told Joe to let him up. And Joe said he wanted to know if he'd had enough before he'd let him up. Anyhow he let him up and brushed himself off and went back to the party.

So the party went on and nothing else was said, but two weeks later he came to a party and the gang decided to put two on him. So they went through the same kind of procedure. Then two hats hit the ground. He didn't hesitate and sailed his on out too. There were two on one. They rassled and boxed around there, and finally old Joe got hold of one of them and threw him over his shoulder. The old boy hit the ground and had the wind knocked out of him and he couldn't get up. Joe and this other one continued fighting, and Joe finally pinned him. To make a long story short, they both agreed to let that one up. They'd had it. So Joe kind of cleaned himself up and went back in the house.

I don't know how long, maybe two or three weeks, Joe had been to a party. He came in. I learned recently he had dated a girl that night. That infuriated this gang. They had already planned to do it anyway. He had gotten home, unsaddled his horse, and was putting the saddle in the crib where they kept the corn. While he was doing that, while he was in the crib, that gang showed up. And they got him as he came out of the crib.

He did everything he knew to try to get them to leave him alone. They told him they were going to kill him. So they carried him off, out to the road about a hundred yards. Grandma Pinson followed, begging them not to take Joe off. And one of them hollered, "If you don't go back we'll kill you too." So she went back to the house. 'Long about this time, one of the men had a beard and evidently he and Joe had had a pretty good round that night. And Joe hollered to her, "Next time you see —— he'll need a shave." Joe identified one of them to Mrs. Pinson.

Now, there's a conflicting story on that. The little house down on the camp road—it's not there now—well, he lived there. And he was supposed to have tried to discourage the men. They went on anyway. But I was told this recently that this man really was in on it.

But anyhow, they went on over a hill and down across a branch and out to the woods. They first hanged Joe to a dogwood tree. The dogwood tree wouldn't hold him and bent. So they took him off and to an oak tree. I had one party tell me that on the way to the red oak tree Joe offered to fight any two of them. If he won they were to let him go. He offered to fight any three of them. They turned him down. They hanged him to a limb on this red oak tree. The tree is still alive. It's in a pasture down in the woods.

There were a lot of pines with a cross made in them. Most of them died off. There are two or three still alive there. Why that was done I don't know. The marks might have been put on by the posse the next day. The next morning they got enough together to go find him. Grandma Pinson had walked two miles to a neighbor during the night to tell them Joe had been taken.

There was one party who was supposed to be implicated in it. The story on him I heard might not be true. That is, later on he got sick and was delirious and was talking and telling the whole story and telling the names of the people involved. His wife called the doctor. She wouldn't let anybody in the room. The doctor put him under sedation until he died.

The violence was a way of life for those people. They took the law into their own hands. They were not going to have an outsider come into the community and mess with what they had going. It was jealousy most of all. Joe apparently had a good personality and was a good-looking man. He met every challenge they threw at him. If they'd whipped him in one of the fights, the hanging probably never would have happened. They decided to get rid of him, and that was it.

In my time I've seen two hangings. It was just a way of life. My daddy used to operate a gin. And there was a gin over on another road leading to Timpson. A fellow had gone down into the colored quarter, and I understand he got into a spat. A colored man was trying to protect someone. This colored man picked up a board and whacked the drunk man. The law came out and arrested the fellow and carried him to jail. They resented the affair. They changed jails. It upset a lot of people. Word got out the fellow was going to be turned loose. He had to take one of those roads past the gins. So there was a mob, and I heard them talking. He didn't come down our way but the other road, and the son of the man he killed shot him in the leg. So they carried him back and locked him up. A mob gathered, and they got a big pole and banged down the jail door. Then they took him out and hanged him right there on the courthouse square. But that's just one of several things that happened around. It wasn't peculiar just to that community. That was a way of life—violence and secrecy.

J. B. Sanders

Loblolly—Do you think times have changed as far as people's attitudes about hangings from back then?

J. B.—I don't think things have changed as to the curiosity about it. People would attend a hanging or run to a shooting scrape. People would still go, but the attitudes to hangings have. I think that in the book *Hangings in Shelby County* there were more whites hung than blacks by considerable number. Of course it was wrong with either of them. Mob rule is not the way for people to live.

J. B. Sanders

Loblolly—Mr. Sanders, will you tell us about this fellow Truitt—how he gathered his information when he was trying to dig out some information about the Joe Shields case?

J. B.—Well, it's rumored that in trying to get this information he tried to eavesdrop around all these houses of those who he thought might be connected or who might talk about it. And it's said he'd crawl up under a house until the whole family went to bed. He was hoping to get some little bit of information he could use in court. And he eventually got himself so worked up in this case that he committed suicide in one of the old-time gins up near Timpson. Mr. Truitt was a member of the Legislature and also a prominent lawyer.

Brother Bob Rhodes

This man that was in the school group came down here when he was hanging in the tree. That's the only thing I could go along with for sure. He was a little schoolboy then, but he was a grown man when he told me. The teacher brought the whole school, which was just up here the other side of the church, to see him hanging there in that tree. He was still hanging there. He said it was the worst thing the teacher could have done. It's a place of no good feeling.

Rusty Marshall

I first became familiar with the Joe Shields story in the spring of my senior year of high school in 1977. I had heard a little bit about Joe Shields while growing up in the Timpson area. But I became really familiar when our school got a state grant to do a film project. Our group chose as its project "Hangings in East Texas," particularly in Shelby County.

We interviewed several older people in the community, and one story kept coming up again and again. That was of the hanging of a young man named Joe Shields. We did an in-depth study of Joe Shields. We made him the focus of our hanging films. Then I have done some personal research and talked to several different people. These people were either very young at the time or whose parents were living in that area and were familiar with what was going on.

In the late 1800's there was an older couple living out of what is known as the Bueno Vista community. That was Mr. and Mrs. Pinson. He became ill and died during the winter of that year. Mrs. Pinson had a daughter living somewhere back east. I believe in Georgia. She wrote her daughter and said that she needed some help. So the daughter sent her son, Mrs. Pinson's grandson, to Texas to live with her and to help out on the farm. This young man's name was Joe Shields.

When Joe came into the community he was a popular boy right off the bat. He was a good-looking fellow slightly over six feet tall, with dark hair and muscular in build.

Back then the only entertainment they had was to go to parties. They would have parties and dances nearly every weekend. Joe got invited to these parties, and he started seeing a couple of the young ladies there and dated one of the more prominent young ladies in the community. And the story goes that as the parties continued, his success with the ladies continued. And that even included some of the married ladies. This went on and on and finally some of the boyfriends of the single girls and husbands of the married ones had had enough. They decided to put a stop to it.

There are conflicting stories from this point on. You hear that they just jumped him. I've heard this story from a reliable source that they challenged him at one of the parties. Joe was an outstanding boxer, and he whipped the biggest boy they could put up against him. Later they brought two men up, and he whipped them both. They saw right away they were having no success fighting the young man Joe Shields. He could whip as many of them as he wanted to that they could put against him.

So, one night after a party, several men went over to the barn where Joe kept his horse. That night he came in after dark. And as he pulled his horse into the crib in the barn where they keep the tack, he was going to unsaddle his horse, and a group of men, a mob, jumped Joe and started dragging him off. It started a great confusion and a whole lot of noise. His grandmother came outside with her lantern. The men told her, "Go back old lady or you'll die too." Of course she was greatly frightened and went back into the house. After a couple of hours she could stand it no more and went to a neighbor's house, and they contacted the sheriff.

By the time the sheriff could get out there it was morning. They got to the farm and followed the tracks to where they found Joe Shields hanging in a tree. It wasn't the type hanging that you'd think of today where they break their neck. Joe was really choked to death. Many say he was already dead before they hung him in the tree. That's because of the torture and abuse he went through—things like having his fingernails pulled off and massive sexual abuse they put on him. Mutilation would be a better word, I'd think.

The next day the local school dismissed school, sent the girls home, and took the boys down to see Shields hanging in the tree. The word I got from an older gentleman who was in that group that day was that it was the most terrible thing he'd seen in his life, and he wouldn't want to see that again.

It was said that several people were invoked but that only three or four were implicated, and it's said that two went to the penitentiary. Later the lawyer figured a way to get them out, so really no one was punished for what turned out to be the murder of Joe Shields.

One man late in his life was sick and in bed. He started talking names and telling the truth of what happened. Several people who were involved with the mob heard about it and called the doctor out. And the man was given a sedative so he gently went to sleep forever and ever, the secret with him. That's basically the story of Joe Shields as told to me by older people.

I currently work during the summers at a camp. And this camp covers a lot of acres. The limb that Joe Shields was hung from has rotted off. People still go by today to see that tree and get a bit of the history behind the Joe Shields hanging.

A Friend

Joe Shields was a relative of a woman by the name of Mrs. Pinson. He came to live with her and help her farm. Her home was in the Prospect community. A creek was named after Mrs. Pinson, and it runs through our home place.

Back then dances were very popular. Joe went to most of the dances and was very popular with the women. He was a very handsome and good and honest young man. This was one reason the men were jealous. A girl named Molly McCauley was also said to be one of the reasons Joe was killed. He had been dating Molly, but they had broken up, or one was going out with others. He stopped dating her anyway. She was jealous, so it was said she was an instigator in his death.

So some of the men were angry with him. The men had divided into two groups. The first group took him and were going to whip him, but the second group wanted to kill him. When the second group arrived that evening, the first group left. Mrs. Pinson followed the second group, begging them not to hurt Joe. The group leader told her he would kill her if she did not leave. The gang leader was in his fifties or sixties.

Mrs. Pinson identified the gang leader to the sheriff. She said, "You will know this man because he will be clean shaven." The man had always had a thick beard. His name was Fayette Harris. The gang leader was a very influential man. He had Negroes working for him and was very prosperous. His youngest son took the punishment along with a Negro man who worked for the gang leader. Both men spent years in the penitentiary.

The gang leader had gotten Mrs. Pinson's daughter pregnant. She had a baby boy, then left town. The gang leader was jealous because Joe had lived in the same house with Mrs. Pinson's daughter. The gang leader later remarried his wife [the daughter].

That was a rough time, and people got by with most anything. Everybody was running scared at that time, but one woman remembered a hen crowed the morning Joe Shields was killed. She had always heard that when a hen crows there will be a death. Her daddy was a deputy sheriff at that time, and he was present at Mrs. Pinson's statement.

Garland Bailey

My mother's name was Fanny Harris. Her brothers were Ike, Bill, and Ed.

Joe Shields was a fine-looking man back in those days. He always rode a good-looking horse and had a good rig. He was pretty popular among the women. These folks who killed him didn't like him for some reason. Now, I don't know the reason. But anyhow, my uncle Fayette Harris and Bill Harris, who wasn't much more than a kid of a boy, were down in San Augustine County where they had them in jail.

So Joe Shields had been hung, and they were down there, and these folks laid it off on Uncle Fayette Harris and Bill Harris, my mother's brother. I can't recall who put the blame on them. They proved it in court that Uncle Fayette Harris and Bill Harris hung Joe Shields. Well, Uncle Fayette Harris was my mother's daddy's brother. Bill Harris was his nephew and had gone to spend the night with him, and they were just as innocent as me and you. Anyhow, they sent Bill Harris to the pen for life. This old man on his deathbed confessed to it, but Bill Harris had had to spend five years in the penitentiary. He was tried down in San Augustine.

Now, why they never did try Uncle Fayette I don't know that, but they kept him in jail. I don't think he ever went on trial, and he never did go to the penitentiary. He fiddled his way out of jail, I guess. He could really play the fiddle and was a good mixer. He was kind of a comedian and everyone liked him. He had lots of visitors in jail who'd come by, and he'd tell them all about it and that he really didn't know how he got involved. People had sympathy for him, and his case never did come up. Then this old man confessed on his deathbed. I guess Uncle Fayette just stayed in jail in San Augustine for five years, but his case never did come up. He made friends everywhere he went. I never met him, but I remember my mother talking about him. I know they turned Uncle Bill out of the pen with a suit of clothes for the five years work he did, and his girlfriend waited for him and when he got out she married him. They moved down to South Texas at Three Rivers in Live Oak County. I only saw Uncle Bill two or three times in my life but knew his three boys. Bill Harris was elected commissioner for as long as he wanted, and one of his sons succeeded him. They did well down there.

The Joe Shields hanging was a bad thing. The men who did it were sharp. They had it all planned, cut and dry and everything. And they made the court believe it. They framed Uncle Bill with that crooked-footed horse or mule. Uncle Bill Harris, that was my mother's father. He owned a big farm up here around Timpson. He had to sell everything he had to fight the case with. The older Bill and Fayette were brothers. And Bill had to sell everything to defend his son. The older Bill was my grandfather Harris. Bill was a brother to my mother.

Galveston Daily News, Thursday, February 18, 1892,
"REMANDED WITHOUT BAIL"

"Four of the Accused Remanded and the Balance Discharged—A Synopsis of the Evidence.

"Center, Tex., Feb. 17—On the night of the 28th of January last, about ten miles northwest of this place and about seven miles from Timpson, there was committed the foulest murder that has ever darkened the fair name of Shelby County, as already reported in brief dispatches to THE NEWS.

"Joe Shields, a young man who had been living in this county for more than three years and against whom no one knew aught, was rudely taken from his home, dragged about three-quarters of a mile from the house and hanged to a limb.

"Suspicion at once fell upon Fayette Harris, a man who lived about one mile from where young Shields had made his home since he came to this county, and he, together with Billy Harris, his nephew, who also lived in the same community, and two negroes, Charley Peddy and Jim Stanton, were arrested, charged with the crime; and on the Saturday following, Jim Harris, a son of Fayette, was also arrested, and the five were placed in jail. Excitement ran very high and threats of lynching were made on all sides, to prevent which Sheriff Garrett kept a strong guard around the jail.

"During the next few days one after another was charged with aiding in the terrible deed and their arrests followed immediately until eleven persons, whites and negroes, were in jail.

"Fayette Harris has lived in this county for thirteen or fourteen years, having come from near Bolivar, Tenn., with a wife and children, and settled near where the crime with which he is charged was committed. About the year 1884 or '85 he left his wife, and she sought and obtained a divorce from him, after which he almost immediately married a Miss Pinson, with whom he lived for a few years and she died, leaving two girl children as the issue of the marriage. Soon after the death of this wife he returned to his first love and was remarried to his former wife, with whom he has since lived. The two children of his Pinson wife have, since the death of their mother, lived with the old lady Pinson, their grandmother. The old lady Pinson was alone save the companionship of the two wee tots, until Joe Shields came to live and care for her. It is said he was sent to care for her by a son. Shields seems to have been very kind to and thoughtful of the comfort of the old lady, and she thought there was nobody like Joe. She was very old and could not be expected to live long, and Harris, it is said, thought that but for Shields being in the way his two children would soon inherit all the property possessed by the old lady, and so there soon sprang up a difference between Shields and himself, and they had frequent quarrels and on one occasion came to blows.

"The people have flocked to the courthouse from all parts of the county, so great was their anxiety to learn all about the terrible murder and to know for certain whether or not the right parties had been caught.

"Mr. Joe C. Shields, an uncle of the murdered boy, and Messrs. G. W. Lindley and J. A. Reed, friends of his, all from Wood County, have been here during the entire trial and have manifested great interest in it.

"The trial ended this evening, and upon the order of the presiding justice Fayette Harris, Billie Harris, Charley Peddy and Jim Stanton were remanded without bail and the case dismissed as to James Harris and all others charged with the hanging.

"Thus closed the most lengthy as well as the most interesting examining trial ever held in Shelby County, if not in the state of Texas. The trial was begun on the 4th and ended on the 17th, and throughout that great length of time Justice J. E. Wright sat day after day, holding in his hands the scales of justice and not allowing a feather's weight to be cast into either side, except such matter as he thought ought to be weighed, and demeaning himself with that dignity and unswerving purpose which should ever characterize the judiciary, either high or low in rank.

"The crime with which the defendants stand charged is the most heinous and inhuman murder which the people of this county have ever known, but the NEWS correspondent desires to correct a matter in connection with the murder which has appeared in several papers, that the murderers not satisfied with their foul deed after they had hung their victim, built a fire under his feet and burned the corpse. There is nothing in the evidence indicating such a fact, and those who were at the fatal tree first next morning say such was not the case.

"The state has been ably represented by County Attorney C. B. Short, assisted by Messrs. Wheeler & Wheeler, while the interests of the defendants have been well guarded by Messrs. Truit & Espy and Hon. J. W. Truit present member of the legislature from this district.

"J. B. Waller, Dud and Aquilla Bell, Steve Stanton and Jim Powdrill, the last two negroes, were also jailed charged with the crime, but were arrested after the five whose cases have been disposed of.

"Statements from the most material witnesses will perhaps give a better insight into the crime and the motives prompting it than could be otherwise given, and therefore the following facts are given as stated by the witnesses.

"Mrs. Pinson's Story

"Mrs. N. M. Pinson testified: My name is N. M. Pinson; know Fayette Harris, Jim Harris, Bill Harris, Charley Peddy and Jim Stanton, alias Jim Needham. Have known Fayette Harris thirteen or fourteen years; has lived twelve or thirteen years about one mile from my house. Jim Harris is a son of Fayette and Bill a nephew. Jim Stanton and Charley Peddy lived with Fayette Harris on the 28th of January last. Was acquainted with the deceased, Joe Shields. Fayette Harris married my daughter and has two children by her. She is dead, but the children are living. I own three mules, one horse, several head of cattle and 390 acres of land. The value of my real estate is about $2,000, personal property $500; knew Joe Shields for three years; he had lived that time at my house; the feeling between him and Fayette Harris was not very good for the last two years; last Christmas a year ago Fayette Harris came to my house and talked to me about Joe destroying my property; I told him that was nobody's business but mine; he said it was his business; told me Joe Shields had to leave my house; I said he would not leave till he got ready; Fayette Harris said, 'Damn him I will make him leave;' he stamped his foot on the floor and said he would blow his damned brains out; he tried a number of times to get me to turn Joe off. The last time he tried to get me to turn Joe off and let him have possession of the place, said he would take the place as Joe had it and take me and the children (his two children by my daughter) and support us and give me a bale cotton extra. I told him no, I would keep Joe. The next morning after Joe and Harris were said to have a fight (which was about last Christmas) Jim Tyer came to my house before sunrise and called for Joe. I told him I did not know where he was. He then got up and left; as he went off our gallery I went to the other where I could see, and there stood Fayette Harris, and he asked Tyer, 'Where is he?' Tyer replied, 'Mrs. Pinson says he is not here.' They then walked off toward Harris'. At that time Joe was at home in bed. The defendant, Charley Peddy, lived at my house last year and made a crop. Jim Stanton lives with Fayette Harris. I am well acquainted with the voices of Fayette Harris and Charley Peddy. (Witness pointed out all the defendants in court.) The last time I saw Joe Shields alive was at my house on the 28th day of January, between 12 and 1 o'clock in the day. He was in company with Bill Harris and Charley White. Bill Harris and Joe left together. Joe returned between 11 and 12 o'clock that night. He came to the horse lot gate; I heard him when he rode up; heard him throw his saddle in the crib. I next heard an alarming voice call, 'Mrs. Pinson, run here.' I ran toward the lot and cried, 'Joe, oh Joe; what is the matter?' He replied, 'Harris is killing me.' I saw the bulk of three men, the best I could tell; they seemed to have him down on the ground. They did not stay there more than an instant. They then took him around the crib from me. The next I heard Joe's voice say, 'Oh, boys; don't.' They got him over the fence and went off. I recognized the voice of Fayette Harris when they were down over him. I followed them on and asked several times where was Joe. They made no reply. I kept on asking, and they finally told me to go back. I repeated the question, 'Where is Joe?' and they replied 'I tell you to go back.' I asked them to tell me what they had done with Joe. They replied, 'We threw him in the crib, and if you don't go back we will kill you.' It was Charley Peddy who used this language to me. I followed them 300 or 400 yards, and then turned back and went back to Jake Ross' and requested him to notify the people.

"Other State Witnesses

"Randolph Tyer said: I went to Mrs. Pinson's on the morning of January 29; went very early; by Mrs. Pinson's directions as to course I went in search of Joe Shields, and saw his dead body hanging to a limb four or five hundred yards from Mrs. Pinson's house.

"Arthur Tatum, a negro boy about 18 years old, said: The next morning after Joe Shields was hanged I heard of it; was standing in the road. Dud Bell and Jim Stanton met in the road where I was standing. Dud Bell said to me and Jim Stanton: 'Have you heard the news?' We replied, 'We have not.' Dud then said: 'Mr. Joe Shields was taken out and hung last night.' I asked Jim Stanton to let me ride in his wagon; he said all right. I got in, and after riding a short distance Jim Stanton said to me: 'I will tell you something if you won't say anything about it.' I made no reply. He then said, 'I was into that.' We had been talking of nothing except the hanging of Joe Shields. When I went to leave him he said to me, 'Don't say anything about what I told you; if you do I will get into it.'

"Randolph Tyer, recalled, said: I saw Smart Bell pick up a watch chain in Mrs. Pinson's lot the next morning after Joe Shields was hung. The chain handed to me now is the same chain. About one week before Shields was hung I saw this chain, to the best of my recollection the defendant Jim Stanton had it on.

"Charley Reed said: I saw the defendant, Jim Stanton, some time in the fall of 1891 buy a watch chain from my brother. The chain now handed me looks like the one. The one sold to Jim Stanton by my brother had a little stirrup on it like this one.

"A. W. Ballard said: I know Fayette Harris; met him last fall. He said he was going to let Joe Shields stay at Mrs. Pinson's until he gathered his crop and got it off, then he was going to him (Shields) and give him a certain time to leave the country, and if he did not leave, G—d, d—n him, he was going to put him to a limb. Said the old lady Pinson was getting old and would not live long, and that fellow (Joe Shields) was staying there and making way with her property. He had two children there who would at her death be heir to all she had; said that was his reason for wanting to get rid of Shields. I know Billie Harris. Days before the killing of Joe Shields he was telling about a fuss Joe Shields and his uncle, Fayette Harris, had a short time before that. He said his Uncle Fayette had been accused of shooting at Shields, but it could not be proven on him; said Shields was a G—— d—— black hearted s—— of a b——, and if he didn't mind his light would be put out.

"Lee Brown said: I know Fayette Harris. Knew deceased. Saw them together at Jake Ross' on the Saturday night after Christmas. I heard Harris say to Shields: 'You have not paid Mrs. Pinson's doctor bill, not her tax;' that he had made away with her property and that he (Shields) was making away with his (Harris') children's property. Shields said, 'I don't know they are your children. I hear folks say so.' Harris said, 'You are a d——d liar, you know they are my children.' The next I saw they were fighting, and Shields had Harris down. Harris said, 'Let me up and I will let you alone.' Shields got off him, and went out the door running. Fayette Harris shot at him as he was running out of the door.

"Thomas J. Clements said: I am justice of the peace; I held an inquest over the dead body of Joe Shields; first saw the body hanging to a limb with a rope around the neck, his hands tied behind and his feet tied together (produced cords with which hands and feet were tied). After being shown a rope, says: From the best of my knowledge, this is the rope that was around his neck; it has what I take to be blood on it, and so had the one taken from Shields' neck; my best judgment is that this is the rope I gave after the inquest to Z. Booth, deputy sheriff.

"Z. Booth said: Was at the inquest over the body of Joe Shields. Thomas J. Clements told me where the rope was which was taken from the neck of Joe Shields. Being shown a rope, says it is the same rope.

"Thomas Reed said: Know Billie Harris; saw him Thursday night, January 28, at my house; came to bring a horse I had bought from him; led the horse with a rope; had seen him in daytime with same horse and same rope round his neck; the rope now handed me is similar to the one he had that night. If there is any difference between the rope that was around Joe Shields' neck, the one Billie Harris had on the horse at my house, and the one now handed me I don't know it. Then he left my house; he said he was going to his Uncle Fayette's.

"Arch. McLaughlin said: I know Charley Peddy; saw him the evening before Joe Shields was hanged; had a conversation with him in which he told me that Fayette Harris and Joe Shields had had a difficulty some time before that; said the people thought it was settled, but that Shields was liable to be taken out and hanged or mobbed at any minute.

"The Defendants' Witnesses
"The state's counsel here began to introduce the defendants' witnesses and began with Mrs. Emma Waller, wife of one of the parties in jail but not on trial. She said: On the night Joe Shields was hung Fayette and Billie Harris came to our house between 7 and 8 o'clock. After sitting awhile Fayette Harris said our clock was too slow. We moved it up to 9 o'clock, which was fifteen minutes behind Harris' watch. They remained at my

house till five minutes before 11 and left together. I think it is about three fourths of a mile from my house to Fayette Harris'.

"Pinkey Harris, daughter of Fayette, 12 years old, was next introduced and said: I was at home the night Joe Shields was hung; father returned from Timpson between 7 and 8 o'clock; we had eaten supper; while he was at the lot putting up his mule Billie Harris came; father and Billie ate supper and after a short while went down to Mr. Waller's. They returned home that night fifteen minutes after 11 o'clock.

"John Bell, father of Dud and Quilla Bell, in jail but not on trial, said: Was at home the night Joe Shields was hung. Dud and Quilla went to a party on Judge Wheeler's place. In going from my place to Judge Wheeler's and returning one would pass directly by Mrs. Pinson's. Dud and Quilla returned home ten or fifteen minutes before 11 o'clock. They told me the next morning about hearing someone halloo at Mrs. Pinson's when they were about one fourth of a mile from her house but that they thought nothing strange of it at the time. At 20 minutes after 12 o'clock Smart Bell came to my house and said Mrs. Pinson had come over to his house and said somebody had come to her house and had taken Joe Shields off, and she wanted the neighbors to come in and see what they had done with him. Dud and Quilla told me next morning that they met Joe Shields about seventy-five yards from Mrs. Pinson's horse lot.

"Dud Bell, one of the accused, was next placed upon the stand by the state, and said: On the night Joe Shields was hung Quilla and I went to a party on Judge Wheeler's place; left there short while before 10 o'clock; came home via Mrs. Pinson's. About seventy-five yards from her lot we met Joe Shields. We spoke and halted a minute; and went on directly home, about two miles from Mrs. Pinson's; got home a few minutes before 11 o'clock. When we got about a quarter of a mile from Mrs. Pinson's place we heard someone call Joe two or three times; it was not a man's voice.

"Frank Whiteside, said: I was at John Bell's the night Joe Shields was hung. Willie Hughes and myself were in the room by the fire; the family had retired. Just as I was preparing to retire, I looked up at the clock and said to Willie Hughes, 'It is about 11 o'clock, we had better retire.' Dud and Quilla Bell were not in that room when I retired. It was twenty or thirty minutes after I retired before I went to sleep. I never heard Dud and Quilla come in the house before I went to sleep.

"The above is a synopsis of the evidence of but few witnesses; in fact it would require almost an entire issue of the NEWS to contain it all, but a great deal of it is unimportant and would not be of interest to the general reader."

Harris v. *State*

Court of Criminal Appeals of Texas. Jan. 7, 1893.

Homicide—Evidence—Acts and Declarations of Co-Conspirator—Instructions.

Appeal from district court, Shelby County: George F. Ingraham, Judge.

Prosecution of William Harris, Jr., for murder. Defendant was convicted, and appeals. Affirmed.

Davis & Garrison, J. E. Truitt, and F. L. Johnson, for appellant. R. L. Henry, Asst. Atty. Gen., for the State.

. . . It was evidently the theory of the state that Fayette Harris, the uncle of the defendant, was the instigator of the whole matter that, fearing that Joe Shields would get a large share of Mrs. Pinson's property if he continued to live with her, he (Harris) first tried to get her to discharge deceased, and, failing in that, he began a systematic plan of trying to turn the whole neighborhood against him, and had succeeded in getting a mob of six or eight to assist him in carrying out his plan to murder. The primary question, then, being the guilt of Fayette Harris, neither reason nor common sense required that evidence tending to prove that guilt should be excluded but, as has been well said, "When a foul assassination like this has occurred, and the circumstances attending it are shrouded in mystery, the command of the law is, 'Turn on the light.'"

. . . Appellant complains that the court erred in not permitting him to prove the ill feeling and threats of Ardis Page and others against deceased. Conceding that the court should have permitted this testimony, we cannot see how it would have benefitted the defendant. The fact that Ardis Page and others were present at the homicide in no way tends to prove that defendant was absent. Indeed, the testimony seems clearly to indicate that there were others present besides those indicted in this case. Mrs. Pinson says, when they were dragging Joe Shields up the road, she heard a considerable noise in the bushes on the same side with the lot, and it sounded like horses. Again, Randolph Tyer, a witness for the state, declares that the tracks show that seven or eight men were present. Again, the identified tracks of the "Tobe" mule and other mules coming from the direction of Rainsville, and hitched near the scene of homicide, indicate with strong probability the presence and identity of other parties who came to take part in the bloody drama. But if Mrs. Pinson is to be believed, Fayette Harris was one of the parties present, and from defendant's own lips comes the confirmation that he was with Fayette Harris at this time.

Appellant insists that this case ought to be reversed because there is no evidence directly or indirectly connecting defendant with the homicide. We do not agree with him. Not only does defendant's own testimony, with that of other witnesses introduced by him, prove that defendant was with Fayette Harris on that fateful night, and irrevocably binds his fate to that of his uncle, but there are independent facts in the record strongly tending to corroborate that statement. It seems that Fayette Harris first married Mrs. Pinson's daughter, by whom he had two children, who at the death of their mother, and upon their father's second marriage, resided with their grandmother; that the deceased, Joe Shields, three years before the homicide, rented Mrs. Pinson's farm, and took charge of it, and supported Mrs. Pinson and her grandchildren. The kindness of the old lady to young Shields aroused the bitter jealousy of Fayette Harris, who saw in the intruder a possible heir and owner of the old lady's property, worth $2,000, and he began planning to drive him out of the property, to which he probably felt he had the better right. He endeavored to do this by compelling Mrs. Pinson to discharge Shields, by trying to drive him away through fear, and finally destroyed him through a mob. His repeated efforts to induce Mrs. Pinson to drive Shields away failed; so did his efforts to drive him away. Indeed, a month before the homicide he attacked the deceased, but was severely handled, and his whiskers torn out. On being allowed to rise, he suddenly shot at deceased, but missed him. He then strove to excite the ill will of the neighborhood against deceased, and openly spoke of his preparation and intention of killing him. He not only threatened him in conversation with neighbors, but even spoke to parties with whom he was not on intimate terms, and told them the story of his wrongs, to wit, how Joe Shields was getting away with his children's property. It seems too clear for doubt that defendant knew of and shared in the ill will of his uncle, and indulged in bitter denunciations of the deceased, regretting he was not present at the fight; stating he was going to see his uncle, and the —— of a —— ought to be hung; and on another occasion stating that his light would go out if he did not mind. On the morning of the homicide, defendant dined with the deceased. The ostensible purpose was to get a favor from Joe Shields. They rode off together after dinner, and, when separating in the evening, defendant was twice heard to ask Joe Shields if we would return home that night. Defendant on the day of the homicide, in desiring one White to arrange a credit for him with Joe Shields, requested to arrange it that day, as he (defendant) would have something to do the next day. After separating from Shields, and two hours before the homicide, defendant delivered a horse that he had sold to one Tom Reed. There was an old three-quarter-inch grass rope, 15 feet long, around the horse's neck, which was taken off by Reed, doubled up, and handed to one Louis Tyer, who delivered it to defendant, who tied it to his saddle. Both of these witnesses, while they cannot identify the rope, state it resembles in length and appearance the rope with which Shields was hung; the witness Tyer stating he had often seen a similar rope about the neck of defendant's horse. Defendant had a newer rope and one of the same length on his horse's neck the next day, which he proved by a witness and his own testimony was his rope. So it is to be noted that, at the lot fence where the mob lifted Joe Shields over, they picked up, next morning, a steel watch chain, with a stirrup charm. It was shown that defendant Jim Stanton had purchased a similar chain and charm; yet on the trial another chain was produced like the one found, but with a different charm. These may be slight circumstances, but perhaps the facility with which the duplicate of the watch chain was supplied created a doubt in the mind of the jury as to the genuineness of defendant's disclaimer of the rope found around the neck of Shields.

Again, the morning after the homicide, before the fate of Joe Shields was known, defendant stated to Bud Powers that Shields had been taken out and hung. He claimed the news was obtained through Firman. Yet, as a fact, the only statement that had been made was that three men had carried Joe Shields off. Defendant claimed an alibi for himself and Fayette Harris at the time of the killing. He says, after delivering the horse to Reed, he rode to his uncle's, and remained with him till after supper. They left the house at 8 o'clock, and did not return till 11:15. This is fully corroborated by Mrs. Fayette Harris. It was during this interval Joe Shields was killed. It was one mile to Mrs. Pinson's. Defendant claims that he and his uncle spent this interval in visiting Warren's house, who lived three fourths of a mile off, and this is corroborated by Warren and wife. But apart from the bad reputation of Warren for truth, and their finding at Warren's house a light-wood splinter like those found at Joe Shields' body, the testimony of Mrs. Pinson, stated with vivid recollection and exactness, seems to have caused the jury to utterly disregard the statement of Warren and his wife. She says she was sitting up awaiting the return of Joe Shields, who went off after dinner with defendant. An hour before his return (about 9:30) she hears a hello at the lot, which she thought was Joe's voice. It was probably the parties on watch signaling other members of the mob just arriving. Mrs. Pinson finally hears Joe Shields coming home. He was whistling. She hears him riding in the lot, and throws his saddle on the floor of the crib, when suddenly she hears him scream, "Oh, Mrs. Pinson, run here." She hurries out to the lot, and in the starlight she sees three men in the lot bent down over Joe Shields, on the ground. She cries, "Joe, what is the matter?" He replies, "Harris is killing me." Joe Shields always spoke of Fayette Harris as "Harris." It was too dark to distinguish the forms with certainty, but she hears and recognizes Fayette Harris' voice giving orders in a low tone. She is within five feet of them, the fence between them and herself. They take him up and carry him across the lot, and she gets around as they are lifting him over the fence. She hears Shields say in a choked voice, "Oh, boys, don't." Again, she hears and recognizes Harris' voice. She follows them, and as they jerk and drag him along the road for 300 yards, sometimes she gets in 10 steps. Three times she is warned back by one of the parties, whose voice she clearly recognizes as Charles Peddy's, with which she was perfectly familiar, he having lived on her place, and was then in the employ of Fayette Harris, and living on his place. She then turns back and tries to arouse the neighborhood, but in vain. The next morning the search begins, and the bloody corpse of Shields is found about three fourths of a mile in the woods, hanging to a tree, with arms and feet tied. The statement of Mrs. Pinson as to the manner of the murder is corroborated in the strongest manner by the tracks, the evidence of struggle, the unsaddled mule in the lot, the traces in the road of the dragging. The presence of Fayette Harris is not only betrayed by his voice, familiar for 14 years to Mrs. Pinson, but by the evidence of the dying Shields—"Harris is killing me."

The record is very voluminous. We have carefully examined it to see that no injustice has been done to the defendant. He has been most ably defended. There were 17 bills of exception reserved, and every defense interposed that the evidence would justify, but the facts were too strong to be rebutted. The reason why the penalty of death was not inflicted seems to have been that the jury believed that the defendant was led by the influence of his uncle into this bloody crime. We see no error in the case, and it is affirmed.

Box Suppers

In earlier times there were fewer opportunities for boys and girls to get to know each other, assuming they didn't attend the same rural school. Social ideas and attitudes were different, and it was a time before most young people had access to automobiles. The date out on one's own, unchaperoned, was more or less unheard of.

Still, boys and girls managed to get together. Two socially approved institutions for this purpose were the play party (described at length in *The Loblolly Book*) and the box supper. In both these, older persons arranged a safely chaperoned way for young persons to meet and to have a good time in each other's company.

Box suppers also had other purposes. They were often held at the rural school or the community church, with the school being the common location. Usually, the lion's share of the profits from the sale of the box lunches went towards the purchase of academic or recreational supplies for the school. The older members of the community took an active part, meeting and greeting each other outside the school building, trading information on farming, the weather, hunting, and fishing. While the men and women gossiped, the young people pursued the exciting business of trying to get their (the girls') box suppers in the right hands or trying to get their (the boys') hands on the right suppers. It was far from a certain transaction, of which interested and amused older onlookers were well aware. *Loblolly* staffers gathered many vivid and pleasant memories from their informants about the box suppers of days gone by. In fact, we were so intrigued that we held a box supper ourselves!

Georgia Gonzales

In the course of history there have been many conniving methods used for a girl to meet a boy and capture the man of her dreams. One of the most popular was the sale of the old-time, famous box supper. The young lady would slave all day over a hot stove and prepare a meal fit for a king. She was careful always to choose to prepare the dishes she was best qualified to prepare, for the way to a man's heart is through his stomach, and this would be a perfect opportunity to land her man. The meals were taken to a community center along with a dressed-up box and auctioned off to the highest bidder. Tension was great as the biddings began. With a red face and fingers crossed and heart pounding, she would stand as the bidding came to her own box. Almost afraid to look to see the bidder, she would wait and pray for the right man to do the highest bidding. The money would go to a community charity. But so what—if the right man was the highest bidder, they could have the money. Many times, the meal spread on the ground and shared by the bidder and the cook was the beginning of a long and happy marriage. So, the box supper played a big part in the history of our country. Just think, we may still be just thirteen colonies if someone hadn't invented the box supper.

Omie Webb

We used to have what they called box suppers at school. We fixed up boxes real pretty. Crepe paper was used for covering them. All different colors were used. Tinsel was added to the crepe paper for additional decoration.

The boxes used for box suppers were many different shapes. Some of the shapes used were round, square, heart-shaped, diamond, or no particular shape at all.

Girls prepared the meal for two people. Meals usually consisted of fried chicken, sandwiches, fruit, cake, or most anything used in packing a picnic basket.

Box suppers were auctioned off to the highest bidder. Prices ranged from fifty cents to three dollars. In your box brought three dollars, you had gotten top money. Girls brought the boxes, and boys would bid on them.

We were not supposed to know whose box it was when they bought it, but sometimes word got around whose box they were bidding on. In a way this was good because it would make certain that boxes brought more. In another way, it was a little boring because it was no surprise whose box you got. After you bought the box you would find out whose box it was that you bought and you would go eat supper with them at school. It was a lot of fun!

I didn't make too many; they were hard to make. We'd pad the tops of 'em with cotton and cover 'em with that pretty old crepe paper with reds and pinks or whatever color we wanted. It would be mounted up so pretty, just the prettiest thing you ever saw. So the boys would go buy the boxes—the prettiest boxes—and bid on the prettiest boxes. And the boys wouldn't know who made what box, you see, unless you'd tell somebody you know. They'd just all bid all kinds of prices on the boxes.

No, we didn't have much money; we just had to make 'em. The boys just wanted food! We'd just fix a real pretty box. Some of the men would auction the boxes off. They would say a dollar, two dollars, three dollars, and it just would go from there. Just like making a wedding dress or something. We'd just go get some ruffles and put 'em on top. And then we'd just line it with paper and put it on the bottom too.

The most beautiful box that I remember was my sister's. It was a house with real-looking windows made of isinglass. It did not bring what I thought it ought to have with a price of seventy-five cents. They had these box suppers about one or two times a semester. It was usually when the school needed money.

All the girls in the school that were old enough built a box. Sometimes that was the only way we had of catching a boyfriend. You started building box suppers at about the age of twelve. I was thirteen when I built my first box. The boy that bought my box wanted to walk me home, but we had come in the truck, so I told him he could walk me to the truck.

My sister, my niece, and I all had coats that were alike. So I came in and hung my coat up, my niece came in and hung hers over mine, then my sister came in and hung hers over ours. When I started to go this boy reached up and got a coat and helped me on with it. I looked down and saw it belonged to my sister, so I pulled it off and said, "I got the wrong coat." I handed that coat to my sister and reached over and got the next one. He helped me put it on. I looked down and saw that I had my niece's coat, but I wasn't about to say so because he had already helped me on with two coats. I wore it home, and my niece wore my coat home.

I never did go to that much trouble fixing my box because I never did have the patience. My sister always had the prettiest box at school. They always had a big turnout at these box suppers. They had other events at the box suppers too. They had a prettiest girl contest. They usually had two contestants, and these were out of the old girls in the school. It cost a dime a vote at that time. That was another way of making money for the school. The girl that got the most votes won a title of being the prettiest girl whether she was or not.

Sybil Whiddon

In the 1920's box suppers were the rage. My school days were during the twenties, and there wasn't a dull moment during that time. I loved going to my little country school and had many friends. But my very best friend was Almeeta Barnett—"Meeta" we called her. We had many good times and never got mad at each other or pouted as some good friends do. Meeta was very popular. I never was popular like she was.

We had many box suppers at Mount Pleasant School at Logan, Texas. And all the girls would try and outdo the others, decorating our boxes with white or colored crepe paper. Some were very beautifully decorated. The boxes were large enough to put lots of goodies in. It was for two to eat, but sometimes two girls would fix one box large enough for four to eat. As an example I'll tell you of the time Meeta and I went home with our teacher Mrs. Ethel Yarbrough and her sister Miss Cleo Powell. She was also a teacher, teaching the little room, fourth grade on down to primer. I assume the primer was kindergarten as today.

Mrs. Yarbrough lived in Shiloh, and they were having a box supper at the school there. So they invited Meeta and me to go home with them and go to the box supper. Meeta's boyfriend lived in Shiloh. I didn't have a boyfriend myself. But we had a huge box all decorated in green crepe paper and filled with the most delicious food: cake, pies, delicious fried chicken, sandwiches, all kinds of fruit like grapes, apples, bananas, or anything that you wanted to put in that box for four to eat. Of course, girls were very timid and didn't eat much, as they wanted the boys to think they were very dainty. But on this particular occasion, Meeta's boyfriend had this friend who knew that two girls had this box together. And they went in together with the money and bought our box, and we ate together. It was so much fun. After the box supper the two boys escorted us back to Mrs. Yarbrough's. There Meeta and I spent the night and went back to school the next day. I'll always remember that box supper.

There were lots of others that we attended at Logan. The purpose was for making money for anything we needed at school. And one was to hire a bus to take us to the fair at Shreveport. And there were other things the teachers and trustees decided we needed for school. Now they call the trustees "the school board." Things are much different now than when I went to school.

Who bought the boxes? Boys and men. Most knew whose boxes they were buying, but others did not and took a chance on who they would eat with. I never disliked anyone who bought one of my box suppers. All were very nice and enjoyed the food and the company. Although I was too young to date at some of the times, I would carry a box. My mother and sisters would fix my box and food, and they put my name in the box, and whoever bought the box would be very nice and compliment the good food, although I was a mere child. Then as I grew older I did not have a steady boyfriend. My cousin was the teacher for a few terms there in Mount Pleasant school, that's the only school I ever attended, and they would have a large box of chocolate candy for the one voted in for the most beautiful girl. Well, most all the time my cousin would win the most votes and get the candy, although several girls would be running. Then my cousin refused to have her name on the list to give us girls a chance to win. And guess what? I won the five-pound box of chocolates! Was I proud of that box of candy. I was about fourteen years old at the time. Then when I was fifteen years old I fell in love and got married. And my box suppers came to an end.

I do wish the schools would start having them again. It's fun and a good way to raise money for anything they want to buy for the school or money for an organization or for someone who needs help in the community, even the fire department.

Eva Hunter

We would have boxes, and we'd make pretty boxes out of crepe paper and just cover the box so pretty. And generally, they'd put in enough sandwiches and cake for two. Our boyfriends generally bought our boxes, but we had box suppers a lot of times along election time, and the candidates would come and give a lot for our boxes just to get us to vote for 'em. They would just keep a-bidding on! We'd have 'em on Valentine's Day in school, 'cause we'd want to make up some money. We'd just have us a good old box supper, and we'd fix up some of the most pretty boxes you ever saw. We'd put sandwiches and cake and pie and anything we wanted to.

We'd hope our boyfriends would buy our boxes, but sometimes those old candidates would get it and we had to eat with 'em. I won't ever forget which one bought mine, and it just embarrassed me to death to have to eat with him. I had to just sit there with that old boy and eat with him. Mr. Laransa Hunt was our sheriff, and one time he bought one of mine. Some people paid a lot for the boxes, ranging from five to ten dollars at a time. Some of 'em would just bid so high!

Dorothy Sartor

In the old days the woman would cook all they wanted for a box supper so she could help raise money for churches and things like that. After she would cook, she would take it to the sale. The preacher or sheriff of the town would sell it for the highest bidder.

It was a good way for a boy to see how good the girl could cook. Most of the time the girl didn't get to eat with the one she wanted. People lived so far away from each other, they never saw each other but once in a while. That was a good way for the youngsters to get together and have fun. The old people would sit and talk about box suppers in times gone by. Most of the time the people had to get married after the box suppers because some fathers felt that it wasn't right for them to eat alone and not get married.

Wild Game Recipes

Human beings have been hunters for a very long time. Although today East Texans hunt mostly for sport, in our grandparents' and great-grandparents' generations the hunting of wild game was a means of survival. Store-bought meat was so hard to obtain and expensive that hard-pressed rural families often fell back on the resources of the woods, fields, and rivers. Over generations, many excellent recipes evolved in the kitchens of early housewives. The *Loblolly* staff, assisted by other Gary students, has compiled a collection of various ways to prepare wild game from the woods and waters of East Texas.

ARMADILLO MEAT PIE

Boil armadillo until done, then cut meat off into small bite-size pieces. Cook vegetables (bell peppers, green onions, tomatoes, corn, celery). Make your dough and put into the bottom of a pie pan. Fill with meat and vegetables and place a dough layer on top. Bake for 30 minutes or until it turns brown on top. (Harold Whitehead)

POT ROAST OF BEAR

Dredge a 4 1/2 or 5-pound roast in flour. Brown all sides in hot fat. Season with salt and pepper. Add 1 cup of water, 1/2 bottle catsup, 1/4 cup vinegar, 2 bay leaves, 2 stalks diced celery. Cover and cook slowly until tender, about 3 to 3 1/2 hours. Add quartered, raw peeled potatoes and carrots and cook about 25 minutes. Thicken gravy with flour and cold water. (Joann Whiteside)

PLAIN BLACK ROAST

4 to 6 pounds of bear roast

Rub roast with flour, salt, and pepper. Brown in hot fat. Place in roasting pan with 1 cup of water and 2 bay leaves. Cover and roast at 325 degrees for 3 1/2 hours. (Joann Whiteside)

BEAR DUMPLINGS

2 1/2 pounds bear meat cut into small pieces
1 1/2 teaspoons salt, plenty of black pepper
2 1/2 tablespoons bacon drippings
2 tablespoons butter
2 cups water
1 recipe of biscuit dumplings

Brown meat in bacon drippings, 2 tablespoons butter. Cover and cook slowly about 20 minutes longer. Thicken gravy if necessary and serve.

To make the dumplings use 2 cups of sifted flour, 1 teaspoon salt, 2 teaspoons baking powder, 1/2 cup shortening, 3/4 cup milk. Combine dry ingredients, sift together, and cut in shortening. Add milk to make a soft dough. Roll out half an inch thick and cut into one-and-a-half-inch pieces. Drop into the boiling bear meat. (Joann Whiteside)

BEAR STEW

3 pounds cubed bear meat	2 bay leaves
2 tablespoons fat	Salt
5 medium potatoes	Pepper
3 carrots	1/2 cup catsup

Brown meat well in hot fat. Season with salt and pepper. Cover with hot water and simmer 1 to 1 1/2 hours. Add cubed vegetables and cook slowly for 25 minutes. When meat and vegetables are tender, thicken slightly with flour mixed with cold water. (Joann Whiteside)

SAVORY BEAR

Cut 3 pounds of bear meat into serving pieces. Dredge with flour and brown in hot fat. Season with salt and pepper. Brown 4 sliced onions in hot fat. Add 2 1/2 cups beef stock, 2 bay leaves, 1/2 teaspoon celery salt, 2 tablespoons vinegar, 3 tablespoons catsup. Cover tightly and simmer about 2 hours until meat is tender. Thicken gravy. (Joann Whiteside)

VENISON STEW

2 cloves garlic
1 sliced onion
3 tablespoons shortening
2 pounds venison
1 can tomato sauce
1 cup water

4 chopped green peppers
3 potatoes, quartered
6 carrots, halved
2 bay leaves
6 medium onions
Salt and pepper

Fry sliced onion and garlic in shortening. Add the meat and brown. Cover with tomato sauce and 1 cup water, then simmer 1 hour. Remove garlic; add carrots, pepper, potatoes, and whole onions. Add more water, if necessary, and seasonings and cook about 30 minutes until vegetables are tender. Serves six. (Lucille Hancock)

DEER

Take the deer pieces and salt them and flour them. Then put the meat in a skillet with lard and fry until brown. When brown, pour water in the skillet and cover with lid. Let it steam. When tender take it up. (Vivian Jenkins)

DEER MEAT STEAK

Sprinkle 1 pound of meat or steak with salt and pepper, roll in flour. Put in bowl and cover with buttermilk until ready to fry. Put 1/2 cup of grease in an iron skillet and heat. Take steak out of buttermilk and roll in flour. Fry on each side until golden brown. (Nadine Chadwick)

VENISON MEATBALLS

1 pound ground venison
1/4 pound ground pork
1/2 cup milk
1 cup bread or cracker crumbs
1/4 cup fine chopped onions
1 egg
1 teaspoon salt
1/8 teaspoon nutmeg, dash allspice
2 tablespoons shortening

Put all ingredients in an electric skillet, just like you cook spaghetti. Mix the venison with pork into some balls, just like regular meatballs. (Carlene James)

SMOKED VENISON ROAST

3 to 5 pounds venison roast
1 envelope dried onion soup
Salt and pepper to taste

Lightly salt and pepper venison roast. Put on grill over hot charcoal fire. Smoke and brown meat about 1 hour. Place roast in enough foil to completely wrap. Pour envelope of onion soup and about 1/2 cup of water over roast. Seal foil tightly and cook 2 to 3 hours until tender. (A. L. Penn)

MARINATED VENISON

Chop 1 onion, carrots, and 1 stalk celery. In cheesecloth combine parsley, thyme, bay leaf, and a few whole cloves. Cook onion, carrots, and celery in hot oil 1 to 2 minutes. Add 1 cup vinegar and the cheesecloth mixture. Bring to boil and simmer 20 minutes. Strain and cool. Pour over venison. Let stand 12 to 24 hours, in either glass or earthenware (DO NOT USE METAL). After you marinate, take meat out and cover with lard or oil and a few pieces of garlic. (Spread oil and lard thinly.) Roast on a rack in a shallow pan in a 350-degree oven. Allow 30 minutes per pound of meat. (Example: cook 3 to 4 pounds for 2 hours.) Baste frequently with drippings. (Patti Hunter)

VENISON

Field dressing
Quarter steaks
Soak in ice water 2 or 3 days to tenderize
Debone and clean meat
Slice your steaks across the grain

Soak steaks in beaten eggs and milk mixture. Dip in flour and deep fry in hot oil, until golden brown. (Sandy Bennett Templeton)

VENISON ROAST

Season meat with salt and pepper. Place fat side up on roasting rack. Lay beef suet or bacon strips across the meat. Do not add water and do not cover. Roast at 300 to 350 degrees, 20 to 25 minutes per pound. (If roast becomes too brown on top side, turn to aid uniform cooking.) (Lucille Hancock)

VENISON POT ROAST

Season roast with Lowrey's salt to taste. Roll in flour to cover. Melt small amount shortening in a Dutch oven or other large heavy skillet. Sprinkle in garlic powder to taste and about 2 tablespoons sugar.

Brown roast in this mixture on all sides. When roast is brown add enough water to cover. Reduce heat to low, cover roast, and cook from 1 to 2 hours until tender. (Barbara Anderson)

CHICKEN-FRIED VENISON

Soak meat overnight in bowl of water, covered, in refrigerator. Remove from water; rinse well. Pound until tender. Salt and pepper to taste. Dip meat into a mixture of milk and egg and roll in flour. Repeat this procedure twice and fry in deep fat until done. (Barbara Anderson)

VENISON CHILI

2 pounds venison
1 pound fresh pork
2 teaspoons lard or bacon fat
1 medium onion, chopped
2 cloves garlic, chopped
1 teaspoon oregano
1 teaspoon cumin powder
6 teaspoons chili powder
1 tablespoon flour
1 1/2 cups water
Salt
1 can tomatoes

Cut venison and pork into small cubes or run through grinder. Brown onion and garlic in saucepan in lard or fat. Stir in oregano, cumin powder, and chili powder that has been blended with flour. Add salt to taste. Cook 5 minutes. Add meat mixture and tomatoes, cook over low heat, covered, for 40 to 50 minutes or until meat is very tender. Add 1/2 cup hot water and cook 10 minutes longer. May be served with or without beans. Serves six to eight. (Patti Hunter)

SMOTHERED VENISON STEAK

6 to 8 venison steaks
Salt
Meat tenderizer
Garlic powder
Lemon pepper
Worcestershire sauce
1 can mushroom soup

Season steaks with salt and meat tenderizer; let stand for 1 to 2 hours. Beat meat on both sides. Cover with garlic powder, lemon pepper, and Worcestershire sauce; let stand another 30 minutes. Place steaks in crock pot. Mix mushroom soup with 1/2 can of milk in saucepan; cook until warm. Pour this over the steaks. Cook on low for 5 to 8 hours. (Pattie Hunter)

SCRAPPLE

1 deer liver	1 pint corn meal
3 sage leaves	1 red pepper pod
1/2 teaspoon salt	1/2 teaspoon pepper

Boil liver in water with pepper until tender, then grind it up. Stir meal in boiling stock; cook slow until meal is well done. Take pepper pod out and drop in liver, sage, salt, and pepper. Chill. Slice and cook in oven until brown. (Virginia Holman)

SMOTHERED DOVE

1 stick butter	1 tablespoon Worcestershire
2 tablespoons flour	sauce
2 cups water	Juice of half a lemon
Salt	6 doves
	Pepper

Melt butter in skillet. Add flour and cook until smooth and browned. Add water gradually, stirring well until thickened. Stir in salt, pepper, Worcestershire sauce, and lemon juice. Arrange doves. Cover. Bake for 2 hours in 350-degree oven. Baste occasionally, adding water if necessary. Serves six. (Mrs. E. Risinger)

DOVE AND DRESSING

12 dove breasts	1/2 cup cooking oil
Salt	4 cups poultry stuffing mix
2 teaspoons dried parsley	1 teaspoon pepper
1 teaspoon minced garlic	1/2 teaspoon ground thyme
1/2 cup melted butter	
1 teaspoon paprika	

Rub dove with oil. Sprinkle lightly with salt and remaining ingredients. Spread layer of stuffing mixture in greased shallow casserole. Arrange dove in casserole. Spread dove with remaining stuffing mixture. Cover casserole with foil if browning too fast. (Mrs. E. Risinger)

WILD DUCK DRESSING

Take 1 wild duck and boil until tender. Combine 1 cup celery, 1 cup onion, 1 teaspoon salt, 1 teaspoon pepper. Add 2 pans of cornbread crumbled up. Debone duck, then mix all together. Bake at 325 degrees until firm. (Mrs. T. B. Nutt)

WILD GAME GUMBO

2 or 3 ducks or squirrels or about 12 doves or quail or a combination
    of any of these
1 pound pork sausage, cut into slices
2 onions, chopped
1 bell pepper, chopped
3 celery stalks, chopped
3 quarts water
1/2 cup oil
1/2 cup flour
Salt and pepper to taste
Red pepper to taste
Bay leaf

    In pot with water, salt, pepper, and bay leaf, boil game until tender. Remove and discard bay leaf. Remove meat from broth, let cool, and remove meat from bones. Heat oil in a skillet and add flour. Stir constantly until about the color of a copper penny. Add onions, bell pepper, and celery. Sauté about 3 minutes. Mix with broth in pot. Add sausage. Cook on low fire about 1 hour. Add meat and cook another 1/2 hour. Serve in soup bowls over rice. Season with filé, if desired. (Mrs. Ken Irby)

SMOTHERED WILD DUCK

1 duck	1/2 cup flour
1 teaspoon salt	1/2 cup fat
1/4 teaspoon pepper	1 cup milk

    Cut duck into 6 or 7 pieces. Season with salt and pepper and roll in flour. Fry duck slowly in hot fat until brown on both sides, about 30 minutes, turning only once. Add milk, cover tightly, and simmer slowly for 1 hour or until tender. Bake at 325 degrees. (Ivie Nelle Stephenson)

ROASTED WILD DUCK

1 1/4 pound duck	2 cups quartered apples
1 sliced onion	2 teaspoons salt
1/4 teaspoon pepper	

    Clean duck, wash thoroughly. Fill duck with peeled, quartered apples. Truss duck. Rub with salt and pepper and sliced onion. Roast uncovered at 325 degrees. Allow 20 to 30 minutes per pound. If desired baste duck every 10 minutes with 1 cup orange juice. Basting is not required. (Deann Jones)

FRIED FISH

Fillet and wash fish. Soak in salt water 2 to 3 hours; pour off water. Then pour bottle of Louisiana hot sauce over fish, leave for 15 minutes, pour hot sauce off. Meal fillets and fry. (Allyne Cassity)

SAUCE PECON

2 cans tomato paste
1 bunch garlic, chopped fine
2 bunches green onions, chopped fine
1 bunch celery, chopped fine
2 bell peppers

Mix all the above together. Then add 6 medium-size catfish heads, 1 teaspoon salt, and pepper to suit taste. Put all the above in 3 quarts of water; cook until fish is done. Serve over rice. (Uncle Levi)

STUFFED WILD GOOSE

1 goose, 6 to 8 pounds
Juice of 1 lemon
Salt and pepper
1/4 cup butter
1/4 cup chopped onion
1 cup chopped tart apple
1 cup dried apricots
3 cups bread crumbs
1/2 teaspoon salt
1/8 teaspoon pepper
4 to 6 slices bacon
Melted bacon fat

Sprinkle goose inside and out with lemon juice, salt, and pepper. Melt butter in large saucepan. Add onion and cook until tender. Stir in apple, apricots, bread crumbs, salt, and pepper. Spoon stuffing lightly into cavity. Truss bird. Cover breast with bacon slices and cheesecloth soaked in melted bacon fat. Place goose breast up on rack in roasting pan. Roast at 325 degrees for 20 to 25 minutes per pound or until tender, basting frequently with bacon fat and drippings in pan. If the age of the goose is uncertain add 1 cup of water into pan and cover last hour of cooking. Remove cheesecloth, skewers, and string. Serves six to eight. (Imogene Morgan)

BASIC WILD PIG

Take one wild pig; be sure that it is very clean. Add salt, pepper, garlic, and butter. Place over open fire and cook until done. Be sure to turn often. (Beth Newman)

HOG HEAD SOUSE

Trim hog heads and feet. Remove all the hair. Put in pot and boil until meat falls from bones. Remove bones. Mash and mix meat. Add ground red hot peppers, salt, and sage to taste. Put into pans about size of dinner plate. Place plate on top, right side up. Place heavy weight inside of plate. Let set until firm. (Omie Webb)

CHITLINS

Take the inside of an animal (any) and cut out the small intestine. Put in washpan and wash the outside and then turn inside out and wash. Then cut them open into two sections and soak them overnight in salt water. Parboil first and then dip into egg and milk batter; salt and pepper and fry to a golden brown in lard. Raccoon and rabbit are best. (Virginia Holman)

CRACKLIN' BREAD

2 cups of cracklin's (wild hog)
2 1/2 cups cornmeal
1 teaspoon salt
2 1/2 cups water

Put water in saucepan and put cracklin's in it, bring to a boil, then pour over meal and salt. Stir until well mixed, then make out in pans and put in a pan and bake until done. (Clara Jones)

POSSUM

Put possum in a big pot of water and cook until you think it's tender. Then take out and put it on a pan in the oven and add sweet potatoes, sage, and pepper. Cook until it gets brown, then serve. (Grandma Ball)

POSSUM DUMPLINGS

Put possum in pot; boil until it cooks off bone. Then put about 6 cups of flour and 3 cups of water, salt, and pepper in bowl. Mix well. Then put it in with possum. Cook about 30 minutes more and then eat. (Mrs. Rhodes)

BAKED OPOSSUM

Skin and cut up possum. Layer in 9-inch-by-13-inch pan. Pour a little water over possum. Sprinkle with 1 teaspoon salt and pepper. Spread 1/4 cup chopped onions over it. Boil until about half done.

Drain water off and refill with more water. Add 3 peeled and quartered sweet potatoes. Sprinkle with 1/4 cup sugar. Bake until tender at 350 degrees. (Ozella Weir)

OPOSSUM PIE

Clean and cut up one opossum and cover it with water, salt and pepper, and cook until it's almost tender. Now place a layer of opossum in a deep pan; salt and pepper and butter. Next lay strips of pastry over this. Add another layer of opossum and more seasoning. Pour 1 cup of cow's milk in the broth over the opossum. Cover the pan with pastry, put a little butter around on top, and cook in a moderate oven until done. (Virginia Holman)

BASIC POSSUM

1 possum
Salt to taste
Pepper to taste
4 or 5 medium sweet potatoes
Boil possum and salt and pepper. Take out when tender; put in sweet potatoes. Cook until tender at 450 degrees for about 30 minutes. Put sweet potatoes around possum. (L. B. Hodge)

PORCUPINE

Skin by hanging back legs from hooks. Remove kernels in small of back and under forelegs. Hang in a cool dry place 48 hours. Soak overnight refrigerated in salted water. In the morning, bring this water to a boil. Drain and immerse porcupine in cold water again. Bring to a boil and again drain. Place the meat in a Dutch oven. Add:
3 cups water or light stock
1 rib celery, chopped
1 sliced medium onion
1/4 teaspoon pepper
1 teaspoon salt
Simmer until tender, about 2 1/2 hours. (Richard Kennedy)

FRIED QUAIL

8 quail (whole)   2 cups lard
4 cups flour   Salt and pepper to taste
Roll quail in flour until thoroughly covered. Lay in skillet of hot lard; cook over medium flame, approximately 20 to 30 minutes. Serve with desired vegetable. (Betty Woolam)

DEEP DISH QUAIL

Put quail in a mixture of cornmeal and flour. Have some grease pretty hot in a Dutch oven. Brown the quail. Add a little bit of water, then let them simmer for an hour. (Mildred Beueler)

QUAIL AND RICE

3 to 5 quail
Salt and pepper
3/4 cup flour
5 tablespoons shortening
1 cup rice
1 medium onion, chopped
2 chicken bouillon cubes

Season quail with salt and pepper to taste. Place the flour in medium-size bag; add the quail. Shake until well coated. Melt shortening in iron skillet and fry quail until lightly browned. Remove quail and set aside. Add rice and onion to drippings; fry until golden brown, stirring occasionally. Add bouillon cubes and 2 1/2 cups water; mix well. Season with 2 teaspoons salt and 1/2 teaspoon pepper. Place quail on top of rice; cook covered over low heat 20 to 25 minutes until tender. (Barbara Anderson)

BAKED QUAIL

6 quail
Water
3 teaspoons olive oil
Juice of 3 lemons

1/2 stick butter
2 tablespoons molasses
Salt and pepper
1 teaspoon mustard

Put quail in roasting pan with water to cover the bottom of the pan. Cover and put in 300-degree oven. Combine the ingredients and blend together over low heat. Let quail cook for 30 minutes and then pour sauce over them. Place back in oven for 30 minutes. (Elaine Barnes)

QUAIL

Cut bird in half or leave whole; season to desired taste. Place on sharp stick, then cook over fire. (Grace Davis)

STEAMED QUAIL

8 quail
1 stick oleo
Salt
Pepper
Flour

1 cup hot water
2 chicken bouillon cubes
1 teaspoon dried parsley
1 can mushrooms

Salt and pepper and flour birds. Heat oleo in skillet. Brown birds on both sides. Mix together water, bouillon cubes, and parsley. Pour mixture over, lower fire, cover, and simmer 1 hour or until tender. Add mushrooms and, if desired, 3 teaspoons cooking sherry. Cook uncovered about 5 to 10 minutes. (Mrs. J. R. Beebe)

STUFFED QUAIL IN MUSHROOM SAUCE

6 quail
2 cans cream of mushroom
1 cup milk
1/4 cup melted butter
2 three-ounce cans mushrooms
4 cups soft bread crumbs
1 chopped apple
1 stalk chopped celery
1 teaspoon sage
1 onion, minced
Salt
Pepper

Combine bread crumbs, apple, celery, butter, sage, onion, salt, and pepper; add enough water to stuffing to moisten slightly. Pack stuffing into cavities of quail. Place quail breast-side up in deep baking dish. Combine soup, milk, and mushrooms. Bake covered at 300 degrees for 4 hours. Serves six. (Mrs. E. Risinger)

RABBIT AND HERB DUMPLINGS

1/3 cup all-purpose flour
1 teaspoon paprika
1/2 teaspoon salt
1/8 teaspoon pepper
2 1/2 pounds rabbit, cut in pieces
1/4 cup shortening
1 cup water
1-pound can small drained onions
10.5-ounce can condensed cream of chicken soup
The dumplings consist of:
1/2 cup dry bread crumbs
1 teaspoon poppy seed
1 teaspoon poultry seasoning
1 teaspoon celery seed
1 package buttermilk biscuits
1/4 cup melted butter

FRIED RABBIT

1 rabbit. Skin and cut it up like a chicken. Dip into flour, salt, and pepper, while grease is heating. Place in hot grease and fry until golden brown. Take and serve while hot. Average rabbit serves four to six people. (Charles Lyons)

RABBIT STEW

1 rabbit disjointed

3 tablespoons shortening

1 onion, finely chopped

1/4 cup chopped celery

2 tablespoons tomato paste

1/2 cup wine

1 teaspoon mixed spices

1 clove garlic

Salt and pepper

2 teaspoons vinegar

Brown rabbit in shortening in large skillet. Add remaining ingredients except vinegar. Simmer until rabbit is tender, adding water as needed. Add vinegar; cook for 5 minutes or longer. Serves four. (Mrs. E. Risinger)

WILD RABBIT PIE

1 dead rabbit

4 slices fried bacon

1 teaspoon chopped parsley

2 sliced boiled eggs

1 pinch of sage

1 onion

1 dash pepper

1/2 teaspoon salt

1 pie crust

Undress rabbit and wash it. Take meat off of the bones and wash it, soak in cold water, drain. Put in a pan; cover with water and boil for about 15 minutes with salt, pepper, and onions. Then put in pie pan with bacon, parsley, eggs, sage, and a little stock. Cover with pie crust and bake for 1 hour in moderate oven. (Virginia Holman)

B-B-Q RABBIT

Place B-B-Q sauce in deep pan with white or red wine, salt, pepper, garlic, or garlic-flavored vinegar. Soak the rabbit overnight. Cook in oven at 450 degrees or on the grill outside, until tender and juicy. (Charles Lyons)

BRAISED RABBIT

1 rabbit

Skin, clean, and cut into pieces. Dredge with seasoned flour. Melt in a pot or skillet 3 tablespoons butter. Sauté rabbit in butter until brown. Cover with sliced onions. Pour over them 1 cup cultured sour cream. Cover and simmer 1 hour or place the pot in a 300-degree oven and bake until tender, about 1 1/2 hours. (Richard Kennedy)

ROASTED RACCOON

Leave a 1/4-inch layer of fat on raccoon. Cover carcass with cloth dipped in fat. Place on roasting rack in a shallow pan. Do not cover or add water. Bake at 275 to 300 degrees for 3 to 4 hours. Remove cloth the last 1/2 hour; baste several times with drippings and dust with flour after each basting for a crackly and crisp crust. (Ivie Nelle Stephenson)

FRICASSEED RACCOON

1 raccoon
1 teaspoon salt
3 tablespoons fat
1/4 cup flour
1/8 teaspoon pepper
2 cups water

Remove fat from lean meat. Combine flour, salt, and pepper in a bag. Add meat; shake bag to coat. Fry in hot fat until brown. Add water; cover and simmer 2 hours or until tender. (Deann Jones)

FRIED SQUIRREL

1 squirrel, cut up
1/8 teaspoon pepper
1 teaspoon salt
1/4 cup flour

Combine salt, pepper, and flour in paper bag. Drop squirrel in bag and shake bag to coat meat. Brown on all sides in 1/2 inch hot fat. Reduce heat and cook 20 to 30 minutes or until tender. Serves two to three. (Lucille Hancock)

SQUIRREL AND DUMPLINGS

2 to 4 squirrels cut up and boiled in salted water until tender
1 1/2 cup flour
1 teaspoon salt
3 tablespoons melted oleo
5 tablespoons water
1 egg

Combine dry ingredients. Beat egg and add water and butter. Add liquid to dry ingredients and blend with fork until moist. Roll out and cut in 2-inch squares. Drop into broth. Cook 15 to 20 minutes. (Mrs. W. H. Penn)

BROILED SQUIRREL

1 squirrel
1/8 teaspoon pepper
1 teaspoon salt

1/2 teaspoon fat

Clean the squirrel; rub with salt and pepper. Brush with fat and place on a broiling rack. Broil 40 minutes, basting every 10 minutes with drippings. Serves two to three. (Deann Jones)

SQUIRREL MILLIGAN

2 squirrels
3 cups meal
2 pods of red peppers
Onion
Salt and pepper to taste

Cook squirrels until tender. Add meal and chopped red peppers and chopped onion. Then add salt and pepper. (Jessie Rudisill)

BROILED SQUIRREL

1 squirrel
1/8 teaspoon pepper
1 teaspoon salt
1/2 teaspoon fat

Clean the squirrel; rub with salt and pepper. Brush with fat and place on a broiling rack. Broil 40 minutes, basting every 10 minutes with drippings. Serves two to three. (Deann Jones)

SQUIRREL CHOWDER

6 squirrels, cut up
4 large onions
5 cups peeled tomatoes
2 teaspoons salt
4 quarts water
10 large sliced carrots
8 quartered potatoes
5 cups corn
Freshly ground pepper, to taste

Add all the above to large pot. Cook over low flame for 1 1/2 to 2 hours. Serves eight people. (Betty Woolam)

BAKED SQUIRREL

2 squirrels
1 medium onion, chopped
3 medium potatoes, chopped in cubes
5 small carrots, chopped
1 teaspoon salt

1 teaspoon pepper
1 green pepper
Clean and cut squirrels up. Combine ingredients and cook in oven until tender at low to medium temperature. (T. O. Hodge)

OVEN-BAKED SQUIRREL BAR-B-Q

Cut up a small squirrel; salt and pepper to taste. Place on a baking sheet and baste with vinegar. Bake in a slow oven at 350 degrees until done. Baste with your favorite bar-b-q sauce and bake 5 minutes more. (Barbara Anderson)

TURKEY HASH

1/2 cup butter
1 cup flour
2 cups milk
2 cups stock
2 cups chopped celery
1/2 cup grated onion
1 teaspoon white pepper
Salt to taste
8 cups turkey cut into bite-size pieces
Melt butter into saucepan. Add flour and stir over medium heat. Let brown. Add all ingredients except turkey and cook on low for 20 minutes. Add turkey and simmer for 30 minutes. (Elaine Barnes)

WILD TURKEY

Preheat oven to 350 degrees. Wring turkey's neck and pluck. Rub down with salt and pepper. Place in roasting pan; put in oven and cook until done, juicy, and tender. (Nadine Chadwick)

FRIED TURTLE

Cut the turtle up into pieces. Put it in a skillet with lard in it and fry it until brown. After it gets brown, pour water over it and put a lid on it. Then let it steam until tender. Then when tender take it up. (Vivian Jenkins)

TURTLE STEW

Pour boiling water over turtle while still in shell. This makes the shell come off easier. Put turtle in pan of water. Bring to a hard boil, then turn fire down. Add:

- 1 teaspoon salt
- 1/2 cup chopped onions
- 1 clove garlic

Boil until meat is tender. Mix:

- 1 cup meal
- 1/2 cup flour
- 1/4 teaspoon salt

Add boiling water and make thick dough. Drop small balls into water. Cook until bread is done. (Ozella Wier)

Hog Killing Day

Killing and butchering the home-raised hog was a winter ritual at many an early farmstead in East Texas. Pork, not beef, was the mainstay of the rural diet, and the butchering and proper preservation of the meat was a critical task of the yearly round. In the following accounts, Mildred Abshier remembers the vivid details of hog-killing day at her family's farm sixty years ago, and Clotille Nutt of Panola County describes how hog killing and butchering is practiced in 1985. Nothing much has changed, it seems, but one thing is sure—folks who go through this process are well aware where their bacon comes from!

Ms. Mildred Abshier

Early in the fall Papa always penned up a shoat to fatten for fresh eating when the first norther blew in. Hot weather tended to cause meat to spoil quickly. And come the first norther, the shoat was butchered and we had fresh pork for the table and about half of it was parceled out to neighbors. Without refrigeration, this sharing not only helped to prevent loss from spoilage but also insured that neighbors, when they butchered an early shoat, would likewise share with us. But winter was the big time for hog killin', when cold weather was an aid to preserving the meat and when hogs were fat.

In summertime swine were razor thin, deserving the appellation "razorback," as they survived on what roots, berries, herbs, and animal carcasses the wooded range afforded. When Papa raised watermelons, or when corn was plentiful, he often gathered the thinnest of the thin ones, especially the little pigs, herded them home, and kept them alive on melons and corn. The sight of a drove of hogs eating watermelons does help one to understand the use of the word "hog" with reference to greed.

When autumn came and the mast fell, it was a different story—a heyday for swine. Roving under the oaks that grew in profusion in the creek bottoms, they ate their full of acorns and grew very fat. It was during this season that Papa rounded up the fat hogs and sent them to market—keeping back some eight or ten of the best to fatten further for the year's supply of meat for the family.

Those kept back were penned up at home, and the fattening process continued with a diet of corn, bran mash, and slop from the kitchen. Mama preferred a diet of corn for the fattening hogs, as corn-fed hogs yielded nice, white solid lard from their fat, whereas lard from mast-fed animals was near-liquid and slightly colored. When those destined to grace the family table at mealtime were quite fat and a cold spell that promised to hang on a few days blew in, it was time for butchering—time to put away the year's supply of meat.

Usually a neighbor or two came in to help, and they received a parcel of fresh meat for their helpfulness. Early in the morning on butchering day the big black wash pot was filled with water and a roaring fire built about it. The scalding barrel was set up nearby, the back end slanted into a shallow hole at about a twenty-degree angle and the open end low and convenient for receiving the carcass of the slaughtered animal.

Slaughtering was done by a blow on the head with the butt of a poleax or by a twenty-two rifle shot to the head. Either way, the downed hog received an immediate knife stick to the jugular vein, and the throat was cut from ear to ear. This allowed the blood to drain freely from the body and made for a less bloody dressing later on. With a man at each hind leg, the porker was dragged to the scalding barrel and heaved in, headfirst, hind legs protruding slightly.

When the water in the pot reached the right temperature, not quite boiling but scalding hot, big bucketfuls were heaved into the barrel, dousing the carcass, which was then rapidly turned and rolled about (hind legs serving as handles) so as to give all parts a good exposure to the hot water. Only the extreme rear portion missed this hot bath, as it protruded from the barrel.

During the scalding process there was a frantic snatching at patches of hair, from moment to moment, to determine at just what point the hair began to slip well. Water not hot enough was ineffective; too hot, it set the hair; underexposure failed to loosen the hair and overexposure would set it. Both timing and water temperature required careful judgment.

When the hair slipped easily, carcass ends were exchanged in the barrel, a bit more hot water added, and the rear end soused and doused in the hot bath until hair slippage was just right. At this point, the whole thing was hastily pulled from the barrel onto boards or a sheet of tin, to keep it out of the dirt, and the men set to with scraping knives. Scraping had to be done in a hurry, for, once cold, the hair set. But when timed just right, the hair and the outer layer of skin yielded to scrapers' knives, leaving a beautifully clean and white carcass.

Next came the call for the gamlin stick, a small, strong stick, about two feet long and sharpened on both ends. At the hock [gambrel] slits were made in each hind leg between the bone and the big tendon and the sharp ends of the gamlin stick inserted in each. The stick served two purposes: it stabilized and held apart the hind legs, an aid to dressing [disemboweling]; with a rope attached at the stick's center the carcass was hoisted, head down, by means of a pulley [most often by manpower alone] to a scaffold or a tree limb and anchored at just the right height for dressing.

A tub was placed under the hanging carcass, and Papa, with a sharp knife and the meticulosity of a surgeon, laid open a thin seam down the belly from anus to throat. Then, beginning at the anus, he completely opened the belly, very slowly, placing one hand carefully inside to hold back the entrails, for a cut or torn gut would allow the contents to spill out and contaminate portions of the flesh it touched, to say nothing of the terrific odor. And always, on male hogs he carefully cut away the genitals, giving particular attention to the urinary apparatus to prevent ruinous spillage there.

The major portion of the opening completed, the insides were cut from their moorings and let fall into the tub below. Liver, heart, lights [lungs], and melt [sweetbread] were removed—heart and lights thrown to the waiting hounds, as Mama would not allow us to eat the heart, and the lungs were waste. Intestines were set aside to be ridded of fat for lard or soap grease and cleaned for sausage casings. Chunks of liver and melt quickly found their way to the bed of coals around the wash pot, and shortly those who chose were munching on roast liver and melt. I never liked either.

With processing well under way, helpers would start the scalding procedure with the next animal slaughtered—and so, killing, scalding, scraping, dressing, and cutting up proceeded throughout the day, with a break for dinner. If all went well, six to eight animals could be butchered on one day.

Meantime the hanging carcass at hand was doused with clear, cool water and rinsed free of blood. It was then removed to the smokehouse and placed on a table of thick, heavy boards, where Papa deftly and precisely did the cutting. The order of his cutting procedure has vanished from my memory, if, indeed, I ever knew it, but I have a vivid recollection of those big beautiful hams he so expertly cut out, running a knife around the bone to make way for handfuls of curing salt. Shoulders were separated, being prized right next to ham, and the head and feet removed and sent to the kitchen, where Mama minced the ears, tongue, and trimmings, mixed this mess with spices and vinegar, and packed it in a crock where it would set for several days. The result of this mixture was souse, or headcheese, which turned out to be a hellified mass that could be sliced as if it were cheese. Some liked it. I could barely tolerate it. Sometimes, but not often, Mama pickled the feet, and sometimes all scraps and trimmings were converted to sausage instead of souse.

In the smokehouse, Papa, with a regular wood ax, chopped the ribs loose from the backbone, which he lifted out and cut into chunks sized in accordance with what he calculated would fit into and season a pot of turnips and greens. Spareribs, flensed from belly portions called middlings, or side meat, provided the fare at dinnertime. Fried brown and served with milk gravy and hot biscuits, they were delicious.

A great deal of the fat was cut away from lean portions to be rendered next day into lard. Hams, loins, shoulders, and middlings were salted heavily and let set a day or so. Later, shaken free of the damp salt, they were re-salted, sometimes with a mixture of saltpeter, and packed away in great wooden boxes, which Papa made and which he called meat boxes. After some time, perhaps about two weeks, selected portions were removed from the salt pack and hung over a slow smoldering hickory fire from which rose a pungent smoke that completed the curing process.

It was most interesting and inventive, the way Papa hung the meat for smoking. From the yucca plant (he called it bear grass), he gathered long slender leaves and cast them into a bed of hot ashes. This softened and toughened the leaves and left them most pliable. Through a hole pierced in the corner of a piece of meat he threaded a yucca leaf, tied the ends, and slipped the yucca loop over the horizontal smoke pole stabilized a few feet above the hickory coals.

Thus, our meat supply for the year—hams, loins, shoulders, middlings, and sometimes sausage—dangled in the rising smoke, was cured and at hand for sustenance for the family throughout the year. It goes without saying that toward the end of the next summer, what was not eaten by that time became a bit rancid and smelly. But Papa's philosophy was that it was better to have rancid meat than no meat at all.

Mrs. Clotille Nutt

You shoot them and stick 'em and you let them bleed, then you haul them to the vat to scald 'em. You have to put the water at 145 degrees. This man we had this year put four sprigs of pine tops and three tablespoons of soda to make the hair slip easier. They put the hog in the vat and roll him over the chains so the hair slips good on all sides. After they get the hog where the hair slips real good, then they roll him out on some board and scrape all the hair off. After the hog has been scraped completely, it is then gangled. Gangling is where you cut through the skin of the back of the leg and pull the tendon out so you will have a place to hang the hog by. Then the hog is hung on a singletree from its tendons and lifted in the air. After the hog has been hung up, it is then gutted and all of its insides are removed. You are then ready to cut it up and prepare it for butchering. Charles, my son, wanted his cut into pork chops. But then you have to saw down the back-bone on each side. We had to have our chops cut at a butcher shop because we're not equipped to cut them ourselves. If you save the backbone, you scrape it down, then you cut the tenderloin, or backstrap. I wanted the tenderloin and backbone out of mine. Then you are ready to cut the mid-dlings, hams, shoulders, and cut the head off.

When all the parts have been cut, we roll them in the sugar cure. We then place it on a board with the skin up so that it can drain overnight. The next morning we rerub the meat and hang it up so the wind can dry it out.

When we have this taken care of, it is time to take care of the sausage and lard. The sausage and lard parts had been separated as we cut the meat, so when we get ready to stuff the sausage all we have to do is grind the meat and stuff it. The lard is put in pots and allowed to cook on an open flame. We scrape our own casing and stuff our own sausage. I take care of all the casing even down to the chitlins. I also take care of all the feet and heads, even on down to making cheese out of the hog's head. The head made some fine cheese; you can eat it with crackers and vinegar over it. You just don't know how good it is. It's made out of the hog's head and feet. The feet is what really makes it stick together.

I was raised up growing hogs and living on the farm. My daddy had us four or five cows. We had to milk every morning. My daddy ran a sepa-rator. We fed the hogs skim milk, and that's how we had our meat and lard to help with our living and all. Back then it was a depression, and I remem-ber many a day when I would chop cotton for fifty cents a day. And I worked in the field and at the house too. I tell you, you can't realize the difference in time from now till back when we were growing up. We worked for fifty cents a day because there wasn't any money back then. My sister and I worked for a man by the name of Millard Robinson, and he said he'd rather have those two Pass girls to lead a pack of colored hands than any other girls he knew. He knew his workers had to put in a day's work if they followed us. He always hired us to chop his cotton and lead his colored workers. We were just real glad to get the job. We would pick peas for fifty cents a hundred pounds, chop cotton, and we were proud to just be able to work.

1. The hog in its pen.

2. The hog being washed down.

3. Building a fire to boil water in the vat.

4. Preparing to roll the hog in the vat.

5. Scalding the hog.

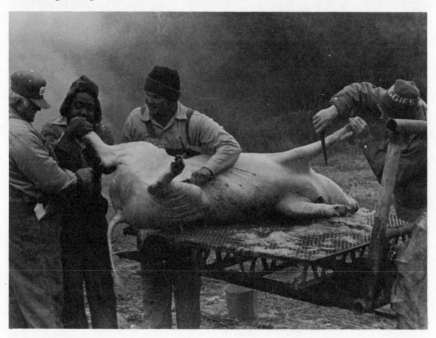

6. Scraping the hog.

7. Mrs. Clotille Nutt with the freshly scraped hog.

8. Hog hooked on the singletree.

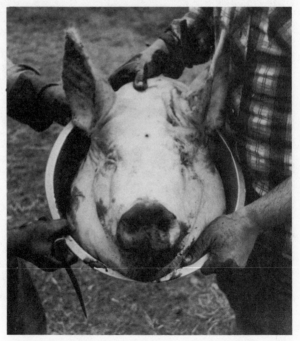

9. The hog's head in a pan.

10. Cutting into the hog.

11. The halved hog ready for butchering.

12. Removing the hip joints from the hams.

13. The cured meat being hung.

14. Cooking out the cracklins to make lard.

15. Straining the cracklins from the lard.

Big Black Wash Pots

In earlier times in East Texas, store-bought tools and utensils were hard to come by, and when you did acquire such an item for use in the home or on the farm, it had to be used to the fullest. The black wash pot, or yard pot, was part of the basic household gear of every rural home and farmstead as late as the 1940's, and perhaps no other utensil was ever put to as many different uses. Some of those applications of the black wash pot are described below, but we are sure there are many others we haven't heard about yet.

Washing Clothes

We found Marie Bortley to be a good friend and a firm believer in doing things no longer common today. She still washes clothes in the old-fashioned way—outside the house in black wash pots heated by a wood fire. She keeps busy washing for herself, her husband, daughter, and grandchildren. Even her washboard is one of a kind and was homemade for her. She makes her own lye soap to use during washing, and she believes her way is still the best for getting the job done right. We also thank Mildred Abshier for her excellent account of childhood wash days in Southeast Texas.

Marie Bortley

I start by putting water in the pots and heating the water. I wash in the first one. Then I clean the clothes on the rub board in the second one and rinse them out good in the third one. I move them from one pot to another on a stick because they're hot. Then I wring out the clothes and hang them on the line to dry.

My memories of washing clothes goes back before my own time. My uncle was born back in the days of slavery. He told me how special days were set aside for the slaves to wash clothes for their owners and for themselves. They were given so much time during the day to get the job done. If they didn't finish in time they were in trouble and were whipped. They sure learned to work that job fast.

Before we got running water I used to take the pots down by the creek and do my washing there. I'd just get a bucket and go back and forth between the creek and the pots to fill them up. I'd start the fire under the pots and go to washing the clothes.

If you didn't have a washboard you'd lay your clothes out on a plank and get a stick and beat the dirt out. Then you'd rinse them and hang them up to dry.

I have a washboard though that's handmade. It's shaped like the ones you buy at the store. You have a board with ridges on it made by using big spike nails. You pound them in and bend them around in the back. It sure does the job.

For soap I usually use my own lye soap that I make myself. I make it using grease and also use old cow bone sometimes. The soap is usually hard so you can rub your clothes with it. What I have right now is soft but all gets the clothes real clean.

Pouring lye soap into the wash.

Beginning to take the clothes from the wash pot.

It's easier to wash clothes now that I have running water. I don't have to take the pots down to the creek anymore. I just leave the pots in the yard by the house. That saves a lot of steps and a lot of time. I just use a hose to fill up the pots as much as I want. I heat the water, which doesn't have to get real hot. Then I just start washing, then rinsing, then hanging them up to dry. I wash several times a week. There's lots to be done because I wash for lots of folks—me and my husband, my daughter, then my grandchildren. Using the laundromat is too expensive. I enjoy doing it here the old way. And we sure do get our clothes clean.

To make the soap I put three gallons of water in the pot. Then I add two gallons of the lye and a gallon of grease. I stir it up real good and let it come to a boil. Then I boil it for five hours to make the soap. Sometimes if I have something to pour it into I will. Otherwise I just let it stay in the pot, and the next morning it's hard and ready to cut out. Sometimes it comes out brown and sometimes white. For the grease I used fried meat grease. Sometimes I'll have old bones I throw in. It depends on whatever I have.

Mildred Abshier

Wash day rolled around once a week, usually on Friday, barring inclement weather. Why Friday, I never knew, except that it insured clean clothes in case we got to go to town Saturday or to church on Sunday. When bad weather did interfere, the dirty-clothes pile grew unmercifully, for keeping clothes clean for a farm family of five, plus the hired hand, was some chore and was best taken care of on a regular basis.

It was helpful if on the preceding day at least part of the wash water was drawn. This task was accomplished by means of a hand-operated rope, which was threaded through a pulley and to which a well bucket was attached at one end. The bucket had a valve in the bottom, and when let down into the well, contact with the water pushed open the valve and allowed the bucket to fill. Water pressure inside the full bucket forced the valve shut, and all that remained to be done was to haul up the filled bucket, hand over hand on the rope—extremely tiring work when one considered the amount of water required for a washing of clothes.

Come wash-day morning, the wash pot, which sat outside the backyard gate in close proximity to the well and the woodpile, was filled with water and a roaring fire built around it. Into the pot went a huge chunk of home-made lye soap, chipped into small bits for quick melting. The fire, powered with pine knots and oak chunks, soon had the soap melted and the water boiling.

White things came first. If you were really on the ball, they had been put to soak in cool water the night before—Mama said hot water set the dirt, cool water loosened it. Soaked or unsoaked, they were soused in a tub of warm sudsy water, and the battle with the rub board was begun.

Washtubs rested on a bench at just the right height to accommodate access to the rub board from a standing position. Near the top of the board was a place for a slab of lye soap—sometimes Octagon if we were out of the homemade variety. From its position on the board the soap was within convenient reach for a generous application to deeply soiled pieces.

Each item of the wash had its individual turn at the rub board, scrubbed up and down, over the board's ridged surface, every stroke powered by the elbow grease of the hapless washerwoman—I having had wide experience in this realm of endeavor. With the bulk of the soil removed or loosened by intensive rubbing across the board, each piece was wrung out by hand, then dumped into the pot of boiling suds. Water and soap were added as needed and the fire stoked frequently.

Punching down was an important part of the cleaning process, maybe stemming from the more ancient practice of using a battling stick for beating dirt from the clothes. The punching stick was a slender board, or stick, two or three feet long, made smooth on one end so as not to snag any clothing it might come in contact with. Mama said that frequent punching down of the boiling wash helped with cleaning and insured exposure of all surfaces to the boiling suds, killing lurking germs. So, smooth end down, the punching stick was applied to the boiling heap—punching, poking, turning, and twisting—as often as Mama deemed necessary or prudent.

As white things boiled, "nice colored things" (Mama's very descriptive terminology for a division of the wash) were given the rub board treatment and made ready for their turn in the boiling pot. Items that faded had to be washed separately and were not subjected to the boil. Work clothes came last—overalls and shirts with ever so much deep down dirt and grime.

These soaked in tubs of suds while white things were renched [rinsed] and nice colored things boiled. An alert scheduling of the various phases of the wash-day work kept the washerwoman hopping but helped to hurry the task along.

Cleaning the work clothes called for the most fortitude and perseverance. Only experience could bring full comprehension of the amount of rubbing and scrubbing on the washboard that was required to dislodge the sweat and grime and grit that only a farmer can impart to the clothing he wears in his daily work. This was where the real rub came in, where both muscle and will of the washerwoman began to wane.

Every time there was a spare moment, more water had to be drawn. This was necessary to comply with Mama's insistence that every item of clothing be subjected to three rinses, the last with a touch of blueing.

When white things had what was coming to them in the boiling pot, the punching stick was commandeered, and they were lifted from the pot and carried, bucketful by bucketful, to the first rinse tub and dumped therein. Nice colored things boiled while white clothes, including heavy and hard to handle bed sheets, were doused and swished and dabbled and squeezed and wrung, piece by piece, from the first rinse to the second and lastly to the third from which they were renched out, or wrung out, and hung out on the yard fence io dry.

There was no clothesline, no clothespins. A strand of barbed wire ["bob wahr"] at the top of the yard fence helped to keep the wash from fluttering to the ground and all too often insured a snag here and a snag there.

Every batch of wash went through the same procedure, and there were days when dress shirts, dresser scarves, dresses, and the like had to be starched, hung out to dry, brought in, sprinkled down, and ironed to a satiny smoothness with sadirons heated in the fireplace or on the kitchen stove. Happily, the washerwoman did not have to do the ironing—not on washday, anyhow.

Washing was an all-day trial, and sometimes, in my youth, I believed it to be a form of persecution. As the waning hours of the day drew on, an aching back, tired feet, and just plain exhaustion lent themselves, I'm sure, to a lessening of the meticulous care Mama desired for the wash. Even in her severe illness she held scrupulously to her standards for family care, including getting the wash done properly.

At times, the supply of water became a problem. When the water table was low or the well went dry, wash pot and benches were set up at the stock tank in the pasture. There the water did not have to be drawn, but we did have to lug the dirty clothes to the tank and drag up wash wood for the fire. Clothes were hung on the pasture fence to dry, where again barbed wire inflicted a snag here and there. When goats were in the pasture, it was not uncommon that pieces of clothing came to be goat-chewed—shredded and fringed beyond use.

In periods of severe drought when well water was low and tank water nonexistent or too muddy to use, we carried everything but the wash pot about a quarter of a mile through the woods to a gully which was spring-fed. Here we rubbed and soaped and rubbed again (in the absence of boiling) and rinsed and hung the wash out to dry on bushes, mostly Spanish mulberries. This arrangement was somewhat less than desirable, but Mama said the soap, water, sunshine, and fresh air at least got the stink out. And I guess it did, to some extent anyhow.

Scalding Hogs

Wayman Walkey

We bring the hog in and build fires around the pots. We have pine out of the woods, enough to heat the water in the two wash pots out there. After we get the water, we build a fire around the pots. It depends on whether the hog had a good bit of age on it, like two hundred or two hundred fifty pounds. It takes a hotter temperature to scald a hog like that than a hundred- or one-hundred-twenty-five pound hog. You just have to have hot water fixed just right so you can scald the hog. At the same time, if it's too hot, it will set the hair on him. This is when the hair will scald and won't come out. The way I can tell when the water is right is to just run my fingers through it right quick to see if it's hot enough. Then we cut the leaders in the back legs, so we can put these sticks in there, the gamblin' sticks. Together all of us catches the back legs and the front legs, so we can hang him up. That takes a pretty good effort to hang up one that weighs over two hundred pounds. With some more hot water out of this wash pot we pour it over the hog to get all the loose hair off. Getting the hair off him is called scraping the hog down.

Making Hominy

Ollie Prince

There are three ways people can make hominy. You cook it the same each time, but what you put in can be different. One way is one pound of soda to one gallon of corn, or one pound of corn to eight ounces of lye, or one gallon of ashes to one gallon of corn. You always use dry corn.

I'm gonna put this water in the pot and let it be getting hot while they coming with the corn. And to two pounds of corn use about a little box like that of sodie, eight ounces at least. Just dump it in there and grind the sodie up in there with the corn. Now, you let that boil in the pot until the husk slips off, which will take about two hours. Then you take it up and pour it in another pot and wash it till all the husk comes off, and then you take the corn and put it back in there and boil it till the water turns white. Then wait till it turns yeller again with sodie. And you wash it again. Then you put it in there and boil it again. Then pour that water off and you pour the water off the hominy until it gets clear, and you take it and cook it till it gets tender. That's all there are to making hominy. I fed my kids a many a meal on hominy when times was hard and we didn't have much money—just go to the crib and get a bushel, a gallon of corn, and make up hominy with it, then we'd eat that for supper.

Making Lye Soap

Bettie Woolam
    5 pounds grease, strained through cloth to take out pieces of meat
    1 can lye dissolved in 1 quart cold water
    2 tablespoons borax dissolved in 1/2 cup water
    1/2 cup ammonia
    2 tablespoons sugar and 1 tablespoon salt
Have the grease just warm to the touch of your hand. Stir into the grease slowly and easily the lukewarm lye. Add borax, ammonia, sugar, and salt. Stir the mixture until it is consistency of thick honey. Then pour into molds to harden into bars of soap. If you don't have soap molds, mixture may be poured into large deep (3 to 4 inches) container, preferably crockery, and after it hardens it may be cut with heavy butcher knife into bars of soap or even broken into usable-sized pieces of soap.

Mildred Abshier
    Soap making at our house took place several times a year, but the biggest batch was made at hog-killing time, when a good supply of fat was at hand. Fat stripped from hog intestines, especially the small ones, was usually consigned to the soap pot—and for a very good reason. More than occasionally guts were torn or cut in the process of butchering, and this allowed the contents to ooze into surrounding fat, contaminating it and permeating it with a strong odor that made it unfit for lard. The same went for fat taken from the urethral apparatus, also for bloody fat and for other waste fat. All that was not considered fit for lard was tossed into the soap pot.
    And pot it was, for Mama used the big family wash pot for soap making. The fat, cut into small chunks, was dumped into the pot, and lye was added in accordance with the size of the pile of fat. Mama's measurements were always by eye, albeit meticulous enough to produce excellent results. With a bit of water added, the whole mess was stirred, and the lye went to work breaking down the fat to liquid. A few hours were required for this process, and bits and pieces of resistant skin, or rind, had to be fished from the pot, else they showed up in the finished product.
    Once the breaking-down process was complete and careful amounts of water had been added, a fire was built around the pot and the stuff was set

to boiling. It was then that the stirring began with the wooden clothes paddle, or punching stick, as we called it.

Oh, that stirring! It had to be continuous and ever in one direction—or at least Mama said so. She always started the stirring, demonstrating the proper technique, from which we were admonished never to depart. She would then turn over that long, drawn out process to my brother Doc, Little Sister, and me, however, casting a fairly regular eye in the direction of the operation. When the contents of the pot had been cooked just enough and the fire pushed away from the pot, the stirring began in earnest. The concoction had to be kept in motion until it cooled and began to solidify, later to be cut into usable chunks.

But we surely disproved Mama's theory that lye soap, to be made properly and of the best quality, had to be stirred in one direction—clockwise, I do believe it was. We stirred clockwise when she was near, then, minus her presence, counterclockwise, by quadrants and fractions of quadrants, jabbed up and down. You name it, we stirred it.

But her soap was almost always good, sometimes fair, in spite of our lack of compliance with her directions. Applied to our clothes, with the aid of elbow grease and the rub board, it cleaned them; highly recommended for washing the hair (we didn't know the word "shampoo"), it supposedly left a much desired auburn highlight, and we often used it for the weekly body scrubbing in the number three washtub, for sweet soap was a luxury not often afforded.

Through the year, grease from the kitchen was saved for making additional batches of soap. Of course, fried meat grease was used over and

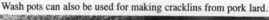

Wash pots can also be used for making cracklins from pork lard.

Moss Heaton stirs the cracklins.

over; you seldom threw it out. But once it became smelly or was burned, it was dumped into the soap grease can, along with grease from super-rancid fried bacon—and bacon got that way in late summer.

Lye soap was a must in our early household. But we all admitted that it was quite a fine thing when Mama could supplement her soap supply with Octagon soap from the country store or with an occasional bar of sweet soap for the family's weekly bathing episodes.

Some Other Uses of the Yard Pot

Making cracklins from pork lard
Scalding peaches to remove skins before canning
Making beef chili
Boiling canned foods to sterilize them
Cooking turnip greens
Making lard
Scalding feathers off chickens and turkeys
Making Mulligan stew
Boiling crawfish
Cooking beans
Washing beans and peas before cooking
Boiling roots to make dye for feed sacks
Heating bath water
Holding apples for bobbing at parties
Making syrup candy
Heating water for scrubbing down the smokehouse
Dissolving block salt to make salt crystals for preserving meat
Melting wax to make candles

Serious Marbles

Marbles and marble games have been around for a long time. Marble games are known to have been played by the ancient Egyptians. They spread from there to Greece and to Rome. The Roman legions brought marbles to Britain and to northern Europe.

From England the movement of marble games coincided with the spread of the British empire. English marbles crossed the Atlantic to America, so the marbles played here are derivations of English games. George Washington was a marble player, as were Thomas Jefferson, John Quincy Adams, and Abraham Lincoln.

Some material on marbles came to us from the people at the Great American Marble Factory, who were a lot of help on some of the games and the rules that follow.

Nucks

Nucks is a hole game, involving three holes, each a yard from the other. The holes are of any dimensions agreed on by the players. A shooting line is established about ten feet away from the first hole. Players lag (roll the marble) to the line, and the closest one has the choice of being first or second. The first player shoots or rolls his marble to get it in the hole. He continues as long as his marbles go in the holes. When he misses, the second player shoots for the hole or tries to hit the opponent's marble. Hitting the opponent's marble gives an extra turn, as does going in the hole. The first player to get in all three holes in the proper order (one, two, three) wins and collects one or more marbles from each of the other players.

Ringer

Ringer is the traditional enclosure game and the one used for championship tournaments. A circle of agreed-upon size (at least three feet and no more than ten in diameter) is laid out, and each player puts an agreed-upon number of target marbles ("miggles") in the center. Target marbles must be at least two inches from each other, but no more than three inches. Each player takes a turn lagging to the edge of the circle from a point ten feet away. The closest to the line has the choice of going first or second, and the others play in order of their closeness.

Players shoot their marbles from outside the ring (as close as can be without hunching over the edge of the ring) to strike the target marbles and knock them out of the ring. Players must shoot knuckles down, with at least one knuckle touching the ground, unless agreed otherwise at the start of the game. If a player's shooter remains in the ring after his turn, it becomes a legitimate target and must be ransomed if captured by another player. The winner is the person who has captured the most marbles when all target marbles have been knocked out of the ring. Ringer can be played "for fairs," in which case the marbles are returned to their owners after the game, or "for keeps," in which case the players retain all captured marbles.

Felicia Wilkerson shows marbles can still be fun.

Chasies

Players agree on the course to be followed. The first player shoots or rolls his marble down the course. The second player attempts to shoot or roll so that his marble hits the first marble. If it does so, or if it comes sufficiently close so that the second player can touch both marbles with any part of one hand, then the first player pays a penalty of one marble. If it does not, then the second player must shoot or roll and the first player must chase. Play continues until all reach the end of the course.

Bounce Eye

A circle is drawn on the ground about one foot in diameter. Then the players put two or more marbles in a pile in the middle of the circle. Each player in turn stands at the rim of the circle and drops a shooter from eye level into the pile of marbles. The object is to hit the most marbles out of the circle. The game is over when there are no marbles left in the circle.

Football

This game is started by drawing a football shape in the dirt, with a line connecting the two ends. Each player puts a marble on the line. In turn each player tries to knock the marbles off the line and out of the football. When all the marbles are knocked out, the game is over and the winner is the player with the most marbles.

Old Bowler

Draw a square in the dirt and connect the corners with diagonal lines. Place marbles down the lines. To determine who goes first, bowl from a starting line; the player who comes closest to the square then tries to shoot the four corner marbles. Players shoot until they miss. Then the center target, called Old Bowler, must be knocked out. If one of the players mistakenly hits Old Bowler before the other target marbles are eliminated, that player is automatically out.

We also talked to others who remembered their marbles-playing days. We discovered a variety of games in a time when young people (and some not so young) created their own entertainment—when marbles were a serious business.

Johnny Smith

They played marbles ever since I remember—way back. I've known my daddy to walk down there [Woods Post Office]; that's about three miles. After dinner on Saturday he'd bathe, put on fresh clothes, and be off for some serious marble shooting. After he got to be about seventy, the playing kind of drowned out over at Woods Post Office and he started going to Gary. He played with Uncle Jim Applegate and Uncle Jesse McGee. Aus

Downing played with them some. Cousin Johnny Hooker was often my daddy's partner. He had a brother named Jed Hooker. He played, as did old Uncle Henry DeBerry.

My daddy used to carry marbles in his pocket, and when he had some free time he'd take 'em out and practice. He was one of the best around. He loved to play marbles any place, any time, and against anyone. It was a pretty big deal in those days. They even went up to Beckville for a tournament one time, but they lost that one. They were serious in their playing. Old Doctor Parker and Cousin Johnny Hooker got into a fight one time. It was some argument about the rules. They made up though. No one got hurt; it was a friendly fight.

The taw was the thumping marble, or the one you shot with. The other marbles were just called ring marbles, and they were larger than the taws. You placed the ring marbles in the playing area to set up your game. The marbles were mostly made of stone and weren't all colors like the glass ones you see now.

To see who would shoot first, the players would toss their taws, to see whose got closest to the center of the square. Then they'd take turns. When they played, it was usually one of two different games. The first one was called Tennessee. When they first started playing they had a big square. Oh, I 'spect it was maybe four or six feet square. They put nine marbles in there, one on each corner, then one in the center of each side, and one in the middle. They played that where the one who got the most marbles won the game, you know. You had to knock at least five out of the nine out of the square. Your first shot would be from about six feet away, and then you'd shoot from where your taw had landed. On that game they could play partners. If the other team killed your partner [hit his taw with theirs], you could give him a marble [a ring marble you had previously knocked out of the square], that is, pay him out. The way they killed your partner, or you, for sure was they'd shoot one of you and your partner didn't have a marble to pay you out. Then you were dead and your team lost.

Well, they'd quit that one and start playing the other game that was called seven-up. They had a little square about two feet square. They put a marble in each corner and one in the middle. You'd have to win seven games to call it seven-up. You had to stand back about ten to fifteen feet away, and if you hit that middle marble and knocked it out of the square, well, you got the game. I've seen my daddy knock that middle marble out seven shots in a row and win. They played partners on that one too. If you didn't hit the center marble out on your first shot you had to try to hit all five out of the square. And if your taw stayed in the square after a shot you were dead, or fat, and were out of the game.

Jim Box

Well, I suppose if you're going to describe how to play marbles, there are all different sorts of games, but the marbles themselves in my youth were called glassies, aggies, crockies.

Crockies were made out of baked clay. They were rounded into pretty fair circles, but they weren't always round, and they were likely to go off in tangents because they weren't completely round. They were made and sold for, oh, I don't know, you could get a big sack of them for a nickel. They were probably made in China, and I'd say there are about two hundred of them in a sack.

Glassies were, of course, made out of glass, and they had a variety of swirled patterns and colors in each one. Some were a solid color, but most of them had some sort of swirl pattern. When you shot the marble, you'd have a nice pattern like a barber pole or something as the marble went toward its target.

Aggies were the best quality, and of course these were the ones we all used for our shooting marbles. There were also steelies, which were made out of steel. They were ball bearings. They were outlawed because when they hit a crockie or a glassy with one of those it broke the marble. You had to have a destructive vent to want to use steelies. Usually steelies were outlawed.

Okay, the aggies—what marked them and made them so pretty was that when they hit another marble, sometimes it would put a little moon in

A variety of marbles.

them. You know, like a little new moon? And so you see a well-used aggie, it would have little new moons under the surface of it all the time. Aggies came in all sorts of colors. I think the rust-colored ones were my favorites. They ranged from some white to some almost pure black. But black ones were pretty scarce. That pretty well covers the marbles.

Playing the game we, as young boys, always decided first whether the game was for keeps. That meant that if you won a marble you stuck it in your pocket and the other guy lost it. The game was over when the other guy lost all his marbles. That's where the expression came from, "He lost his marbles." Usually the game was played by drawing a big circle out in the dirt, and this usually was good old black dirt, like we have here, or sandy dirt. You would take a stick or a pocketknife and draw a big circle on the ground about eighteen inches to two feet in circumference.

There would usually be four or five marble shooters, and each person would ante up a couple or three marbles to put into the circle. This is what the crockies were usually used for, because they were the cheapest and ulti-mately what you wanted to lose the most if you had to lose something. Then the first shooter, keeping his knuckles out of the circle, would shoot. The aggies were what they would usually use to shoot with. He would shoot his aggie into the circle into the other marbles, trying to knock the best-looking marble out of the circle, but at the same time he wanted his marble also to come out of the circle. That's because if his marble stayed inside the circle, then people were privileged to shoot at it, and if they knocked it out of the circle, then they got to keep it.

So they always wanted to make sure that their aggie came out of the circle after hitting the other marble. So you try to make them spin, travel quickly after they hit the other marble, and get out of the circle. If you hit one too solidly, and you had to hit them pretty solid to knock the other marble out of the circle, your aggie would stay inside the circle and you would lose an expensive marble. By expensive I mean you'd pay a nickel for a whole sack of crockies, and you could get probably twenty or thirty glassies for a nickel, and you might pay as much as ten cents for one aggie. So if you lost your aggie by having it stay in the circle after you knocked a marble out, and you lost it by somebody knocking it out, it was the equiva-lent of losing anywhere from thirty to sixty glassies and a couple of sacks of crockies.

We went to a little country school, and during marble season it was not at all uncommon to see boys with their pockets bulging. Marble season is when school started. What was confusing about the bulges in their pockets was in the area around Fort Worth, Birdville, there were native pecan trees, and the pecans were getting ready to thresh. So one pocket would be full of marbles and one would be full of pecans.

Most boys also had a sack they carried around their neck. It was a little canvas sack with a drawstring around the top, and of course you could tell by looking at someone's sack or at the bulges in their pockets and tell whether they had been lucky or unlucky at marbles. Oh, I started to say, you had a pocket full of marbles and a pocket full of pecans, and you could tell by looking at the bulges which was which. The pecans were sharper. The pecan season also was marked by brown hands, because we couldn't wait for them to get ready and fall from the outer shell. We'd shake them down and peel the green shell out from around them and eat them.

Oh, yes, we would determine who shot first by lagging; that is, we'd shoot our marbles toward a straight line marked off about six or eight feet away. The one whose marble was closest to the line was the one who got to shoot first. The first shooter was always at an advantage because he got to shoot at the choice marble.

Ray Arnold

When I was little the kids would play the dog out of marbles. They would go to the store and buy a dozen for a dime. Then at school they would play when the teacher fell asleep.

Rusty Marshall

They would buy them at the store. And when they'd get lucky they would find a paint can and bust it open to get the marbles out of it. If you were to get your hands on one of those crystals, you were really hot stuff. If you were playing and won a marble from the other guy, he would have to give you two or three regular marbles. And those steel ball bearings, we called them steelies. I could get one of those and get up close enough to break a cat-eye marble in half.

One of the games we would play was pot. It was where you put some marbles in a circle. They were the ones you'd keep. The other games were kind of about the same; you hit the other person and you win their marbles.

Rusty Hodge

Well, my grandpa was born in 1901. He grew up in the times where neighbors and friends would usually get together about once every six months. The small children from the age of about six months old to about twelve years of age would go too.

Their mothers would bring blankets for the younger girls to sit on as they watched the smaller children. Our old grandmother would be sitting close by while the ladies were getting the noonday meal together.

The younger boys that were old enough would usually start a game of marbles. This game was played four or five different ways. One way was to draw a round circle, then each player would divide four or five marbles in the circle. They would take their favorite marble, which would be a cat eye, a crystal marble maybe with a solid stripe, or a ball bearing. A ball bearing was a shooting marble.

They would then flip a coin or a log to see who shot first. Shooting was done by putting the marble on the tip of your finger and thumb behind the marble. You had to keep your finger on the outside of the circle. You would shoot and knock as many marbles as you could out of the circle. Any marble you knocked out, you'd keep. That's why they called it keeps.

Another way to play marbles was called chase. This game was played by one player shooting out across the ground, and the others would get after him by hitting his marbles. If hit, the game was over for him.

Another way was a game called holes. This game was played by digging holes in the ground. When you were shooting for the holes, if you could get to the last hole before someone hit you, then you won the game.

Alton Cromwell

I started playing marbles when I was about seven years of age. There were usually fifteen to a sack that they carried around. The marbles were all different colors. At first, in about 1928, they came out with clay marbles but later came out with stone marbles, called white stones marbles. Sometimes the marbles were set in squares with one big one in the middle. In about 1932 they came out with glass marbles.

Usually if it was a group playing there would be from anywhere to two hundred through three hundred marbles in a circle about fifteen feet in diameter. I would take a big agate and stand up and would bust a marble out of the circle. And sometimes I would break them, but they still would go out of the circle. If your hand or your foot went over the line, somebody else would take your turn. The agates that they played with came in all sizes, some up to the size of a five-cent piece. They were made up of a special rock. If you hit the marble hard enough with the agate it would make a half-moon inside. To take the half-moon out, you would soak it in hog lard and leave it over night. The next morning it would be gone. I had to do this a lot.

They had another game called rolly wolly, but the marbles were much, much smaller. You would make holes and would try to get the marble in the hole. But your opponent would try to knock your marble out of the hole and in turn get that marble. All the marbles you knocked out of the circle, you got to keep.

Usually, if you had a good number of kids, ten to twelve would play at once, depending on if they had enough marbles. I used to sell the marbles I would win, one hundred for ten cents. This would pay my way to the show every week.

We used to play where the First National Bank is, the new one. It used to be a wagon yard when I was a boy. They used to make their own marbles, out of clay. We would usually play for keeps; if you got it you kept it. The game, if a good one, would last anywhere from a hour and a half to two hours. The main or favorite marble would be the agate. We would use the agate to shoot glass marbles with. The agate is a little see-through. Only the boys played, no girls played. I was real good. A marble could be an inch away from the line and I would hit it, and my agate would stay inside the circle. At the store, marbles usually cost about twenty-five marbles for ten cents, but I would sell one hundred for twenty-five cents, which was a good deal. We only played at school a little, but we didn't play for keeps. When I had quit playing marbles I had about fifteen hundred of them. My father had played in 1903 and gave me his agate. Marble playing is really a skill and art.

Outhouses

Outhouses, privies, johnnies, biffies, johns—they were known by many different names—were once the norm rather than the exception in rural East Texas. Although they may look primitive from the perspective of indoor toilets with running water, bathtubs, sinks, and the like, the outhouse was an advancement on the toilet facilities our great-grandfathers often put up with. As late as 1935, no fewer than 1219 rural schools in Texas had no toilet facilities whatsoever, according to a survey of that year by the State Board of Education. The rule was "Boys one way, girls the other," and as Mildred Abshier points out in the concluding essay in this chapter, that was often the rule at home as well. One early teacher in a country school went before her three-man board of trustees to lobby for a girl's toilet. She was listened to in silence by one tobacco-chewing old farmer who then remarked, "Not so long as there's all that bresh out there."

The outhouses that gradually replaced the "bresh," or brush, had their own problems. None of the people we talked to missed them or seemed particularly nostalgic about them. All of them had vivid memories of the thing, none of them really fond ones.

Jim Box

The typical country outhouse from the twenties and thirties was a building approximately four by six by seven foot tall with a sheet tin roof. It was weather-stripped with one-by-fours. The door was hinged with a button [small piece of wood] nailed on to it so it could be closed from the inside or outside.

Usually outhouses were classified as one-holers or two-holers. The two-holers' social implications were where two brothers or two sisters could share the Sears and Roebuck or Montgomery Ward catalogues in a relaxed social environment. For preadolescent and adolescent boys, the lingerie and foundation garment sections of the two catalogues often provided a major anatomical and sex education. Needless to say, these young men used those pages last for their original intended purpose, which need not be named. Also in the country outhouse was a baking powder can full of lime. The lime was sprinkled into the pit to reduce the pungent odor from time to time.

The country schools usually had two large outhouses on opposite sides of the campus, one for girls and one for boys. My particular school had eight-holers, which were filled to capacity during the season when turnip greens and poke salad were a staple diet at home.

The graffiti on the walls were written with stolen bits of chalk from the teacher's blackboards. The chalk graffiti showed up quite well on the age-darkened boards of the outhouse's interior.

One serious flaw was inherent in the simple flimsy structure of these small outbuildings. That flaw was that the family outhouse was an easy victim for the prowling predators of Halloween evening. The morning following Halloween found many ill-tempered country folk laboring to restore the family outhouse to its previous upright condition. Victims sometimes seized upon this opportunity to get a fresh pit nearby and move the fallen outhouse to a cleaner smelling and perhaps more sanitary location. The dirt from the new pit was used to fill the old one.

The large eight-holers on the public school grounds seldom escaped the attention of Halloween's marauding goblins either. The morning after Halloween found an irritated but quietly amused principal and superintendent supervising a crew of boys pulling with ropes and pushing on the downed building to restore them to an upright position. It mattered not that many of these laborers had been in the goblin gang of the night before. The labor proceeded with an air of jocularity almost as high-pitched as that of the previous evening.

Alas, the wheels of progress in the 1930's reduced the numbers of the vulnerable target at Halloween. This was accomplished by a WPA program which provided recast concrete floor thrones which were too heavy to tip over. With the passage from the scene of these vertical shrines of meditation and education an era had ended.

Sybil Whiddon

I've seen a lot of outdoor bathrooms in my lifetime, and the cozy plush bathroom of today makes me appreciate the modern time more.

It made no difference if the sun was blazing hot, or ice, snow, or the north wind was howling around the corner, when nature called you had to brave all kinds of weather to make the trip to the outdoor privy. It may not have a top on it, even; a lot had only an unraveled burlap bag for a cover for the door. You would have to replace them, as the wind whipped them into threadbare tatters in no time. There were many more burlap bags, which horse feed and cow feed came in, in those days. Now feed, et cetera, comes in thick paper bags, even fertilizer. No good for outhouse doors!

I've lived in many different houses, and each had a different outdoor toilet. Some were pretty decent, and some were a disgrace. I lived at one place where part of the cover on the toilet was a piece of tin. The other side was open, and when the sleeting rain or snow came I always made sure I got on the side covered by the tin. It makes me shiver to think of the days gone by before we had indoor bathrooms. I don't think we had an indoor one until about in the 1950's.

Before I married, my dad and brother built an outhouse of scrap lumber. It was a good sturdy building, and roomy. We were so proud. We finally had a good outhouse about as fashionable as any in the country. The Sears Roebuck catalogue stayed dry on the inside and so did we. It was a ways from the house, so you got your exercise when you walked there and back in your line of duty.

An East Texas "privy", or outhouse.

Joyce Johnson

Outhouses are outdoor toilets. A long time ago when people who lived in the country had no indoor plumbing, they built outhouses. The construction was built of plain, dressed, or rough lumber, but whatever the case, the seat was always planed.

Outhouses were always built with adults in mind. Usually the overall size was four feet by three feet and about seven feet tall, having one door. The fancier ones had small cutouts for windows. These had no glass panes but were left open for light and ventilation. The cutouts were high on each side. Tin was usually used for the top. Sometimes handmade wooden shingles were split for the top.

The seat was built of a one-inch-by-twelve-inch board having one to three round holes usually nine or ten inches in diameter and about a foot apart. The seat was about twenty-two inches from the floor, and youngsters were sometimes afraid to use them because of the height.

The small building was sometimes called the john and was a necessity in rural areas. Homes, churches, and schools had them. Toilets were built to accommodate the need. There were one-holers, two-holers, three-holers, and so on.

The cleaning of toilets was done by the parents. Shovels were used to remove the waste. Sometimes there was a hinged door on the back to be lifted and propped open while cleaning. Others were built with a permanent opening at the back on the bottom for easy cleaning. After the waste was removed and hauled away and buried, household lime was sprinkled through the holes to disinfect and deodorize. An old worn-out broom was left in one corner for sweeping out spiders and cobwebs.

The Sears and Roebuck catalogue had a dual purpose back then. The out-of-season catalogue was a necessity. If pages were torn out and clinched in the fist, they were much softer for wiping.

Disasters occurred now and then. Usually outhouses were built about one hundred yards from the house, but sometimes you didn't start in time. In summer, wasps, snakes, and spiders were intruders. In winter, rain, snow, and sleet sometimes covered the path getting there—needless to speak of the cold wind after arrival, making your visit very uncomfortable and disagreeable.

I can only guess about the origin of the outhouse. Probably when the first pioneers settled and cleared out surrounding areas of woodland, they realized the need of a place to hide.

The last people to use outhouses were less fortunate people in rural areas.

Joyce Morton

Outdoor toilets were built of rough lumber. They were usually built about five feet by seven feet. You had to dig a large hole that was dug real deep and then build the toilet over this. The inside was built like a long bench with two holes in it. It had to be built a long way from your house for

Inside the privy, equipped with a Sears catalogue, and a shovel for lime.

sanitary reasons. In the wintertime you would think you were going to freeze when you had to go to the toilet. They were usually inhabited with spiders and wasps. It had a half-moon cut in the front of it.

I remember one Halloween some friends of ours would go around and turn the toilets over. The one girl didn't do it anymore after she fell in the toilet hole. She had to tell her parents about it, and her mother had to put bleach in her bathwater to get rid of the smell. And she had to throw her clothes away.

The floor of the toilet was usually dirt, and the building was not nailed down, so they were fairly easy for two people to tip over. The teenagers would go to the toilet to smoke, hoping their parents wouldn't find out. The door didn't lock. They just had a screen latch inside and a wood button latch on the outside. Lots of them were painted brown. That's where they got the title for the song "Ode to the Little Brown Shack So Dear to Me."

Kenneth Whiteside

Once, when my daddy was about twelve and his younger brother was about ten, Daddy locked Steve up in the outhouse. They were outside waiting for the bus, and they had a two-holer. Well, Steve had to go to the bathroom. Daddy thought it would be really funny to shut him up in there where he couldn't get out. So he propped the door shut with a two-by-four, and then he got on the bus and went to school. Steve stayed in that outhouse until about eleven, when his mother finally heard him hollering and came and let him out.

Once some boys were out on Halloween night and were turning over outhouses. This old farmer snuck up behind them and shot them in the behinds with buckshot. They never did go back to his house.

Gladney Burns

When my brother A.D. was a young man he would go to the outhouse to read for hours at a time. One day my younger brother Hilman set out to break A.D. of this habit. He went on to the roof of the outhouse to see if there was something he could do. While he was on the roof he discovered a hole and decided that if A.D. was sitting on the seat he would pour water through the hole straight down the middle of his back. He decided that the very next time A.D. went to the outhouse, he would pour water down the hole in hopes that it would break A.D. of the habit of going to the outhouse to read. So it wasn't too much longer until A.D. came out heading for the outhouse with a book in his hand. Hilman let him get settled in good, then started out for the outhouse himself. Not too much after he got back, A.D. made it to the house. His pants were soaked, and it looked like he had used the rest room all over them! The whole family began to crack up, and he became terribly embarrassed, but it taught him not to go to the outhouse just to read.

Mildred Abshier

Most farm homes in our part of the world had outhouses—some accommodated two users, some three, some only one. Then there were homes that had none, and in the early days of my life, our home fell into this last category.

How did we manage? A profusion of bushes and shrubs grew in close proximity to our house and provided cover for privacy. There were also barns and stables and cowsheds that one might get into or behind. And not to be forgotten were the thunder mugs—ours was always of the common variety, enamelware, nothing fancy. And poor Mama! Why she didn't make all the family take turns at cleaning those chamber pots, I never knew. But she always took that duty upon herself.

But there came a day when Little Sister would have her way, and we would have an outhouse. The baby of the family, born prematurely and held very dear for fear of losing her, she more or less ruled the roost, so to speak. Papa had been brought up so poor that he could never see any sense in wasting money on lumber for a privy, especially when there were adequate means of cover at hand. But Little Sister prevailed, literally bulldozing him into submission.

It happened this way: A school chum was coming to spend the weekend with her, and she simply would not have the family degraded before her friend by not having an acceptable privy. And she told Papa so in no uncertain terms. Anyhow, he got busy with the structure.

The finished product was a double-capacity affair equipped with latches, inside and out. Lacking carpenter skills, Papa had problems fashioning the openings over which occupants would position themselves. They were not exactly shaped and proportioned to that part of the anatomy which they were to accommodate; too, they presented some rough, splintery areas— but those would wear smooth with time and use, he said.

Little Sister's friend came and all was lovely. At appointed times they walked arm in arm to the new structure, Little Sister nonchalant, as if having an outhouse was nothing new in her family.

Often we had a houseful of company, and at such times traffic to the new little building became congested and occupants had to be extra careful to keep the inside latch turned, for privacy. On one such occasion I saw my uncle go inside and pull the door to, but he seemingly failed to turn the inside latch, as the door stood slightly ajar. A few minutes later a scream emanated from the vicinity of the little house. At that moment a young lady, some seventeen or eighteen years of age, slammed shut the door of the privy, flung her arms into the air in a tragic gesture, as if forcing some unwanted vision from sight, and rushed headlong in the opposite direction. In truth, Uncle had not secured the inside latch.

A Final Note From Loblolly

The most celebrated privy in East Texas resides on the grounds of the Rusk County Memorial Library in Henderson. It was placed there by the Rusk County Historical Commission. The historians got the idea for preserving an outhouse when they noticed a gap in the education of school-children, who often asked the guide, "Where's the bathroom?" The guide told them, "They used an outhouse." And then the kids said, "What's an outhouse?"

The Henderson outhouse is commodious, measuring six feet by eight feet in floor space. The steeply pitched tin roof is fourteen feet high at the peak and includes an awning over the three steps leading up to the door. Its red paint is faded and peeling, but the old outhouse is still structurally sound, and a close look reveals the expense and skilled carpentry that went into it.

It features double-wall construction, with louvered windows on two sides. The interior walls are paneled and have fancy wainscoting and trim along the bottom. All door and window facings have intricate milled patterns, as does the ceiling.

The business portion of the outhouse is a simple, unadorned bench along the back wall. The three holes are side by side, each covered with a wooden lid, and each hole is a different size.

White Oak Baskets

Loblolly often hunts for stories on old-time handicrafts, and this time we found Joe Roughely, basket maker. Mr. Roughely lives in the Deadwood community just out of Carthage. He still makes fine, utilitarian white oak baskets from the raw materials he gathers in the woods. The craft of basket making was passed down in Roughely's family from grandfather to father to son, and he intends to see that his generation is not the last to make hand-made baskets.

I been knowing how to make baskets all my life. My daddy did it, and I sat by him and watched. My grandfather did it before him, so it's a tradition passed down in my family. But I only been making baskets seriously for about the last ten years.

Sometimes when I'm out cutting pulpwood I find just the right tree for my baskets. I only use white oak for my baskets. You can use post oak, but I think white oak works better. Also, the tree needs to be six to eight inches in diameter.

When I get the tree home I try and get to work on it while it's still soft and pliable. I cut them into half-inch-wide strips. You don't use the bark or the heart of the tree. I dress the splits down on my leg with my knife. Then you got to edge up the splits.

After that, you take sixteen splits and lay them down. These are the ribs of the basket, and they form the shape of the basket. Then you take another split and move them in and out of the ribs. You just keep on doing that till you get to the top, then take another strip and lace it in. There you got your basket.

Some other things about these baskets are that they last a long time. I've had a large laundry basket for ten years, and my uncle's got one I made thirty years ago! There are a lot of different patterns you can use, too. There's a big square laundry basket, little flower baskets, and just some plain round ones.

People see them and they want to have one. I can't seem to keep many around here. Some of my baskets are in Houston, Galveston, San Antone, and even Kentucky. Most of 'em were gifts.

Any little time I have a few hours, I go out to my shed where I keep all my things and work out a little wood for a basket. I usually have to work outside 'cause it gets real messy. I use this knife I made out of a crosscut saw, and the handle out of some wood.

When you're dressing your splits, the secret is not to move the knife. You just pull the wood under the knife.

Me and my uncle and a nephew is the ones in the family that are left that know how to make baskets. My daddy wanted to keep this tradition going, so I guess it's up to us to teach the younger ones.

1. Mr. Roughely's handmade basket knife.

2. Carrying the white oak splits.

3. Using knife to begin to rive a split.

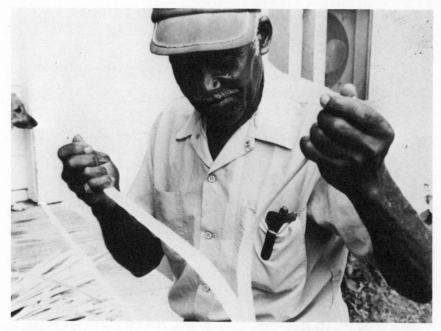

4. Riving a split.

5. Edging the splits with the knife to make them smooth.

6. Laying down the first eight splits for the basket ribs.

7. Weaving between the first eight rib splits to form lower bottom.

8. Continuing to weave lower bottom.

9. After threading eight more ribs through the lower bottom, beginning to weave all the ribs together.

10. Using knife to tighten weaves.

11. Bending ribs up to shape sides.

12. With all ribs bent, basket is ready for work on sides.

13. Weaving the sides.

14. Putting the rim on the basket.

15. Finally, on some baskets he puts a handle.

16. Mr. Roughely with some of the baskets he has made.

Birthing and
Child Care

Today, when a woman is pregnant she goes to the doctor, who gives her a childcare plan for her and the coming baby. She has available books, pamphlets, and classes on childbirth and childcare. A bewildering variety of products are marketed for her and the baby—baby food, baby toys, baby clothes, baby books—the list goes on and on.

But elderly women can tell of a time when mothers didn't have all these conveniences. The rural population had limited access to a doctor's care, and visiting the doctor was unusual except in cases of extreme illness. Often, midwives were the ones who came to deliver babies right in the home. The baby's clothes were homemade, usually long gowns for both boys and girls, and baby food was plain table food mashed fine so the infant could eat it.

In the following accounts, women tell of childbirth and childcare in a time of self-sufficiency without hospitals and doctors.

Suzie Hendricks

I'm eighty-six years old. I live in Huker, Texas. I was born at Merie Hill in Shelby County.

We had midwives because it was very rare for the doctor to make it in time. The women used kerosene lamps, clean sheets, and boiling water. Everything was done very carefully.

The mothers breast-fed the babies, or we mashed up table food real fine so they were able to eat it.

I delivered a baby in 1956; her mama was Connie Bailey. Mrs. Bailey called me real early one morning and wanted me to come over. I went over there, and she was in labor. So I called some other women and we left for the hospital. Mrs. Bailey couldn't wait until we got to the hospital though. I had to deliver it in the back seat of the car. The doctor couldn't believe it.

We didn't have all the different medication there is now. All we had was paregoric. We used flour sacks for diapers. We didn't have Pampers or anything like that.

Things sure were different then.

Sandra Youngblood

Well, you wonder if the babies have it easier now or a long time ago? Today, we have a lot of modern conveniences to make life easier. In the pioneer days, the birth of a baby was a big event. The women had a very hard time having them. They didn't have the medicines we have now. Some mothers and babies didn't make it. The winters were very cold and houses were hard to keep warm. A lot of times they would warm rocks or handmade bricks in the fireplace and wrap them in towels and place beside the babies or at their feet. Most families had cradles instead of baby beds. These were handmade with love. Most babies wore long baby dresses, even the boys. Sometimes they wore these until they were three or four years old. Babies stayed babies longer then. Boys wore foot-length gowns to bed until they were grown. Flour sacks were used as diapers back then. Most of them were folded three corner with one pin. A lot of their clothes were made of flour sacks, too. Sometimes they would weave their own cloth out of cotton or wool from sheep. Later, they could go to the country store and order a soft batiste material. If a baby had to have a bottle they used any bottle they could find and stretched a nipple over it. They didn't have all the baby foods we have now. They ate porridge and mush. When they could eat regular food, the mother would mash it up real fine or chew up little bits and feed it to the baby.

Life was hard for the pioneers. Some women had to work in the fields right on up until the baby was born and then had to return to the fields as quick as they could. Some babies were carried in slings on their mothers' backs, and many were pulled on the end of cotton sacks in cotton fields. Mothers started teaching their young as quick as they were old enough, and if they were lucky there would be a school close enough to walk or ride a horse to when they were big enough. Some kids didn't get but a few years of schooling. As long as they could read and write some, parents were satisfied.

Syble Whiddon

There was an old woman by the name of Grandma Floshire who went all over the country to deliver babies. When she was called upon she usually rode horseback or maybe someone would come in a wagon or buggy, or if in walking distance, she would walk. She had one son who lived with her. She delivered my brother Robert Adams, who was born in 1908. I can remember my mother telling about it. I never heard her mention who delivered her first three children. My sister Modie Irene, the oldest, was born in 1900. Then there was a baby who died at one month of age and my sister Annie Beatrice. When I was born in 1914, Doctor Guy Wenberly was the doctor in Logansport, Louisiana, and he came out to our farm about fourteen miles. We lived in the Logan community. My baby sister, Gertrude Arline, was born in 1918, and Doctor Edd Smart delivered her.

In those days parents did not tell their children of the blessed event that was about to happen, that they were to have a little brother or sister added to their family. You would just be sent to Grandma's house for a day, and when you got back you would be told you had a brand-new baby sister or brother. If it happened at night time, you'd go spend the night with Grandma and Grandpa, or maybe Aunt or Sister, whichever was available.

My mother and one of my aunts were midwives in the 1920's, and I can recall several babies each delivered. They were fortunate to never run into a case where the mother or baby died or had any trouble. My aunt delivered one of my sister's babies. All babies were delivered at home, as there were no hospitals then. We didn't know of any until years later. In early years, baby was fed by breast-feeding, and when a little older, women would chew up food and give the baby or mash it up real fine. They seemed to thrive on feed of that kind, but I never chewed up food for my babies. I've doctored them with various remedies, as people did not go to the doctor then as they do now. Far out in the country, you would rub the chest and bottom of the little babies' feet with quinine and hog lard for a cold, and you'd give them onion tea and catnip tea for hives. One of my brother's babies died with what they called bold hives.

When children had chills and fever, they were given Tasteless Child's Tonic and "666." Three Sixes, we called it. It was sure terrible-tasting medicine. For measles you would be sure to keep the patient in a dark room and give them hot drinks or cold drinks to get them broken out good, and to take good care and not get out in the wind or cold until they were out of danger of a relapse, for relapse was worse than ever.

Nancy Murphy

This woman got sick and they came after me and I went out there. I suspected that this baby would be born that night. And the baby died. We carried it to a graveyard the next day and dug a grave in the snow and buried it. That was tough back at that time. We were in a wagon or something like that. It was real cold. We didn't have a service; we just buried the baby. Its mother got along all right, as best as I can remember. It was a little boy, and it was a long time ago, I imagine fifty years.

I've been a midwife so many times that I really don't know. I've been with a lot of them when the babies were born, back when we didn't have any hospitals. You would have to bathe the baby. They were so dirty when they were born that you had to bathe them in warm water and put something on their eyes to keep them from being so sore. And you'd put something on their bottom so their little panties wouldn't keep them so sore. And the water in the pan, that's what you'd have to bathe the mother in, too. You had to have a pan to carry water in the room. That's the way it used to be all the time.

We carried the afterbirth outside and buried it in the ground. That was the only thing we could do.

Well, back at that time I don't remember us giving them anything, because I didn't have any pain pills. We'd give them chloroform on the woman's nose, when she's going in labor with the baby. Besides that, that's the only thing we'd give them. We didn't know what a shot was, I guess.

We never did have to strap the mother down, never anything like that. They would pass out, some of them. When they were having convulsions they'd say all kinds of things.

We cut the cord with scissors, just old scissors. Nothing sanitary. We just got them out of the drawer wherever she had them and cut the baby's cord. I never did think about it being infectious. Sometimes it would take a good while to get well. None of them died from it, though.

The baby that died the night I was telling you about that was so cold was the only one that died when I was with them.

I was with a woman one night, and I went to her house. We walked, this man walked with me, and this baby was born way in the morning. It came up daylight and we went to get coffee and went in the kitchen, and the only thing this woman had to eat was hot water bread in the oven. Coffee and hot water bread, that's all we had, but that early in the morning it tasted very good if you've been up all night. But the baby lived and it did fine and the mother did, too. It's been so long since I was back there that it's hard to remember everything.

When my first baby was born, I was sick two days and two nights. The doctor that lived at Gary was our doctor. We were having church down there at our church and I was so near to death, but I remember they turned church out and a bunch of them came up there, even the preacher. He came and was in there when the baby was born. They thought the baby was going to be dead. They got it in their arms and walked around the house and did everything they could to bring it to. And they did, they brought it to. It weighed eleven pounds and a half. This was Ollen Bush. My next one, ten years after that, I had a little girl, but everything went fine with her.

I had to stay in bed. We had to stay in bed ten days at a time back then. They wouldn't even let us get out and on the floor for a thing in the world. Now we get up and go places and do whatever we want to, but we didn't back then. They wouldn't let us. We had to stay in that bed.

More
Country Proverbs

Patch grief with proverbs.

—Anonymous

Like other elements of folklore, proverbs well up from some unknown reservoir in the minds of ordinary people. From time to time someone will set down a collection in print as we do here, but the living tradition of proverbing goes on all oblivious. In proverbs, the wit and wisdom, humor and cynicism, of the folk crystallize in pithy sayings that possess a timeless quality.

Proverbs also seem to reach across the boundaries that lie between very different cultures and languages. Here, for example, are five Russian proverbs taken from a column by James Reston in the *New York Times* in 1985. Somehow they sound like they would fit right in with our collection from Panola County!

The cow may be black, but the milk comes out white.
Wash a pig as much as you like, it goes right back to the mud.
The shortage will be divided among the peasants.
When you live close to the graveyard, you can't weep for everybody.
Make yourself into a sheep, and you'll meet a wolf nearby.

A good deed is never lost.

A good name is a second inheritance.

A good name is better than precious ointment.

A howling dog means death is near.

A liar needs a good memory.

A little neglect may breed great mischief.

All is fair in love and war, but in friendship there is truth.

A new doctor, a new grave digger.

Any man who gets all wrapped up in himself makes a very tiny package.

Any woman who doesn't know true value can throw out more with a teaspoon than a hardworking man can bring in with a shovel.

A pinto's a pound, the world around.

A rich bride goes young to church.

A still tongue makes a wise head.

A soft answer turneth away wrath.

Beauty is only skin deep, but ugly goes clear through to the bone.

Better to be a young man's fool than an old man's sweetheart.

Be what you appear to be.

Blood is thicker than water.

Calamity is the test of a brave mind.

Company is like bread. After three days it goes stale.

Debt gives another man power over your liberty.

Diligence is the mother of good luck.

Don't cut down the tree that gives you shade.

Don't ride a good horse to death.

Don't send a fox to watch the sheep.

Eat at pleasure; drink by measure.

Every chimney smells of smoke.

Every man steps to a different drummer.

Every rose has its own thorn.

Every slip is not a fall.

Every tub must stand on its own bottom.

Far fields look greener.

Few words are best.

Figures never lie, but liars can figure.

Give me the roses while I live.

God protects fools, drunks, and infants.

Great men may jest with saints.

He's a fool that makes his doctor his heir.

He that falls in love with himself will have no rivals.

He who holds the ladder is as bad as the thief.

He who never changes, never minds.

He who never fails will never grow rich.

He with lots of money has lots of friends.

If people fought sin as much as they did fat, this would be a moral paradise.

"If's" and "but's" butter no bread.

If you look back too much, you'll be headed that way.

If you want to be poor, grasp.

Inflation is when you finally get the money to buy something and it isn't enough.

Jests breed bad blood.

Joy and sorrow are next-door neighbors.

Keep your mouth wet and your feet dry.

Kindness to the just is never lost.

Life is a matter of living it.

Little boats should keep near shore.

Lost time is never found.

Memory is the watchman of the brain.

Mirth prolongs life.

Moderate measures succeed the best.

Never do anything by halves.

New brooms sweep clean.

Of two evils, choose the least.

Once bit, twice shy.

Once a cowboy, always a cowboy.

One only has to die to be praised.

Pride goeth before destruction.

Promises won't butter any bread.

Quackery has no such friend as credulity.

Quarreling is the weapon of the weak.

Rich get richer and poor get children.

Right is with the strongest.

Short visits make long friends.

Sight is a faculty; seeing is an art.

Sloth makes all things difficult.

Speak of the devil and his imps will appear.

Speak sweetly; you may have to eat your words.

The borrower is slave to the lender.

The cat in gloves catches no mice.

The good die young.

The misfortune of others should make us cautious.

There's no disgrace in poverty, but it is inconvenient.

There's no fool like an old fool.

The used key is always bright.

The world advances by impossibilities achieved.

Tighter than a duck's end, and that's waterproof.

Uncertainty rules from the cradle to the grave.

Until tomorrow, equality is elusive.

Well whetted is half mowed.

What one person doesn't want, the other does.

Wise men learn by others' harms.

You can load a thousand pounds of gold on a donkey, but he is still just a jackass.

You can't make a silk purse out of a sow's ear.

You may wait on time, but time won't wait on you.

Zeal rather than ability is the father of success.

Zeal without knowledge is the sister of folly.

More
Home Remedies

Perhaps nothing from *The Loblolly Book* has attracted quite so·many comments as our compilation of home remedies. Many persons have asked us questions like "Is keeping a Chihuahua dog around really good for my asthma?" and "Can I really cure my inflamed finger joints by squeezing a weasel to death?" To these inquiries we can offer a definite "Maybe."

The reader will have to winnow the wheat from the chaff from the tongue-in-cheek in these home cures. Some of them probably work, and others offer a sense of dealing with one's medical problems while doing no measurable harm. But others should be approached with extreme caution—weasels, we have on good authority, can deliver a vicious bite when aroused! In any case, assuming you failed to cure yourself with our first round of home remedies, you may find just what you need below.

Arthritis
    Squirt the joint with WD-40.

Bee Sting
    Put one teaspoon of baking soda on the sting.
    Rub blueing on the sting.
    Spit tobacco on it.

Black Eye
    Apply raw beef.

Bleeding
>Put kerosene on the cut.
>Take a piece of unglazed brown wrapping paper and twist around cut
>>until bleeding stops.

Blood Poisoning
>Soak afflicted area in Epsom salts and water.

Blood Problems
>Take one teaspoon sulfur and molasses every day for a week.
>Drink sassafras tea in spring of the year.
>Eat a big mess of poke salad.

Burned Mouth
>If you've eaten too much hot pepper in your food, go and sit on a
>>chicken roost to cool your mouth.

Burns
>Rub vanilla flavoring on the place.
>Rub white toothpaste on the burn.
>Put butter on the burn.
>Put a fresh-sliced potato on the burn.
>Put an apple peel on the burn.
>Apply vinegar.

Chest Congestion
>Rub goose grease on chest; wrap with flannel.

Chills
>Drink creek water.
>Boil cow chips and bitterweeds in wash pot to make a tea. Drink it.
>Take a bath in cold water.
>Boil a sassafras root and drink the tea.

Colds
>Put a towel and turpentine in a pan. Heat. Lay cloth on chest, then
>>lay a thicker cloth over the first.
>Put two pieces of garlic on each side of your jaw.
>Hang garlic around your neck.
>Put some grated onion into a bowl of melted Vicks on chest or head.
>Mix dry onions, butter, salt, and pepper. Boil and eat.
>Put a mustard plaster made from turpentine, tallow, and snuff on
>>chest. Let them wear it until they wear it out.
>Take a flannel rag dipped in water and sprinkled with turpentine and
>>lay on chest.
>Drink some buzzard soup.

Coughs
>Dissolve peppermint candy in whiskey and drink.

Mix one teaspoon of sugar, two teaspoons of kerosene, and five
   drops of honey. Take in spoon.
Mix kerosene, turpentine, and some lard on a rag. Put on chest and
   between shoulders.
Let one teaspoon of brown sugar melt in mouth.

Croup
Drink alum and sugar.
Take a bacon rind and melt it over a burning piece of "lighter" pine.
   Add a teaspoon of sugar and take in spoon.
Mix one teaspoon of sugar with eight drops of coal oil. Place on
   tongue and allow to melt and run slowly down throat.

Dandruff
Wash head in warm borax water.

Diarrhea
Drink rice water.
Take a little bit of vinegar with some black pepper.

Diphtheria
Gargle with sulfur and water. Swallow a little of the mixture.

Earache
Put salt in bag and put it on ear.
Heat cornmeal, place in pillowcase, and lay head on it.
Put an aspirin in the ear and let it dissolve.
Warm olive oil in teaspoon, place on cotton, and stuff in ear.

Eye Ailments
Boil elm bark, dip cloth in bark tea, then put wet cloth over eyes.
Put a baby pearl button in eye and rub it around.
Place fresh grated potato on eyelid.

Fainting
Blow in and out of a small sack.

Nail in Foot
Soak foot in cooking oil.

Headaches
Sit in cold water.
Put leeches on your forehead.
Tie a buzzard head around your neck.
Stand on your head and spin around until you're dizzy.
Drink two and a half bottles of moonshine and take two aspirin and
   don't worry about your headache until tomorrow.

Hiccups
Stick your head in a bucket of water. Breathe ten times deeply.

Eat a teaspoon of peanuts.
Put a pencil in your mouth sideways and drink a glass of water.
Drink a little water and salt.

High Blood Pressure
Drink some vinegar.
Drink some tea made of boiled peach leaves.

Infections
Soak wound in very warm water in which Epsom salt has been
dissolved.
Rub sugar and butter on infection.
Apply a milk poultice.

Itch
Mix sulfur and grease and apply.
Boil poke roots and bathe in the liquid.
Rub sulfur on the itch.

Mumps
Eat some hog jowl.
Put grease from sardines on your neck.

Nosebleed
Pour ice water on back of the person's neck.
Hang a piece of lead around your neck.

Poison Ivy
Mix starch in warm water and bathe in it. Stand up and allow the
starch to dry.
Boil whole kernel oats or wheat until a thin paste is formed. When it
cools, apply to affected area.
Dab white shoe polish on rash.
Take a bath with water and vinegar.

Rash
Rub the rash with parsley.

Red Bug Bites
Squirt lighter fluid on them and set on fire.

Ringworm
Use yellow dock steeped in vinegar.
Put green walnut juice on the ringworm.

Sore Mouth
Chew on elm bark.

Sore Throat
Rub oil of wintergreen on neck, then wrap with a washcloth.

Drink honey and lemon juice.
Gargle with a teaspoon of salt and a half a cup of water.
Rub throat with turpentine.
Cut a slice of pork or sliced bacon. Simmer in hot vinegar and apply
    to throat as hot as possible.

Sty

Rub something gold on eye to get rid of it.

Sunburn

Put vinegar on it.
Wash with sage tea.
Lather up a bar of soap, spread the lather over the burn, and let dry.
    This will draw the heat out.

Swelling

Rub area with horse liniment.

Tonsillitis

Put red axle grease around neck.

Toothache

Put oil of cloves on surrounding gum.
Chew on inner bark of willow tree.
Apply a bit of clean cotton and some ammonia to the infected tooth.
Get a peach tree limb, scrape inside bare, and put in hollow of
    tooth.

Warts

Put one aspirin on the wart. Dampen aspirin and cover it.
Sprinkle or rub used snuff on wart.
Steal your mother's dishrag, rub the wart with it, then burn it.

Worms

Take three drops of turpentine in one teaspoon of sweet milk. Skip
    three days, then repeat for one month.
Put one cup of green walnut juice on the worm.
Eat a lot of garlic.

Fighting Chickens

People have been raising and fighting chickens since the days of the ancient Greeks. Early settlers to America brought these birds with them, and like it or not, they have been part of the American scene since. As passengers on the move west across our continent, fighting chickens arrived in Texas. Today, it has been said that in Texas there are more cockpits than movie theaters. But if you think it is strictly a Texas or Southern activity, you are wrong. It was estimated in a recent year that $20 million was bet on cockfights in New York State alone.

Cockfights are illegal in Texas, and people who are convicted are subject to fines of up to $100, but on most any Sunday afternoon gatherings take place on an informal basis. They are called brush fights, and owners fight their cocks more for the love of the contest than for the money involved.

To find out about the world of fighting chickens, we discovered a fascinating gentleman named LeRoy De Loney. We visited with him several times at his home, which is surrounded by an acre of fighting chickens of great variety. He told us of his career with these chickens, of the breeds and breeding, of the care and training involved, and why he loves the fights. We are appreciative of the time he spent with us in sharing his world of chickens.

I started in this business in 1946 after the World War Two. We had chickens on this place ever since I was a little boy. I was born here. Actually what got me interested in fighting chickens happened a long time ago. A horse trader came by here and asked us if they could camp down on the creek below the house. They traveled in a covered wagon. So my father told them, "Why, sure, there's plenty of room down there." They wanted to graze their horses, so we let them have a little grass. The old-timey horse traders traveled through the country in a covered wagon. Men had their horses, which were led behind the wagons.

Well, every once in a while they'd have to let them graze a little green grass. There was a good place down in the bottom, so they stayed down there a couple of days. My father let them put their horses—the extra horses that were too wild to graze outside—in the lot out there. So, when those horse traders went to leave, they asked my father, "How much do we owe you?" My dad told them, "Nothing." Then the man told my brother, "I've got a fighting rooster, young fighting cock down there that I'll make you a present of." So he took it, and that's the original start of fighting rooster blood on this place. That was at least sixty years ago.

That young cock walked a mile and a half through the woods to where some folks lived on our place, some renters. They had three old roosters over there. The young cock went a mile and a half through the woods and killed those three roosters. Well, we had to go get the cock, bring him home, and my father put him in the garden. The cock came up and spurred him on the arm. So my dad killed him; he wouldn't tolerate it.

Fighting cocks was here before my time. Cockfighting has been going on here in Texas since before the 1900's, but it hasn't been big until about the time of World War One. That's when it really developed, and now cockfighting has really come to the front since World War Two. There was lots of cockfighting between the time from World War One to World War Two. I did not participate with cockfighting at that time even though we've had at least some fighting cocks in the family since 1910.

I didn't originate cockfighting; I want you to understand that. Cockfighting was originated in this country by greater people than me. I'll tell you how far back cockfighting goes. George Washington had fighting cocks; that was the first president. I don't know, I don't have the proof to tell you, but Abraham Lincoln had fighting cocks. Lyndon Johnson had fighting cocks, and so did Mr. Kleberg who owned the King Ranch. Those are big shots, people that are up in the world and are great leaders. I don't know whether it was Thomas Jefferson or Andrew Jackson, but one of them had fighting cocks too.

Now these young ones here haven't been trimmed yet, so they don't look like a fighting cock, but they are colorful. These are what we call babies. That cock there is a Commodore Gray because he came from England. If you read the cock magazines you'll find that there's a lot of Grays being fought, but I don't particularly like the Grays. I like the red color the best. We fight some Grays, because they're awfully good-blooded chickens. We have some here that are a very good bloodline.

These are the Claret family. There's some more of those pint-size chickens that I showed you. We like to keep a few extra around in case something happens because they could get killed. Chickens are called stags when they're not old enough to fight. I don't know when the name "stag" originated, but after they graduate to the fighting class we call them cocks. When they aren't old enough, we term them stags, but we do have stag fights. If they're a real good breed they'll fight about as good as the older ones.

The wild animals are so bad to eat up the chickens that we have to store the hens someplace, so we put them together with the cocks. From this situation many good matings are produced. We always try to put in a hen that will match the cock. This one isn't very pretty at all, but he's out of the old-hatch cock and that's the kind we like to breed. Last year we got sixteen of these, sons of the old cock, and fifteen of them lived. We breed the inbred strains to hold the bloodline. You must have the inbred strains while they still fight. They're just as fine a game chicken as you can get, but they cannot withstand rough competition.

The crossbred cocks have more stamina. If an inbred cock gets cut real bad in a fight he can't get back up. A crossbred or one that has more hatch blood in him can get back up once he is hurt.

Inbred means breeding in the same family—maybe the daughter back to the daddy or maybe the young stag back to the momma. Now these chickens have been a family for at least fifty years, maybe longer than that. I don't mean to say I've had them that long, but I've got them from people that have nurtured them for a number of years. We nurtured the strain and crossed it with another strain. That's where your best fighting cocks come from.

This mean son-of-a-gun is a Genet Pyle. Ordinarily they are not as mean as he seems to be, but the reason they bite you so hard is that their feathers are green. Green feathers are feathers that are not mature yet, like a pin feather on a turkey. These feathers on a chicken are actually not green but bloody. It means they are sore and not mature. That's the reason you don't ever want to fight a cock when he has feathers that are not mature.

I have a lot of trouble with wild animals around. I try to keep all the chickens penned up. You'll notice by having them up by the house we've raised all of them. If they run outside the foxes and wolves will bother them. They'll eat all of them but two or three. I lost practically all of mine early when raising them. I was so determined to raise some that I just keep them protected. I'm gonna keep them together here until they get to fighting each other, then I'll have to cage them separately.

A hen would be valuable if you want to reproduce them, but the cocks are really the ones that are valuable, and they are highly sellable. I haven't thought of selling all these, but it's to be considered. Some we have are the grandsons of the big winner. Now we have a pretty good hope for the future. By the way, we've already agreed to send the big winner back to South Texas. He's still here, but they've convinced me that they can do more with him than we can. Of course we can get back anything that we want. They've already sent me two or three chickens that might be just as good as the big winner.

I've had people say to me, "How can you remember this chicken and that chicken?" I've been with them so long they're just like a family. I used to work for Sears Roebuck years ago in Chicago and had thousands of items in a warehouse. Every item had a number, and I knew what it was and where it was. A friend said, "I don't know how you know all these numbers." I replied, "Stay around long enough, you will."

I put my grandson in the business. His daddy got the bug too. I imagine my grandson has as many chickens as I do. He lives right on the border, close to Mexico, where he can sell them pretty good. I've got some cocks here that will go into Mexico, so they'll bring good money.

I feed the chickens every day except on Sunday. That's the only day we don't. It doesn't hurt them a bit to do without a day; they used to do without for two days. It seems to work mighty good. There's a lot to know about feeding, too. You have to learn how much to feed them because that's a part of taking care of cocks. You must not give them all they can eat. If you give all they could eat their old bodies would be too big. Also, the extra food will cost too much. The ordinary amount is about an ounce and a quarter feed a day, and that maintains them. It's like feeding a dog. After he's grown you'll only feed him a moderate amount and feed him once a day.

There's another thing that develops between seasons. The cocks will become wild if not handled between seasons. When you get to handling them again, they'll get more tame.

The more wing they got the better. You want the wings to drag the ground because that helps him to fly. A cock must use those wings in his fighting. A big tail, lots of feathers, and generally a big shawl around their neck is what you look for. Now that's a typical fighting cock.

The Green Legs are one of my bloodlines that we've sponsored for eighteen years. Here are two families that we brought together and had them fought. They're very good fighters but are very hard to raise. But they're excellent chickens. That cock is well bred and he's gonna come on. You don't have to wonder if they're gonna fight, because you know what they can do.

I've got some of them that are hardly worth their feed and some of them you'd give your right arm for. We ought to kill the ones that aren't good; get them out, give them away, or something. Often, a young kid will come along and want a cock to play with, and I will give one of those to him. I shouldn't do that, but they're not good enough to go in competition. Every cock we have here is not good enough to go into good competition. But we generally know which one is good, although sometimes we get fooled.

We start fighting roosters after Thanksgiving and generally go until the Fourth of July. You see, now they're losing their feathers. Chickens at this time of the year are in-between the season of fighting because the chickens are shedding their feathers. The chickens and cocks both will shed their feathers. When they shed their feathers, they lose their spirits. The fighting cocks are a lot the same way. They're not happy or interested in courting the girls, you see, when they got their feathers off. They don't look pretty. Chickens are pretty close to humans in some ways. They are subject to the same diseases that we have. They often pick up your personality.

Now that's the son of the old fifty-thousand-dollar cock. I'll show him to you now, but without his feathers he doesn't look very nice. With his feathers, he's mighty proud and all. You can print this in your story, which is absolutely true, but certain cocks that are produced in Texas often go to the Philippines, Hawaii, Guam, or even to Mexico. Then sometimes they're brought back to this country because they're such winners over there. We brought them back for the purpose of breeding, so we can get more of their offspring.

Now I'll show you a cock there that has won over fifty thousand dollars in the ring. He had nine fights; four with knives, that was the slasher fights, and five with a dagger. He is the daddy of this little cock right here.

This is the old cock that won fifty thousand. It's still a cock, you see! He's a powerful thing. He had a knife fight that cut him about six inches down the side and his insides were coming out. That was in Old Mexico, and my adopted grandson smuggled him back. Once you send them over there you can't get them back unless you smuggle them. My grandson's father owns a ranch right on the border.

This chicken here came from St. Louis. That's what you call a Red Richardson Hatch. He's the best of that type of chicken that I've ever owned, and I've been fighting chickens for about thirty years. I don't know whether that cock up there flew in from Hawaii or the Philippines. I got him back, so I imagine that it was Hawaii. I know that they fought him in Hawaii, Guam, and in the Philippines. Then he was carried to Mexico about two or three years ago. That cock is about six years old.

These are a different breed. This one is a Wyatt Hackle cock. I got these from South Texas. That's another breed that's called the Commodore Gray. They haven't been in this country very long; they come from England.

This is an inbred chicken. A guy brought me two hens with no cocks, but you can breed the mother back to the son and so on. So that's what you call an inbred string. That's a Claret chicken; she's a T. J. Jordan Claret, which people like in this country very much. He's about the last of the pure ones.

We have had our fights around here about two miles away for two years now. I fought over here for about seven years. I fight cocks even though it's illegal; I don't care about that. I fight cocks because I love to see the action, and the cocks love to fight. They're raised for that purpose. They're not like a broiler chicken. You raise a broiler chicken only to kill him when he's eight or nine weeks old. You slash his throat. That's not too kind to him, is it?

You know very well that these cocks here are treated a lot better than a broiler chicken. Sometimes I have cocks here that's twelve or fifteen years old, and they get fed and watered every day. Besides that, they're well cared for. But then if we set them down and let them fight a little, my God!

This is where all your money goes, the feed room. A lot of people ask me if I have ever counted up to see how much it cost me. I said, "No. If I did, I'd have quit a long time ago."

This is where you finish them—get them ready for fights, you see. These is what you call your holding pens where you put them in to rest.

Cockfighting is a big deal, but a lot of people have never heard of it. They tell me, "Well, I didn't even know you ever had any fights; I never heard of fighting." There are thousands and thousands of dollars spent on cocks. I could take you to places in Texas or Oklahoma where they have ten acres of cocks just like I got on an acre here. I got about forty up on the hill there. These cocks, they look so sorry now, I hate to show them to you.

There was a Presbyterian preacher out here the other day; he asked me how much I sold them for. I said, "For about seventy-five dollars, or something like that." He said, "I thought chickens sold for twenty-nine cents per pound." I said, "That's as dumb as you can come!" When they get big enough to fight I'll ask a hundred dollars apiece because those chickens, you can't get ahold of them. The chicken fighters won't let you have them.

The main families of cock are the Hatch and the Clarets and then the Roundheads and White Hackle. You see, lots of other families of chickens have come from them. The Pyle chicken comes from Ireland. Out of this Pyle chicken came what we call the Wild Cat Blues. The difference in the Claret family has produced offshoots of other families. We have what you call the Butcher., We breed the Butcher to the T. J. Clarets. And so it goes.

[*Loblolly* Note: We returned for another visit to LeRoy De Loney and he continued his narration on fighting chickens. He had done some trading since our last visit.]

I got rid of the big winner cock. He had actually won more than a quarter of a million dollars for his previous owners. I have another winning cock that fought in the same contest that the big winner did in Old Mexico. They smuggled him back across the border. We call him the smuggled cock instead of the big winner cock. We also have some very good chickens that we call Valley Roundheads. People that produce these chickens don't want us to call them the same that they call them because they commercialize in those. To me, these four chickens that they gave me in place of the big winner would cost twenty-five hundred dollars if I bought them. He's giving them to me because I let him take the big winner. This cock fought the same time the big winner did. The big winner fought nine times, and this cock only fought two or three. The big winner was like some great race horse that won the Triple Crown, you see; this cock out here has some to go.

The conditioning period, getting a cock ready to fight, takes at least six weeks. You do what we call preconditioning by putting him in a fly pen, letting him fly up and take exercise and jump and fly up. We keep him in there at least two weeks. Then we move him into the cock house for another two weeks of flying and scratching, feeding him in the deep straw or shucks. It increases his exercise, and then you get him a particular feed. There are different kinds of feed, but it's mostly good, wholesome clean grain. Then you give them vitamins and minerals. Now you've got up to four weeks of his conditioning period. Then the last two weeks you change his feed to a more concentrated kind of feed. It's still mostly grain, but you add a little more minerals to it; it's a little more concentrated. Then you can start giving him his exercise. Some people run them on a board, some people fly them, and others put them in the fly pen. I raise a roost pole so they'll have to fly higher and develop their wings. It's a process of exercise, mostly.

If they won't exercise themselves, you have to make them. If they won't jump up and down on the roost pole or scratch for their feed, you have to force them to take exercise. You run them on the board, and that's where the work table comes in. We personally don't like to force a cock to work. We like to have the cocks work themselves. If you have to force them to work, then they might be slow when you put him in the ring. We get our best action out of the cocks that we don't force to work. That's how we condition a cock to fight.

This is the running table. You give them exercise here—run them back and forth nearly every day to get them ready to fight.

When I say good chickens I mean good bred; that's what you're always trying to do, improve the bloodline. If you're successful in doing that, you have a pure chicken. The experts say that if you just have two or three, you can more or less get them mated.

That's what you call a Pyle chicken. They come from Ireland. This chicken didn't, but his ancestors did. They're a high-flying chicken and a good chicken. There are some more of those Hatch chickens. You breed them for the purpose of crossing to get your fighting chickens. You see two or three different strings of chickens here. That's because you need two or three strings to get your fighting chickens. He's pretty, but he hasn't been trimmed yet. He's not old enough to trim, yet you have to trim them at a certain time; otherwise it would grow back.

When fighting, he's up and down and moving over to the right and left. But when he flies up he must land square on his feet.

We always have a referee at all fights. Generally in the big fights we have judges also. The referee is the boss; he has charge of the fights. The decisions he makes are it. If you're having a fight in the yard, get you a referee, somebody to be the boss, because you are always going to be on the side with your chicken. You don't always fight until the death; you can fight for a decision. You can get a decision by a rooster being counted out. If he doesn't continue to fight, in other words, if he just stands in the corner and the other rooster does all the fighting and he doesn't fight back, then the man owning the rooster that's doing the fighting can call for the count from the referee. After a series of three ten-counts and a twenty-count, you can call for the count, a twenty-count. You can win what they call a decision fight. But a good cock will continue to fight. I'd much rather have a death than a decision. The best cock is the one that will get in there and kill him quick. You can also have a draw fight, if both cocks get killed at the same time and neither one's alive at the end of the fight.

The jaggers [fighting implements attached to the cock's legs] are not all the same. There is the slasher knife, then there's what we call the gaff, steel gaff, for sticking. I don't have a knife here, but some of my fighting buddies have some that they fight with. They are from one to three inches long. In the Philippines they fight them with three-inch knives, and in Mexico they fight them with a one-inch knife. The gaff is used mostly in the States. The knife is used mostly in foreign countries. Those are the two systems.

The entry fee in the small fights around here runs up to about fifty dollars. The big fights run from two hundred to five hundred dollars. The regular fights we have around here, our entry fee is most generally five dollars per cock. Brush fights are just little fights where a bunch of people get together and go into the woods and fight. The pit where they fight the chickens can be just a cleared-out area, nothing fancy.

Planting by the Signs

Let there be light in the firmament of the heavens to divide the day from night, and let them be for signs and for seasons, and for days and years.

Genesis 1:14

To everything there is a season, and a time to every purpose under the heavens: a time to be born, and a time to die, a time to plant, and a time to pluck up that which is planted.

Ecclesiastes 3:1–2

Caught completely unaware, we stumbled onto a strange and fascinating idea—at least, it was strange to us. In talking to some men and women of the community we found that planting, harvesting, timber cutting, slaughtering, painting, and weaving were and still are carried out according to the moon and signs of the zodiac.

The zodiac is based on twelve constellations. The moon in its circuit passes through each of the constellations in succession. There is a planet, an element (fire, water, earth, air), and a part of the human body associated with each sign.

We have taken the chart that follows from a booklet, *God's Way*, published by T. E. Black. This chart gives complete information on planting by the signs as compiled from many years of experience. Mr. Black's guide is available from C. J. Black, P.O. Box 785, Andalusia, Alabama, for $1. His chart is reprinted here with his permission. Using a good planting calendar and an almanac, one can follow the rules to insure success. Readers may not credit this, but there are still many believers who attribute much of their success in farming and other activities to following the signs. *God's Way* is a treasure house of advice on the signs and how they touch many of life's activities. The following is a sampling of Mr. Black's wisdom based on his many years experience as a student of the signs.

"My Guide is a lifetime Guide. God made the signs and then gave man the knowledge to make calendars and almanacs to separate the Signs that we could follow them and have a success in this life. If followed they will lead you to all the good things you need. The Signs are always the same. They come around every 28 days, year in and year out. Most times the dates will be different in each month; at many times the same sign twice in the same month.

"Peanuts planted at the right time will grow off faster, vines will be thicker and short jointed, limbs lay close to the ground and with normal weather will produce a full crop. If planted on the wrong sign their growth will be slower, and vines will be thinner, long jointed and vines will stick up at the ends. With normal weather you will get about half a crop. Oats, rye, wheat and millet, along with all other things that grow seed heads planted at the right time will be a third larger than it would be if planted at the wrong time. Tobacco seed beds sowed at the right time and transplanted at the right time will be a third larger and heavier than if planted at the wrong time. Sweet potatoes and Irish potatoes will make 3 to 5 times as many if planted at the right time, and you can gather them when they will rot or when they will keep.

"By planting at the right time you will make 3 to 5 times as many bell peppers, egg plants and tomatoes, and all will be uniform shape and full size. Okra planted at the right time will start bearing when it gets 4 to 5 inches high; if planted at the wrong time it will do well if it ever bears. Corn planted at the right time, worked and fertilized right will stand wet or dry weather twice as long, will not fire up and will make a good crop if you get good weather. If planted at the wrong time and you get the same weather, it won't make more than half a crop.

"When the ground is cool it is okay to start planting the day before the good sign comes in but in the summer and fall plant on the exact days only. I have made tests when 8 hours made twice the difference.

"For rooting flower cuttings, limbs, and vines and for setting out flower bushes and trees the months of December and January when the signs are in the knees and feet. Also for pruning and putting out flower bulbs. Never take up plants of any kind for transplanting when the signs are in the heart or head, known as Death Signs.

"Gather potatoes and all other root crops when the Signs are in the knees or feet or from the last quarter of the moon till the new moon.

"Best time to start to break habits is on the new moon or in the Sign Pisces in the Feet.

"For weaning babies and animals the Sign I give in my Guide are on the New Moon.

"Best time for canning all vegetables, cooking preserves and jelly, and making pickles the Signs I give in my Guide are from the last quarter of the moon to the new moon.

"Kill meat when the Signs are in the knees or feet, or from the last quarter of the moon until the new moon.

"Advertise when the signs are in Libra or Scorpio. Ask for jobs or deal with creditors when the signs are in Leo, Libra or Scorpio. Cut hair to stimulate growth of it when the signs are in Cancer, Scorpio or Pisces."

The people we talked to were Earlie Webb and her daughter Callie Robinson, Lucille Johnson, and D. D. Chadwick. They explained many things about planting, including which signs are best to plant under. Here are some parts of our interviews with these people.

Earlie Webb

Those twelve days at the first of the year or the twelve days after Christmas, according to that it's the kind of weather. Every day represents each month of the year. I didn't mark them down. I usually mark them down every time, but I didn't this year.

And we always farmed, and my husband always planted by the signs. Well, he tried to plant in the old twelve days of the moon—the garden, such as English peas and Irish potatoes and onions and things like that. This is done the dark nights in May. I have *Ladies' Birthday Almanac*, and it tells you when these twelve days are so you plant on those days, usually in the dark nights.

Of course, I've had so much sickness till I've forgotten lots of it. If you plant on the full moon everything will just grow tall and won't bear any fruit. Blooming days, I believe that's on the full of the moon.

Lucille Johnson

I go by the signs here in the *Birthday Almanac*. I go by the planting signs of the zodiac. There are twelve signs. See Mr. Black's chart.

February is a good month for planting beets, English peas, lettuce, onions, radishes, spinach, and turnips. Plant the things that make on top of the ground on the first quarter of the moon when the signs are in the arms [Twins]. Plant things that make under the ground on the decreasing of the moon and the signs are in the knees [Goat]. This is also a good time to kill weeds or prepare soil for planting. Never plant anything on the new moon or do not plant the day that the moon changes. There are also signs for bug day.

183

I use the *Ladies' Birthday Almanac*. That's what my daddy and mother used, and naturally I always got that kind, too.

Daddy, he was a farmer and he farmed all of his life and he went by the signs. He raised cotton and corn and sweet potatoes and everything. Well, I've noticed by planting things on twin days and growing of the moon they come up quicker and better and grow off faster. You plant things on the decreasing of the moon they don't grow off as fast.

D. D. Chadwick

Planting Guide (by D. D. Chadwick):
Plant corn full moon.
Plant cotton twin days.
Plant beans and peas twin days.
Don't plant on virgin days.
Plant spuds on dark nights.
Plant anything on the bowman [archer] sign, the thigh.
Plant watermelon when the sign is in the thigh.
Plant anything to grow fast and tall the new moon.
Plant flowers the virgin days.
Plant grass for hay the new moon.

The signs circulate; the signs of the moon goes with you. On the fish sign [Pisces], the sign is in your feet, then they move up and back again once a month.

Virgin days is blooming days. You see, you read this right here [*Ladies' Birthday Almanac*] and you'll see what that is. Virgin days is blooming days. I just got the signs of the moon, when the moon changes is all. I plant by that all the time.

You see, there's bowman days [archer, Sagittarius], that there is when the sign is in the thighs, and twin days. You take anything and plant it on the twin days, peas or anything, and most of the time you'll bear two at the place. Nothing's gonna make on virgin days. It just don't.

On the new moon, corn grows tall and won't make as heavy an ear. You take watermelon and plant them when the sign's in the thighs, they'll make long, smooth watermelon. You plant them on scorpion days they'll be rotten. They'll have that rotten spot in them. You plant sweet potatoes on the dark nights. You know, they're like Irish potatoes; they make under the ground. Peanuts the same way.

Callie Robinson

The old people believe in the almanac. And it's true! It was hard to get an almanac this year. They have blooming days, and then they have twin days, and that's when the sign's in the knees. If you notice in the front of it, it's got all the signs, and you pull your teeth by those signs. It also tells in there about fishing. And then there's another thing, when you plant, if you're planting Irish potatoes in the wet of the moon, well, you don't plant then because they'll rot in the ground. And I believe in all that because my mother and father farmed all their lives and they always raised a good crop. They believed and went by all that.

It tells in the almanac when the wet seasons are, and you don't plant then. The potatoes, you plant them in the dry season, you know. It tells you where the signs are. Good Friday is a good time to plant, too. We always plant our English peas during the old twelve days of the moon, and they will not freeze. You can set out cabbage and they won't freeze, and you can set out onions, too.

People read their almanac each month to know what to do for the whole year. The old people lived by it because they didn't have all these radios and things to know what the weather was gonna do. It's just real interesting to set down and read. They're getting hard to get. And usually we get a couple of them because we'll want to read and then we'll discuss it.

If you'll just read your almanac by each month and really learn all your signs you'll do all right. I don't know them like I should because I always depended on Mother. She and Daddy would read them and they knew what they were doing, so I just asked them and I didn't have to read as much. Mother will be eighty-four years old in October, and that's the only way we ever had of making a living. It's just really interesting to go by all the signs, and if people would just get back to that, we'd have a better world.

O.T. Baker
A Shelby County
Boyhood

Our friend O. T. Baker was born in Center, Texas, on November 22, 1910. He grew up on the family farm and as will be obvious was a keen observer of rural life at that time. He experienced much and forgot little.

O. T. was a good student who attended a one-room country school and graduated from Center High School in 1928, receiving offers of 22 academic scholarships. He was an excellent artist and cartoonist as well, and having a career in that field was his dream at that time. And he was a good enough athlete to compete in the high jump in the 1932 Olympic trials.

O. T. Baker was a driving force in establishing the Institute of Texan Cultures in San Antonio and also led in beginning the annual Texas Folklife Festival held on the institute grounds. He is now retired but stays active as a consultant on such things as folklore and tourism.

O. T. has shared a lot of time in relating his growing-up years in Shelby County here in East Texas. The following pages are excerpted from a 346-page oral memoir of his early life, a transcription that provided a real test to *Loblolly*'s new information processor! We are grateful to him for relating these fascinating remembrances and pleased to make them available to you.

This is a personal remembering of East Texas and the area of Shelby County where I was born in 1910. My parents were Lem B. Baker and Maggie Crocker Baker. My father was a farmer, stock raiser, and lumberman. My mother had come to Texas in 1883 from Tennessee when she was three years old. My father was born in 1880 on the same farm where I also was born.

My grandfather from Tennessee grew up to be, I guess you would call him, a circuit rider, except Baptist preachers never use that term. He served churches all over East Texas. He usually went horseback, spending two days to get to his appointment. Sometimes he served as many as four churches, none of which paid him anything except maybe sometimes giving him a cured ham or sack of potatoes or something like that.

He became a Christian when he was about forty years old. He became a preacher shortly after and was considered to be one of the outstanding frontier preachers in East Texas. I personally never heard an ill word spoken of him, but many, many people appreciated his work, his honesty, his humor, and kindliness. One merchant, who had been asked by his grandson to fill a considerable bill of groceries, said, "Why, sure, that's all right. I'll give him a whole store if he wants it." Likewise, a president of a local bank had assured the same grandson that he would honor a note of whatever amount of money his grandfather should endorse. So he was honored in every way imaginable.

My own father was a hardworking little man and only five feet six inches, probably weighing one hundred thirty pounds wringing wet. My mother was somewhat taller, five feet eight inches, and when she grew older, he considered her a heavier person than he was. She was highly ambitious and, I would say in retrospect, highly talented. She had artistic abilities, and she had ambition. She always considered living and working on a farm something she had been penalized with and certainly not something she wanted her children to inherit. So she did the very best she could, both of them did in fact, to see that all of us had the best education we could possibly get. It never entered their minds that any of us would become farmers or ranchers, or any work attached to the land.

If any man were asked what would be the highlight of his life, he could truthfully say, no doubt, it would be any time he was eating.

The first remembrance I have of eating anything in particular was eating breakfast in a cold kitchen, which seemed to be a mighty long way from the fire. We didn't have any fireplace in the kitchen. Our kitchen was sort of a lean-to shed built on the backside of the regular house, which had a dogtrot separating the two big rooms. In the winter our kitchen was cold as blue blazes. I ate from a table that my grandfather made, the first table I ever ate from, and it so happened that it was the first table my father ate from. I remember sitting in a chair scrunched up in a sort of a mackinaw-type coat belonging to my dad, pulled around me so tight that I could hardly reach my plate. And what was I eating? Same thing I always ate for breakfast: biscuits, butter, and syrup. The only thing about it was, in East Texas we were a peculiar breed of people. We had our own special way of pronouncing things. If someone had asked us what was "syrup" we wouldn't have

O. T. Baker as a young man.

known. We called it "surp." Anyway, that was the first meal that I remember eating.

I remember at about the same time watching not only my parents but more especially parents of other children that might come visit us. Babies that might be one year old, or less, were fed in part by the parents chewing the food and removing it from their mouth and placing it in the mouth of the baby. I believe this is called pap. Anyway, thinking of it now, that practice is kind of disgusting, don't you think? Anyway this is some of my early remembrances of eating.

Hunting for food was something I remember doing very nearly in the manner that the Indian children would do. Our house was located almost in the middle of a forest. I don't know how many hundreds of acres or thousands of acres belonged to the Pickering Lumber company. They had one of the largest sawmills in East Texas. This was about eight or ten miles east on the Sabine River toward Logansport, Louisiana. Out in these woods that belonged to that lumber company were all sorts of wild nuts, berries, and other things, which I'll get into later. But any time I had the chance, that is, if my mother looked away about two minutes, I went streaking out through the woods looking for something to put in my stomach. I can't think of a better way to come into the world than running around through the woods of East Texas eating grapes, berries, nuts, and other wild things.

Filling my stomach created this delightful feeling, usually after getting away from school. You can imagine with the type of lunch we had, surely children got hungry during the two-mile walk home from school. And it would increase our appetites, getting home about four or four-thirty. We would run to a thing called a safe, which some people called a hutch. We just called it a kitchen safe. It was a cabinet that had two screen doors, a couple at the top, and a drawer where they kept the knives and forks. And after a little bit of experience we could come in and tell whether or not our parents had any company. Normally there was nothing in the safe left from lunch except for a cold piece of corn bread, maybe a bowl of cabbage or beans. But on rare occasions the heavens would shine and the whole world would be different. Just a quick glance at the safe and we could tell that there had been company.

Company always opened the bountiful doors. There might be some fried chicken left. And usually my mother never stopped with just cooking chicken one way; there was fried chicken, chicken pie, or maybe even chicken with dressing. And if you found that you might also find a piece of boiled ham. And if you found all of that good stuff along with some left-over biscuit, you would think that right here is where you spent the afternoon. As I said, I wasn't any dumb cluck. I knew that if they had company that there would be some good stuff down in the bottom of the safe. So quick as a flash I turned to the wooden bottom, opened the front of the bottom compartment, and, sure enough, always there would be a cake or at least one or two fried pies and maybe a custard. I could start with the good stuff. This was a highly specialized occasion, and I didn't let something like that get away. Usually, when there was nothing but a piece of corn bread and a bowl of beans, nobody (and I mean nobody) would have a stomach for that kind of stuff.

So the next best thing was changing into work clothes and striking out for the barn. Why in the world would you go to a barn to get something to eat? Oh, that was easy; that's where we kept peanuts, up in the loft in the barn. We always had enough peanuts to carry us from one year to the next. When I got started on eating peanuts I got hooked on them. And usually if I had to go back to the field or a mile away to the creek to cut some wood or something, you could trail me pretty easy for the peanut hulls.

I would have my overall pocket stuffed with peanuts. I could eat almost half a gallon of peanuts walking a mile. This had to happen every day once I got started. I found this to be true for several things that I've eaten, like pecans. We had a large pecan orchard, twenty or twenty-five trees, so we raised enough pecans to last us most of the year. And if you get started eating peanuts, pecans, or something of that type, about the same time every day, you can't do without them. I guess it's like being on dope.

As I have said, there wasn't anything that could compete with eating for a young boy in East Texas. But there were other things that were of interest, and one was chewing gum. We couldn't afford to buy chewing gum from the store very often, and when we did you could be sure that we didn't throw it away the first day. We would always stick the wad of gum up some place where we would be sure to find it. It might surprise you to know that most kids looked around for gum and it didn't matter much whose it was. If we found a wad of gum stuck somewhere, we might just as well chew it for a while and didn't always remember to put it back.

One tree called a sweet gum had a very fine sap that usually was agreeable to chewing. You could tell pretty easy if this gum was on the sticky side. If it stuck to your fingers when you picked it up then it usually stuck to your teeth when you chewed it. There was only one way to do the sticky gum, and that was to get it cold. If you could find some real cold spring water running in a creek—and that wasn't very hard to find usually—you could hold the gum in the water a few minutes and it would get hard enough to chew it. And sweet gum always improved the longer you chewed it.

There was one little additive that most of us knew about, a berry that grew on a vine that might be called a brier. It grew along the creeks on most of the trees, and it had thousands of little black berries. We called them stretchy berries, because inside the black outer skin was a very sizable inner layer of latex of very fine stretching quality. Inside this layer then was a real hard seed about the size of a BB shot. It was no trick at all to put one of these stretchy berries in my mouth and bite into it, spit out the outer husk, and roll it around between my teeth and tongue and work the latex, the rubbery part, loose from the seed. By the time that I had added about fifteen or twenty of these berries to my chewing gum, I had a very fine quality bubble gum. I wouldn't be surprised if this is how bubble gum originated.

In East Texas we had two or three types of gum trees, mostly the sweet gum. If we wanted to experiment a little bit, we picked a little bit of rosin. We called it "rawzum," from a pine tree. Now if we were real careful we could get some rawzum that chewed, but none very well. Actually, none of them could compete with sweet gum.

Sweet gum trees were both a blessing and a very torturous enemy to us. If you had a sweet gum tree out in the field, it was almost impossible to kill. If you cut the tree down, it would send up a hundred sprouts from the root. It was a very difficult job in the spring to go in with an ax and bust off these sprouts. 'About the only ways to kill this tree were to use poison, which we didn't have in the beginning, or build a fire around it and burn it so that the fire extended to the roots. With oak trees and most trees out in the woods, you could chop a ring around the bark and there wasn't any chance that they would live. Neither would they put out suckers from the roots.

Now there was another gum called the black gum. It had very beautiful leaves in the fall, as did the sweet gum, but there was another use of it. The small twigs or young branches out at the end of the growth made the very best tooth brushes. Nobody that I knew owned a commercially made tooth-brush. I suppose there were such things, but we didn't know about it. Every-body knew about making a toothbrush, called a tooth "bresh"! This tooth-brush was used for more reasons other than brushing teeth. Most people, by the time they were adults in East Texas, had become addicted to dipping snuff.

The toothbrush would be a little twig about five or six inches long, chewed into a kind of a blob on the end, which would be used to roll around in the snuffbox and then put inside the jaw to hold the snuff in place. Often the other end would be sharpened to use as a toothpick. This was one of the main uses of the black gum.

Now I mentioned the fact that many people dipped snuff. Well, it so hap-pened that I never did get addicted to that, but I did learn to chew tobacco at the age of four. My father kept his Brown Mule tobacco in his turtleback trunk, in the same tray where he kept his watermelon seeds and other seeds. I didn't know then that the odor from the tobacco, I suppose, was detestable to any of the insects that might eat the seeds. At any rate, this was the best place in the world to keep seed because nothing would bother the seed as long as they were close to that strong Brown Mule tobacco. And I can assure you that the wrapping that comes around the plug of Brown Mule is actually brown dynamite. I gathered up a little of this out of the tray of the trunk one day when I was about four, put it in my mouth, and by the time I was out in the yard I was sick as a horse. I was spitting up all over the place, going around and around. The world just came up and smacked me in the face. This was as sick as I remember being.

But as the years moved along, I learned to chew tobacco very well. It seems that almost everything that I learned to do when using tobacco made me sick at first, like smoking the first cigar. I'd just finished eating a hot watermelon one summer day, and my older brother had brought in a couple of what he called cheroots, kind of small cigars that came in a package of five. He let me have one, and we sat down under a hickory tree and fired them up. And pretty soon the tree was moving around like the world was with the Brown Mule tobacco. I got very sick and lost all of my water-melon. Then my older brother, being five years older, became rather expert at using some of these things, and I tried to mimic him. He learned to smoke and roll his own cigarettes, and so did I.

Mostly, to start with, he was smoking the leaves from a plant we call rabbit tobacco. I don't know really what the name of the plant is, but it grows about two feet tall, has little leaves that curl up and look kind of like little rabbit ears. They weren't too bad. We smoked everything, I guess: cotton leaves, corn silks, grapevines, and tie vines. The only trouble about smoking the vines, they really would bite your tongue.

But the worst smoke that I ever had in my life happened when I was about twelve or thirteen. I found a can of snuff, and just to smell the stuff was enough for me. But I had heard the other boys talking about smoking cigarettes made from snuff, so I tore off a piece of brown paper bag and got off in the cow shed and rolled it the best I could. If you never tried rolling a cigarette with snuff, this is not as easy as falling off a log. I finally made it by twisting one end and rolling the paper around a stick, making it round and then licking it down tight, then pouring the snuff down this tube. The only thing that I failed to do was to somehow or another let the snuff know that I was going to smoke it. I struck me a match, started sucking on this tube, and since I had the end twisted where I fired it up, it took just a little bit to burn enough to have air through it. Once it had burned through to the snuff, I sucked about a teaspoon full of it down my throat! I still gag from that. It took me at least two days to get all of that stuff out of my throat. I cried and rolled and ran and jumped and squalled—and everything else— but that's the worst experience I ever had with tobacco.

Now, I said that I chewed Brown Mule because my dad had it in the trunk, but when I got to be about ten or a little more I learned that there was better-tasting tobacco than Brown Mule. The other boys would bring some to school, and we would slip off down in the woods. The school we attended had rest room facilities for girls but not for the boys. We were out in the woods to begin with, and so we would just slip off down there to chew our tobacco. I became a pretty frequent user of one kind in particular called Spark Plug. This was a sweet tobacco, with plugs about half an inch thick, and it came in what they call a pound plug of tobacco. This consisted of four layers, and you could get a quarter of a layer for a nickel. See how expensive it was? I could manage, somehow, to get hold of a nickel. I'd go by the store every week and buy me a cut of Spark Plug for a nickel. Also, there was a thicker plug, about two times thicker and even sweeter, called Star Navy. Now, Star Navy was more expensive, so I hardly ever managed to get any of that.

I'll never forget one spring I came in from school with a big chew of tobacco in my mouth. I came on back about a mile from the house, where I picked about two handfuls of dewberries, which naturally I was not eating because I had this tobacco in my mouth. As I came along, my dad stopped to talk to me about something. Well, naturally, in my telling, answering the question he asked me, the saliva of the tobacco got to working up so I either had to spit right in front of him or swallow it. I didn't know what to do! So I desperately started throwing those berries in my mouth. Before I knew it, I had about a dozen berries all chewed up with that tobacco. And there wasn't anything in the world for me to do but swallow the whole mess, which I did. I think my dad was having one whale of a time. I suspect he'd had experiences like that too. It took me at least a couple of days to get my natural color back after that.

People in the early days mostly all used tobacco. We had the picnic twist, one that had kind of a hank or twist of tobacco that had been sweetened. There was whiskey twist, a kind of a dark twist that was somehow soaked in molasses and whiskey—very popular. Then there was a real rugged type of man that would grow his own tobacco and add nothing to it, just raw grain tobacco. It would take something worse than a mule to chew that, I can assure you.

Tobacco was good for many things. For a wasp or a scorpion sting, there was nothing better than a wad of chewing tobacco as a poultice. I don't know what property of the chewing tobacco would do it, but this was just about as good a remedy for an insect bite as anything we knew. I didn't know of any ladies who chewed tobacco or even smoked, but quite a lot of the ladies used snuff. They did it kind of on the sly, mostly.

I had an uncle who was a pretty heavy dipper of snuff. He was over at the house one day kind of low-rating a friend of his that he'd seen at a party. This man was dipping snuff, and since they didn't have a fireplace in the room (that's where they usually spat if they were dipping snuff), this guy didn't have any place to split. It was too far from the window, or somebody was sitting in it, probably. So what did this guy do? He just spat on his shoes! My uncle Henry was laughing at this man and low-rating him, but at the same time what was he doing? Why, he was spitting in his shirt pocket! Everybody has his own viewpoint, naturally.

I remember one man who came into the store to buy his year's supply of groceries. He had it all written out on a piece of paper and handed it to the store man because he himself couldn't read. It was for ten cents of sugar, a dime's worth of flour, and three caddies of Brown Mule. Now a caddy had about forty pounds in it. That was a year's supply of groceries for this guy!

I remember one time I found a can of smoking tobacco; I believe it was Prince Albert. Now, I have no idea what it cost at that time, but probably ten cents, which was an enormous price. But I found this can, and it had just barely been opened. So I figured it would be a shame to waste all of that and decided I'd make myself a pipe. I was just out of school for the afternoon, and I went right by the barn and picked up a corncob to make the pipe bowl. Then I started to the creek about a mile back of the house, where I was going to get a little switch cane to make a stem. In fact, I crawled over in a neighbor's field because he had switch cane a little closer than where ours could be found. So I was over there in his field with the sedge grass about waist high all around. Anyway, I pretty quickly got the cane stem ready and set into a hole in the side of the cob, which I had cut about two inches long and had it already rounded off and ready to go, packed with tobacco. Well, like any beginner pipe smoker will do, I had it overpacked. So I struck a match on my pants and made a try. But it was in the spring of the year, and the wind was blowing pretty strong, so it just blew my match out. I struck three or four matches, but as I said, I had the pipe packed pretty tight. Then an alarming thing happened. I realized I didn't have but one more match! I said to myself, "To be sure I'm going to smoke, what I'll do is make me a little fire out of some of this grass, and I can light my pipe at leisure." So I squatted down and started a little fire with the grass. I took a stem of burning grass and started puffing on my pipe, but about the third puff I realized something had gone wrong. The wind blowing hard had caught this grass, and the fire already was leaping as high as I was. I figured right away that the smoking would have to wait! I started running for my life. I had enough judgment, however, to be careful which direction I ran. I ran away from the house—way around. I came around about four miles, I guess, and came back from another direction. By the time I got to the house it looked like the whole world was on fire back there. As it so happened, the next day after this—I was eighteen or nineteen years old at the time—I had a job offered me down the other side of Houston. So I left the next day, and I suppose to this day nobody knows who burned up about four miles of fence and all of the timber along that creek.

Now usually, in the country churches that I attended, most all of the young men in their teens and twenties, even some of the married men, felt compelled along during the services to get up and stomp out of the house and get outside and roll a cigarette. This wouldn't have been so bad if they had been quiet out there, but there was a pattern of telling dirty jokes right there in the door of the church. More than one time my father, being a deacon, had to go out and pretty well quiet down the group. This seemed to be an accepted custom—anybody who smoked had to get up and stomp out of the church at least once during the service.

I was told that one preacher in an East Texas church had a carpet put on the floor. Now, I have never seen a church over there that had a carpet, but this is how the story went. The preacher didn't want anybody spitting on the carpet, so he pleaded with everybody who chewed tobacco to leave it outside. And it would be, he thought, a request they would heed, since he certainly wasn't trying to keep anybody from chewing, he was just trying to protect the carpet. Anyway, he told them that he knew no dog would run off with the chewing tobacco, but they had better mark the chip they put it on because some other friend of theirs certainly might get it!

Also, one guy over in East Texas told me how he used Brown Mule chewing tobacco to catch catfish. He said he would cut this Brown Mule up into little chunks and get out on a log around the fishing hole. And he would pitch this Brown Mule out there, just scatter it around on the surface of the water. And pretty soon the catfish would come up and grab a piece of tobacco. Then all he had to do was sit there with a pole, and when one of these critters came up to spit, he'd hit him right between the eyes.

O. T. Baker, 1984.

My folks, my mother's side, came from Tennessee as I mentioned, and the story in Tennessee and other parts of the country was that East Texas soil was bountifully rich. All you had to do was just throw the cottonseed out and then jump back, for it would grow all over you. You can see right away that not all the tall stories originated in Texas; some of them were brought to Texas. Anyway, this was one of the prime selling points for people to come to Texas.

Now, the cotton grown in East Texas, that I can early remember, was a short-stapled variety called half-and-half, this being derived from the fact that approximately half the weight of the cotton would be lint, or the cotton part, as opposed to half being seed. This was quite an improvement over most of the cotton grown across the South.

There was a long-staple cotton and a big-boll cotton called Triumph, but this cotton only had about one third the amount of weight in lint to the amount of seed. So you can see the difference in growing half-and-half as to Triumph. There was, however, a difference in the amount of cotton you could grow per acre, so it fairly well leveled out. The Triumph cotton sometimes made a very big stalk, perhaps as high as your head. Half-and-half usually was not much more than waist-high, making it hard on the backs of pickers.

Most of us despised working in cotton. It was difficult to chop, which was done when it got up about four or five inches tall, chopping out all excess amount. Today they don't do that; they let cotton grow much thicker. We also had to weed cotton. Crabgrass is very difficult to get away from cotton. I always considered myself to be a good cotton chopper, able to keep up with the best of the men even when I was a young boy. This was a matter of pride on my part. And when it came to picking, I could pick more than anyone in my family. My older brother was kind of slow, plodding and deliberate, spending most of his time daydreaming, I think. But he would pick the cotton clean. He would reach down, pick a boll of cotton off the stalk, and deliberately pick the locks out, one at a time. There's four locks in a boll of cotton. He picked them out one by one and dusted off any amount of sand or picked off any amount of foreign matter that might be there. For that reason he was not asked to pick much cotton.

However, there was a practice in those days of saving back a bag of perfectly clean cotton if you had it. It would run through the elevator last, so that the sample of cotton on the outside would be nice and pretty and clean. I don't know how well this worked, but it was an effort to outguess the cotton samplers, who always cut the bagging on the side of the cotton, pulled out some of it, and looked at it. They felt of it and checked the length of the fibers and all those things; then they would make their bid on it. So my brother had the honor of supplying the sample cotton, or at least we thought it would work out that way. With me, I couldn't care less. My idea was to get the stuff out. I have known some real high-powered cotton pickers, including one of my cousins who confessed that he did pick one day in a race with a girl who was eleven years old. They started about sunup and stayed until dark, and each one of them picked about a bale of cotton. She beat him by just a few pounds, but between them they picked around twelve hundred pounds in one day. That was considerable picking.

I myself have picked close to six hundred pounds over in East Texas. This was considerable picking too, especially because our cotton was not consistently the same size. You need cotton to be uniform if you're going to pick the most. And the idea of anybody getting down on his knees to pick cotton is ludicrous if you are going to really be a cotton picker. Anybody who would wear knee pads should admit to being on the lazy side. A real cotton picker will pick just one row at a time, never two rows, because you waste time swinging from one side to the other. What you do is get astride one row, never look up, and have several bags of cotton-picking sacks spaced so you don't have to spend too much time taking a bag to the weighing wagon or shed, wherever you are taking it. Now, if you really want to be a cotton picker, that's the way you do it. Don't waste any time doing anything else; stick with it. Of course this takes a considerable constitution to do that, and today it makes my back hurt just thinking about it. But if there's anybody that really remembers what it was like to pick cotton, I do.

I remember many times it rained a lot during cotton-picking time. We often had to quit picking because we didn't want to pick cotton wet and bring it in; it would tend to sour and start turning blue and ruin the seed and the cotton too. Finally, one year it rained so much that I felt a little bit conscience-stricken that I would feel so good about it raining. But this stopped altogether when my father decided we would put on raincoats and rain hats and pick in the rain. We then spread the cotton out in an old house we used as a barn, let it dry like that, stirring it up about twice a day. So this put a stop to my feeling good about rain.

Over the many years, the practice of farming in East Texas has changed drastically. In fact, I doubt anybody in Shelby County really farms at all. When I grew up, most people were either farmers or cattle raisers or lumbermen. There was quite a lot of timber, since most people who owned land had most of it in timber. They cleared some land every year.

Clearing land was quite a tedious process. Most all the trees cut left stumps, and hardly anybody bothered to dig stumps out; that was just too much work. A settler could spend all his time digging and finally might have to burn them out. And around the stumps and even among the cotton and other plants there was quite a lot of noxious-type weeds and grasses, especially crabgrass. One of the ways that we combated crabgrass was to raise geese, turning them into the cotton fields.

Now, if we did this as a regular practice, we had to plant our cotton so that we had it in a fenced area, because geese would just as soon eat corn and sugarcane and watermelons as they would crabgrass. If we had a pretty good-size patch we had a good fence around it. Most of our fences were made with railing in a zigzag pattern. As long as we kept them patched up and old rotten rails replaced, these fences were pretty good against hogs and geese and anything of any size. And geese were pretty good at keeping the cotton clean, for they would not eat the cotton but would keep the crabgrass eaten down so that we could plow around the cotton, eliminating quite a bit of the hoeing.

Now the geese we had were good. Though I am not a connoisseur of geese, I think all the male of the species were white and the females usually had what we called a pied color. They had kind of a grayish blue on the back and sometimes kind of a light color on the front. The old gander, the male, was considerably larger than the goose.

As I said, we kept geese primarily to keep crabgrass out of the cotton, but we also harvested the feathers about twice a year. We'd pick all the underside feathers off their bodies in early spring and then again in the late summer or early fall. This gave them plenty of time to cover up for winter.

We made feather beds and pillows and all those things with the feathers that we picked, and we sold some to people who bought them at pretty good prices.

We had a particular way we picked our geese. We'd drive them into a chicken yard, then take the ones that had not been picked into the chicken house and button the door. And my mother sat out under the shade of a tree, wearing something a little bit on the order of a nail apron, made from the top parts of a pair of men's pants. She just cut off the front part of a pair of pants and put her some strings on it to make a tie string around her back. And sometimes she would leave one and sometimes both of the pockets on the apron—the front pockets that went way down deep.

I'd catch a goose or a gander, either one, and bring them out, holding their feet because they had sharp claws that could rake down my arm and leave a bunch of bloody stripes. I'd catch these geese and bring them out, with one hand holding their feet, and holding them around the neck close to the head with the other because they could saw into you with those teeth too.

Then Mama would stick the goose's head down into her apron pocket, put the body of the goose between her knees, and, holding its feet with one hand, start pulling its feathers out of the front part of the body. And she'd pick this goose all the way across the breast and all the way up the neck within about three or four inches of the head. We put all those feathers in a bag hung on the tree, and once the feathers were pulled off, the goose still had a covering of down left. They weren't totally nude. Actually it was a relief for the geese during the hot summer to have the feathers removed. When she got through I'd take the one that had just been picked and put him back out in the field, where he could go ahead and eat his crabgrass or whatever. Then I'd go back and get another one.

My mother had seven or eight beds filled with feathers in the mattresses. All of our beds had at least one feather mattress on it. There were six of us children, and she gave each one of us a big feather mattress but still had some left. All of our pillows were big, heavily stuffed, delightful things. Nobody ever slept on a pillow unless it was filled nicely with feathers from the geese we raised. This was a matter of pride with my mother. All of our beds were feather beds, and under the feather beds was a cotton mattress and then the springs.

The goslings, the baby geese, were interesting creatures but very stupid. Even though geese are normally at home in the water, the little babies, if it came a rain storm and rain came down pretty heavy, would stand there with their mouths open, and if you weren't careful they would drown. I don't know how that could happen, but this is true.

So if we saw a big cloud coming up, we had to go out in the field or wherever the geese were and herd them back. And we'd put them in a chicken yard where we had a chicken house. That's where we encouraged our chickens to roost, and we'd put the geese in there so the babies would be out of the rain. Many a time, if we were a little bit late getting them there or maybe if it rained during the night, we'd have to jump up and go out and gather the goslings. My mother usually wore an apron, and her customary way of rescuing the goslings was just to reach down and pick them up and put them in her apron. She'd bundle it up just like a basket, having thirty or forty goslings in her apron. And they weighed forty of fifty pounds wet. Then she'd bring those little rascals in the house, and we'd take some cloth towels and dry them off. Some of them we'd think were already drowned, but we'd rub on them and put them up by the fire, and pretty soon they'd start wiggling and come back to life. This was always surprising to me because they were supposed to be waterfowl and at home in water.

As I mentioned before, fooling with geese was about as interesting as anything I know. I had a younger brother who spent most of his time as a little kid, say, four or five or six years old, before he started to school, watching our geese. He'd go out in the morning wrapped up. My mother would wrap him up real warmly the best she could, and he'd go out and just sit and watch the geese, especially if they had babies. He dearly loved them. He came in one time and was so cold he just backed up close to the fire and caught his pants on fire. He didn't even notice it. He just started back out to watch the geese again with his pants leg just blazing with fire. Mother had to run and catch him and throw some water on him.

Most of the ganders were pretty ferocious-type creatures. One of the most interesting parts of working with geese had to do with getting to see several ganders fight every day. They made a considerable noise to it, so we could hear them for a half mile. When they started fighting, two big ganders began flopping their wings and beating each other. All the other geese would form a circle around, cheering, and it sounded very much like a championship football game. There was a great hubbub going on, loud shrieking, screams and squawks, thumping and flopping—everybody seemed to be involved in it. The ganders sometimes would fight for an hour, and usually it was a pretty hotly contested duel until finally one would suddenly tuck what was left of his tail and run. The other gander would emerge to be king of the roost.

Now, we had one particular gander that stood above the rest. He stood tall. His head must have been four feet off the ground, and he had a long twisted neck, with the feathers coming down the back side of his neck in rolls, making almost a full half turn.

He was the king for quite a long time, four years at least, and we referred to him as Old Twisted Neck. Most of the ganders had names given for one reason or another, but Twisted Neck was the cock of the walk, ruling in a pretty stern manner. Not only would he bite his adversaries but he would jump up and scratch them with his claws. And not only did he herd the other geese around, keeping them under his control, but he also was a mighty good watchdog. Nobody invaded his territory, horses or mules or cattle, or anything like that. They were afraid of Twisted Neck because he would fly up and scratch the living daylights out of their eyes. He could catch them by an ear with his beak, which had teeth almost like a handsaw. This is what they cut through grass with. They just sawed grass in two, and Twisted Neck might do the same thing if he got a dog by the ear. He might just nip off a piece of it.

Twisted Neck was particularly respected by all of us kids. We raised about twenty-five or thirty adult geese, always keeping about three ganders and about twenty or twenty-five females.

One particular time I remember Old Twisted Neck was herding his family out close to the house, and it came up a big cloud. I ran out to see if I couldn't get them into the chicken yard. And we were coming across the cotton patch, which was up pretty close to the house, where it pretty well got fertilized more than others. That's because if we had any cans of trash or anything like that to dispose of, we'd just throw it out in the field close to the house and plow it under. And as a result the cotton stalks got bigger there than they did back down in the field.

We had a practice of cutting the cotton stalks with a stalk cutter. Now, sometimes the stubble or the stalks would be cut off three or four inches from the ground, and a kid running across the field not watching his step might stump his toe on one of these cotton stalks. And that's just what I did—I was looking back at the geese. It scared the living daylights out of me when Twisted Neck started chasing me.

The king gander was like the top dog of any family, who had a protective sense over his group. He had a warning routine, a loud hissing noise, like a shrieking squeal, flapping his wings against his chest. It was a fearsome sound that he made, especially since it was directed at me. I was running, looking back at Twisted Neck, and hung my toe on one of those cotton stalks, landing about six or eight feet in front. I had been running full blast, and before I could recover and get up, he got right on top of me, on my back, almost scalping me. He was grabbing my hair, sawing it off in big chunks, flopping me in the back with his wings, and clawing my shirt into shreds with his bloody claws! This was a fearsome thing or situation to get into. If it hadn't been for my older brother being close by, running out and kicking him off, no telling what Twisted Neck would have done to me.

As it was I had some pretty good sizable gaps cut in my hair from the back. He had been sawing off big chunks of hair each time he bit. He pretty well put the fear of God in me right then. The next week I had an occasion to try and round them up again, so I decided I wasn't going to run any more chances like that. We had a rake that the handle had come out of it. It was pretty near six feet long, and this made a pretty good weapon for me to go out and to drive the geese. There were thirty or forty of the creatures out there, maybe more than that, and they had a bunch of little goslings.

When they had babies, the overseer or the king of the group got a little more dominant then he did otherwise, and a few days earlier we had had this little encounter in which he cropped my hair. So I think he thought he had the fear into me and could do it again. But I was ready for him this time. He caught sight of me about a hundred feet away and headed at me just like you would launch a torpedo. He had his old crooked neck stuck out about as straight as he'd ever get it, letting out his war hoops and cries and hissing sounds and looping his wings and heading right at me. I swung back with this rake handle and hit him right in the middle of the neck. His head was sticking up from where I hit him, oh, about fifteen inches I guess—he was a long-necked rascal.

But his head just spun around that rake handle about three times and cracked against the handle. Well, he just flooped over; I'd just cold-cocked him—that's what I did. He finally got up. I had thought that I had killed him. And he started moving and kicking and flopping around and finally got himself where he could stagger around, getting up on his feet so he could see who I was. He stood there and looked at me and just straightened up his neck, then turned around and sort of replaced his wings to natural position and walked right on back to his little herd. He never did bother me anymore, and I guarantee you this was a relief for me. If I ever had a time when I was almost scared to death, that was it. I shall never forget Old Twisted Neck.

Now, another thing to look forward to was sugarcane. I remember back that once I got started to chewing sugarcane everyday, it also got hold of me, and I just couldn't wait until my usual time to get sugarcane. Most boys in East Texas who grew up around the turn of the century probably would concur that sugarcane was the outstanding thing that grew, the most enjoyable. Most everybody I know probably grew sugarcane, and I suppose most of us concurred that the neighbors' sugarcane always tasted better than ours. Part of the enjoyment would be the excitement of slipping across the creek, maybe at night, going coon hunting on a cold night, building a big fire, getting enough firewood, sitting down around the camp fire to listen to the dogs chase the coons, almost drowning out the fire with the peelings of sucarcane.

Sugarcane is a grass, and the sweetest grass in the world. It was brought to Texas in 1731 by the Canary Islanders who settled in San Antonio. Sugarcane had also come in to Florida, Alabama, all along the Gulf Coast. So by the time my parents arrived in Texas, sugarcane had become a general crop that everybody depended on for one of their main sources of food, and a very popular one. It was the most important one single food in the South because it would not spoil very regularly and could be depended on as a food. If you ate a good plate of biscuits, butter, and syrup, you could work all day.

In addition to raising corn and peas, everybody had patches of sugarcane because syrup was the one most dependable food we had besides bread. The sugarcane we grew by dropping the stalk of cane in the furrow and covering it good. We usually selected stalks of cane, put them in an earth-covered mound, and then planted them around the first part of March. We always selected a piece of new ground, we called it, the bottomland that often still had trees on it. This was a practice that was fairly common, but being able to dig up tree stumps and remove all of the evidence of trees like they do today with huge implements, tractors that have big knives that cut them up and move them out, was unknown to us. What we had to do was cut the low branches off and leave the tree standing, which, as the years passed, would drop part of its bark and part of the limbs. It was a job every spring to pick these up and burn them, and you can very well imagine that the person had to stay pretty alert to plow around those trees. All the roots were still underground, just ready to grab you at any moment. To plow and strike a root, if you were about half asleep, would wake you up very suddenly. You could have your jaws popped together, and the plow line might just drag you right on over the plow into the horse. These would cripple you up pretty good. I guarantee you, I know! Mostly, you would put a cutting blade on the beam of a plow, which is made at a blacksmith's shop with a sharp edge forward. The purpose of this was to cut roots, so the plow following would move right between the roots. On a given piece of land in maybe five or six years, you would get most of the trees out, all except sweet gum, which you never got out. It just kept putting up shoots and sprouts from the bottom. Eventually you would have to build a fire around it to kill it. But this was where we put our sugarcane, always in new ground. The humus of all the rotting leaves, twigs, and things like that was a type of food that the sugarcane liked best—sandy soil filled with humus.

And we very often had sugarcane that would mature, I'd say, at about ten feet tall. It would be so high that a man on a horse couldn't reach the top of it.

In the fall you tried to cut the cane before frost. If you cut it down and stacked it, frost wouldn't hurt it. But you didn't want to wait so long because it tended to dry out. If you left the roots, stalk, and stubble in the ground, the next year when it came up there would be a tremendous number of stalks growing up from the roots of this cane.

Now, there are many things that we as growing boys liked to do, but I suppose none that I can think of gave me more pleasure than what happened in the fall of the year: making syrup. As I said, we didn't call it "syrup," we called it "surp." My father owned a cane mill, which was located about a mile back of the house on the creek. The reason for having it isolated like that was not the isolation, I guess, but the need for being close to a source of water. We had a spring back there on the creek, and it gave us a good supply of fresh water, which was essential to keeping all of the syrup pans clean. Also, it was just a good place to set up operations because we needed a storage place. We made syrup for all the neighbors around, and sometimes we might have stacks of sugarcane all around the woods. Each person would haul his cane and stack it like cordwood. We might have many piles twenty feet long and six feet high, just stacked between some trees. Each one, according to the time the owner got there or made prior arrangements with my father, would be made into syrup.

The farmers, they were fighting one thing. That is, they did not want their sugarcane to be frostbitten. Pretty good syrup can be made with frostbitten cane if it is made immediately, but a few days' wait and it would start souring, and then the syrup was no good. You see syrup, in my opinion, was the one most important food in the frontier South. The main reason for this was that it would keep without spoiling for a long time. If you got the moisture out of anything—meat, fruits, or vegetables—it would keep so long as you kept the moisture out, but that's difficult to do. In the case of syrup, it might revert to what we call rock sugar, but it would still be edible. So, syrup had a very important part to play, especially since it was made to use not only as a food on the dinner table but also as a medium of exchange. Most of the cotton that we had was chopped and picked by the Negro families that lived in the town about six miles away, and these people were quite willing to work for syrup. Depending on what the going rate was, it might be one gallon of syrup for a hundred pounds of cotton picked. In rare cases when we were in the tail end of the picking and the cotton was pretty scrappy, we might have to pay three gallons per hundred. Nevertheless, it kept us from having to use money.

Now, the reason I enjoyed the syrup making was that, like everybody, I liked to have company. Always there would be a group of people either standing around watching or helping around the cane mill. Now the cane mill we had set up was a device made of cast iron, with the housing of the cast iron enclosing three rollers made of steel. These three rollers were so situated that they had a cog fitted to the top so that it would turn each one of the rollers. On top of this cog was a long stem that stuck up and fitted to a gin pole about twenty feet long and so balanced that the long end would reach out about fifteen feet from the mill. And this was the end that the horses or mules were hooked to, usually two horses. We didn't use mules much. And they were trained to go around and around all day.

My job at first was to take the mash, which is the stalk of cane after it went through the mill and dropped out on the opposite side. Soon and often it would be a big pile that had to be removed. It was a continuous operation, and we would just stack it in a circle just beyond where the horses walked. We had a big stallion that we worked quite a bit, and he was so full of mischief, he and I had quite a game we played. I don't know really what he or I would have done had he ever caught me, but he—lucky for me— never did quite catch me. He'd spot me going across in front of him with a load of mash, and he'd make a lunge for me. I'd jump over the big pile, clamor over it with my load of mash, and roll down the back side, which was located on the side of a hill going down to the creek. I might roll about fifty feet before I got to the bottom. But this kept it from being a job of boredom.

When I got a little older, my job was feeding the sugarcane into the mill. As I said before, sugarcane was probably the most popular crop grown on an East Texas farm. Most of the kids that I knew grew up chewing sugarcane before they had teeth almost. It was something that all of us enjoyed doing. I in particular enjoyed it.

Also I enjoyed it more if I got a supply of sugarcane out of a neighbor's patch. I'm sure that he was aware of that. More than likely his boys would cross the creek and get into our patch too. I found out that the best time to cut a supply of chewing cane was Sunday morning early. I'd go back down about a mile behind the house over there and cut about a dozen stalks of cane, then I'd bring them all the way back to the barn, where we had a big room full of cottonseed. We kept this cottonseed to feed the cows, and it was pretty easy to ram these stalks of sugarcane back into the cottonseed. And you might be surprised to know how much the taste of sugarcane improved by being stored in a place like that. By the end of the week this cane seemed to me to be about twice as sweet as it was to start with. It had a kind of mellow taste that was hard to resist. Like many other things, I got into the habit of chewing one or two stalks of cane a day, and then I couldn't do without it. It was something that I really got addicted to.

But making the syrup, as I said, was a fascinating thing because of all the things we did there. It also was an occasion like an everyday picnic. My dad would send somebody to the house in a wagon along about noontime, and my mother always would have lunch ready. Of course we didn't call it lunch; we called it dinner. We'd have a tubful of real good stuff to eat. We'd bring it back down to the mill, and it was just an everyday picnic. We always had a big Dutch oven filled with hot biscuits, which with some of the fresh syrup right out of the pan was pretty hard to beat.

Now, many people never have seen a cane mill work. The juice from the sugarcane, when it came from between the rollers, poured out into a box. We had a wooden box that would hold about forty gallons of juice. And from the box, a one-inch pipe came out at the bottom and ran underground over about thirty feet to the furnace. Now, this furnace had a shed over it to protect it from falling leaves and rain. See, there were trees all around, and you didn't want to get trash in the syrup. And this furnace was made without rocks because there weren't any rocks in East Texas. It was made with mud—mud and straw—like most of the chimneys. This furnace was about twelve feet long, leaving room for an eight-foot pan, which was about eight by four feet in length. Then we had what we called a separator. This was a pan that had partitions about every one foot, with alternating gaps on them. The gaps were about four inches wide on alternate ends.

The juice would pour into the front end, where we had a faucet on the one-inch pipe. We let about fifty gallons of juice run into this pan when we started, and as it cooked we'd move the juice back toward the rear. As we cooked the juice, impurities in the juice—of which there was quite a bit— would rise in a kind of foam. We called it skimmings. Now a lot of people who had cane mills would throw the skimmings into a barrel, and this would ferment and make sort of a home brew, which would be pretty heavy in alcohol. But as I said, my father was a Baptist deacon, and he didn't believe in doing this, so we threw our skimmings into pits, one on each side. A pit would be a couple of feet deep and about six feet long, I guess, and maybe about thirty to forty inches wide. And being in this pit did not keep the skimmings from fermenting. We'd shut down at dark, and at night our hogs, which would run around in the woods, knew where to come for a party. The next day we would have a bunch of drunk hogs. This made for an exciting little sideshow for us.

What we had to do when the syrup got the right color on the far end, and free of any skimmage, would be to draw it off from a bunghole into a tub, which had a red flannel cover on it to strain the syrup. This syrup then was dipped out of the tub and put into buckets, jugs, or gourds, just depending on what we had. The syrup was immediately capped and sealed and ready to be hauled away.

In the very early days syrup would likely have turned to sugar, rock sugar, we called it. After the syrup was poured out, the rock sugar was chipped from the side of the bucket, or in the case of a jug, hot water was poured in there and sloshed around until it melted. Then it was poured out into a pan and recooked. This was the best-tasting syrup in the world. I dare anybody to find anything to taste any better than rock candy syrup! It was almost pure cane sugar and didn't have any of the dark taste. It was much lighter, almost like honey, making eating it a delightful thing. However, after World War One, there was introduced a method of smoking syrup with sulfur fumes running through the juice. And this somehow kept the syrup from going to sugar. At the same time, it never did taste quite the same, either. I personally would just as soon go ahead and do it the old way and come up with some very delightful rock candy.

Now, there were different ways of eating syrup that changed it a little bit. Many people had a practice of pouring brown ham gravy into it, or maybe putting the syrup in a plate, which had some fried ham gravy. This changed the taste of it a little. Some people actually cooked it together like that, but I never did like it that way myself.

My older brother had a little technique. He would take syrup and a glob of soft butter and just beat it with his fork into a froth on his plate, making kind of a foamy mess out of it, I thought. Then he would spread it on the biscuit with his knife. He thought it was a manly thing to do, I guess, to see how much he could put in his mouth at one time. My mother always cooked big biscuits—oh, I would say three or four inches in diameter—which he would take in about two bites to a side to show me what a big man he was. I remember admiring the dexterity with which he would spread this frothy-looking buttered syrup onto that biscuit, then cram it into his mouth, and I tried it myself without the success I saw him having. But we really liked syrup, and I know that some members in my family would never finish a meal except with buttered biscuits or a piece of buttered bread and syrup. That was a pattern of eating regardless of what else we had. We had eight of us in our family, and if we didn't have company and weren't sharing off to anybody, we might very well have a syrup bucket sitting right on the table.

The people who came into Texas and settled as farmers and stock raisers for the most part let their animals run outside. There was no stock law. Horses and mules were kept strictly for working purposes. And they were the only animals they bothered about building fences to keep up. Cattle and hogs ran out in the woods on the free range. This was something my father never overcame. Texas finally passed a hog law, or stock law, requiring people to keep their animals confined to their own property, but he just thought it was a given right he was born to, that they had free run outside. He couldn't adjust to the stock laws.

Everything that a person had in a way of livestock was free to roam through the woods, and the fences were to fence their crops to keep the animals out. The only animals we kept up in a corral or a pasture were our horses, the milk cattle, and fattening hogs. We didn't brand any cattle; we marked them on their ears, like hogs, by cutting a slit in one ear and a notch or a crop in the other one, or whatever the registered mark was. And if we wanted to get ready for hog-killing time we usually had to go through the woods and try to find our hogs.

Now, corn for us was mostly grown for human and animal consumption. We fed our hogs corn before we were ready to butcher them, after we got them out of the woods. Our hogs were marked with a slit on one ear and a crop and a notch on another. I'm sure other people got some of our hogs. But we might sometimes have gotten a hog that didn't have any mark, always picking out some pretty decent-looking hogs. We drove them in and put them in a pen and fed them out with corn for two or three weeks, plus what we called slop, scraps from the kitchen.

Another practice we had with hogs happened when we gathered our cotton and our corn and everything else we had in the field, including our sugarcane. Then we would turn our hogs and cows in the field. The cattle would eat the corn stalks and the grass and whatever would be left there and the pea vines, which we always planted in our corn when it got about knee-high or a little higher.

Some of you might be surprised to know that people in the earlier days preferred pork to beef, and not just in East Texas. I understand that this is true throughout the country. Many people shot wild cattle, skinned the animals for their pelts, and fed their meat to the hogs. This is quite surprising to us today. Most of us eat more beef than we do pork. But I can remember that we killed sometimes as many as eight or ten hogs in one year and usually not more than one beef. There could be some reasons for this other than just liking the meat. For the most part we preferred to keep pork because it would be more tasteful the way we kept it.

If you butcher a hog in cold weather and salt the meat down and smoke it, it usually is pretty tasty meat. The only way you could keep beef and make it edible would be to dry it, but for some reason we didn't dry meat very well in East Texas. I suppose one reason would be that the moisture content of the air is too great. It is pretty difficult to dry out meat to make jerky in East Texas.

Now, nobody butchered a beef totally for his own use. Usually a family just didn't have that capacity to eat a beef before it would spoil. When we butchered a calf—usually about a six- or eight-month-old calf—we selected the parts that we thought we could eat, and in about a week's time cooked up as much as we could to last a few days and to put about two buckets full of meat down in the well. We filled these buckets with selected pieces of beef and lowered them into the water, which was not too cold but was certainly much cooler than it would have been out of the water. This was the only way we had of keeping anything for even a very few days.

Anytime we saw a wagon roll up in front of the gate with the back bed full of sweet gum branches with leaves on them, this meant one thing. Somebody had butchered a beef and was peddling out to his neighbors that which he couldn't eat. This was always a very welcome occasion on our part because we would get fresh meat. Usually these people carried a little hand scale with them. The lady of the house would usually go out and buy ten or twelve pounds of meat, all her family could eat before it spoiled. In two or three hours, usually, a man would sell out what he had left of his beef.

Over in East Texas we had standard calls for cows that went a little bit like this. I don't know if I can do it because it was always high-pitched, and usually the ladies did it because they had a high voice and it would carry a greater distance. But they went, "So-o-ok, so-o-ok, so-o-ok, so-o-cow! So-o-ok, so-o-ok!" And when calling pigs, they didn't call them anyway like you hear and see on TV. They went something like this: "Pe-o-oh pig, pig, pig! Pe-o-oh, pig, pig!" And this would always rattle them out of the woods. We might have had trouble calling them up if they were in an area with heavy acorn and hickory nut crops, giving them plenty of food in the woods. However, if we got in the habit of putting out a little corn for them, we could train our hogs so they would come up also. And the reason we wanted them to show up in the fall was we wanted to pick out the ones we were going to butcher, picking out four or five at a time and keeping them in a pen close to the barn. We fed them on corn for about two weeks. And the first cold spell, that's when they got it! Feeding corn like that made pretty good meat. Usually hogs that grew up in the woods eating roots and grubs and things like that tended to have flesh that was not considered to be as firm as that which was fed out with corn.

After you fed him corn for a few weeks, this improved the meat. Many people thought killing a hog had to be in a certain manner. I don't know if this is the valid belief or not, but there are some who believe if you are going to kill a hog or any animal, it should be on the full of the moon or the rise of the moon. Now my dad scoffed at this idea just as he did at similar notions about times for marking hogs. Whenever his knife was sharp was the time to do it.

I knew people who would never castrate a hog unless the moon was right; same way about killing hogs if you want real good firm flesh. This is true in killing any animal that's to be tender. You should by all means kill the animal while he is on the increase in gaining weight and never if possible kill an animal that has been agitated. I can for sure testify to this. The thing to do is try to keep the animal in a cool, comfortable place and let the procedure of slaughtering be done as quickly as possible. Meat is always more tender and sweet if you observe those rules. And we never killed hogs unless there was going to be a cold spell. We called it a blue norther. We usually had a blue norther blow in and catch us while we were at school. We always hated to go home because we knew our dad would have three or four hogs ready to scrape when we got there. This was something that nobody really enjoyed doing because the weather would be so disagreeable.

I mentioned that if possible you should never agitate a fowl or an animal of any kind before butchering. I'll give you a case in point. When I was about twelve years old, or maybe ten or eleven, somewhere around in there, it was in the early winter and we had what we called a blue norther. And unfortunately, my dad was serving on the jury, so he got word to us by dropping a card in the mail. We got it that same day because he mailed before the mailman got out. But by the time we got in from school, Mother had the card and everything was ready. She had already built a fire around the wash pot so that the water would get hot. And the card from my dad (just one of two cards I ever saw in my life in his handwriting) said very clearly that my older brother and I were to butcher the hog we had in the pen.

Well, my brother must have been about fifteen, but for some reason he had never before shot a hog. My father really preferred hitting them in the head with a poleax. But we had a little single-shot twenty-two caliber, and my brother got this thing out, making him as nervous as a June bride. He came out to the hog pen, I had the poleax in my hand, and he had the gun. He took a wobbly aim at the hog while it was eating corn in the trough. We had put corn in the trough so it would stay over there so my brother could get a close shot. As I said, he had a nervous, wobbly aim at him, and instead of hitting the hog right straight between the eyes like he was supposed to, he hit him down on the snout.

Well, you can imagine, this did nothing but infuriate that hog. She was mad! She whirled around like a streak of light, tearing out with a squeal and a squall. I suspect she weighed four or five hundred pounds—a pretty big sow—and she had about fifty to seventy-five feet to go before she hit the fence on the far side. Well, she just made a little round hole through that fence. She hit it with such force that she just broke both boards on the fence, rather than push them off, clearing a way through the fence just like it wasn't there. And away she went. Well, naturally, my brother was helpless. He only had one shot in the first place—no more shells available. And he'd left the box in the house.

While he ran back in the house to get another shell for the single-shot rifle, I tore out after the hog. The hog ran back through the field toward the creek, way down into the cotton patch, through a kind of low place we called Old Stumpy, then right through the woods into the back field. I was running as hard as I could to just keep him in sight.

Finally, when a few miles away from the house, I got on the other side of the sow, forcing her up against the fence. I was close enough but about out of breath, carrying that ax and running as hard as I could. That hog was pretty fast. I hit her a lick, but it didn't do anything, just glanced off. Then she started running again, going about a mile east. I circled across another creek, back through the woods again, and about every ten minutes I'd catch up enough to hit another blow. You can imagine how agitated this hog was, and I was not too calm and collected myself!

Finally I headed that old sow back toward the house, I guess close to half a mile, right in the middle of a big brier patch. These were what we called saw briers. They were big enough that when I ran against them, they pretty near sawed my leg off. I got this hog up in the middle of this brier patch, though, and got in a few hard, out-of-breath licks that knocked her down.

So here we were, rolling over each other and me hitting with the ax every now and then. Finally I managed to club her to death right there in the briers. I was so exhausted. My lungs were burning; my heart was racing! I was in terrible shape!

By this time it was getting later and later, just about dark. We had a little old sled—we didn't call them sleds; we called them slides. We'd hook a horse to them and move a few things around, like hauling something into the garden. Because we didn't have a gate big enough to put a wagon through, we'd use the slide instead. We hooked up the sled, came back down into the woods, rolled that hog onto the sled, and got him back up there. You can imagine what a miserable situation we had. Cold, boy, was it cold! And raw and misting rain. And here I had just completely scraped my lungs raw from all that running and beating, also yelling and hollering. This is what I'd call killing nervous meat! That hog wasn't fit for a dog to eat.

Every year we would try to sell a certain number of hogs and calves too, and sometimes an old cow. Usually the cattle we sold were bought by cattle buyers who came through. Might be just one man, might be two, but hardly ever more than three together. They would go through the county buying cattle, and they usually had a schedule, so if we had any stock we wanted to sell we had them penned up. They would offer us a price, and if we took it they got out some things they carried in their saddle bags that they called cattle blinds. A cattle blind was a piece of rawhide a foot square with holes punched in two corners.

The buyers would rope the animal and tie one of these blinds around his horns. This kept him from seeing out front. He could only see from the side. And it was surprising how much easier it was for one man to drive a bunch of cows when they had these on. One man could drive as many as twenty-five or thirty animals, heading them out and driving them six miles into town without a problem. If he ever got them started they would follow the leader. They just trailed right along, making it much easier. And the strange thing is that never, in all the movies and stories that I've seen about cowboys and handling cattle, have I seen any treatment of driving cows with blinds on. But I've watched driving like this many a time.

In general, driving cattle through the brush country or open country was nothing at all compared to driving them through the deep woods of East Texas. If you ever let a cow jump out of the group, especially where the under brush was so thick in hills and that type of thing, all entangled vines, well, within less than a half a minute this animal could be totally lost. You had to keep right on top of the group of cattle that you were driving or you could wind up several head short.

And you might wonder how people could tell their own cattle from others if they were running around through the woods. For some reason we didn't brand cattle with a branding iron; we did it with a pocketknife, by making marks on their ears. Now our brands, registered just like brands used with a hot iron, were registered in the courthouse. Our brand was a cropped left ear. (That meant the point of the ear was cut off just square across. That's a crop.) And we had a slit on the other ear, about a three-inch split right down the middle, with an underbite—that's a notch cut out of the bottom. We just pinched the ear up between two fingers and cut out a little chunk of it from the underside. That's called an underbite. Now, some brands might have two underbites or overbites, overbite being a notch cut from the top of the ear. Sometimes a crop and an undercut or underbite was on the same ear. But our brand was a crop on the left ear with a notch cut out. Now, on the other ear, the right side, we had the slit right down the middle and the underbite.

You might imagine that this type of branding or registering of animals could be pretty easy to alter, and that is true. I am pretty sure that many people lost cattle or hogs in this manner. It was also true that most people kept dogs that were trained to be cow dogs or hog dogs. We always had hog dogs, and we'd train our dogs to catch the hogs by the ear. That was the place where they could catch them and hold them without much injury. However, with a hog that was fairly good size, say about three to four hundred pounds, and you had one or two dogs ahold of it, they might tend to chew that ear up or split it pretty bad. And in so doing, you might alter the earmarks with your dogs.

We had the problem of give-or-take a few in raising hogs out in the woods. In fact, it was not uncommon for people to go out and help themselves if they needed some meat. They'd take a bead on a likely looking hog and look at the ears later. Besides, anyone could alter ears pretty easy with a pocketknife, and nobody could prove anything. I've just talked to a lawyer who grew up about four miles from where I did, and he said he had a couple of clients who were accused of hog stealing. And by the time he got through with the jury, talking about overbites, underbites, double bites, slits, crops, and all of that, he had them very confused. They were ready to throw up their hands and quit. So, you can see that raising hogs back in the early days was a thing of trickery, to say the least.

One of the most exciting parts of having cattle run out like that would be the frequent bull fights that I could witness. I mentioned earlier all of the country out north of our house and to the east and west as well belonged to a big lumber company. I don't know how many thousands of acres. And there were cattle and hogs and other animals running all over the country, belonging to many people and some belonging to nobody for certain. Occasionally some person would keep a pretty good-size bull for his own breeding purposes, but running at large, he often moved around from one group of cows to another.

And somehow animals like that can develop an acute sense of smell. They scent other animals a long way, and a familiar sound was the noise of bulls challenging each other. They started off from a distance with a kind of low rumble, and I could tell if it was coming my way by the increase in the sound. And if I really wanted to get into the deal and had nerve enough, I'd take off through the woods and try to anticipate where the battle was going to happen. Once I got closer to it I could hear the other cows running through the woods, all the cows and the calves and other bulls. There might be a bunch of young bulls along with the others, and even steers. They all got excited. I could hear them running through the woods, breaking dry brush and crashing through the other vines and timber, making a terrible noise. And things got real exciting because I had to be close to see the action. That's because there was always a bunch of low brush obstructing the view. So there was a little bit of risk involved trying to get a grandstand seat. What I wanted to do was get up a tree right over the fight if I could, and this was not always possible because I didn't really know exactly where the meeting would take place. The eerie sound of all the moaning and bawling and shrieking, the noises of the cows and the calves, would be loud. And the bulls, they tended to circle once they got up close. They didn't come at each other all at once. They would get about a hundred feet apart and stop and throw lots of dirt up into the trees. I could hear the dirt hit the leaves in the trees as it went up and then showered all around.

This was about the most exciting thing that happened to me in my growing-up years, jockeying for a position for a ringside or over-the-tree look at a bull fight. Usually if I were lucky I could scale up a tree where I could get a good look. I might have to hang down from a limb with one hand and a foot in order to see. But usually, when the bulls finally made a dash at each other with loud roaring, snorting, squalling, pawing sounds, well, they didn't stay right in one spot. They pushed each other all around through the brush and into trees. Eventually one of them would get the other one down, and sometimes, if he were lucky, ram a horn right up to the hilt in his adversary. When that happened, if you've ever seen one gored like that, you never forget it. And then usually the fight would be over. Sometimes this didn't happen, though, and they might push each other around there for thirty minutes, tearing up the whole countryside, neither one winning the battle over that length of time. On rare occasions they might just finally fall to their knees and give up out of sheer exhaustion. But for most part, all of the bull fights that I saw, one would wind up being the victor, with the other one disappearing into the brush.

In a book called *The Revolution of the Texas State*, there are many things about Texas as a nation. One of the things that I recall was of interest was the first road contract given by Texas. This occurred during the time that Texas was a nation, and it was for the construction of twelve miles of road. One stipulation in the contract was that there would be no stumps left standing taller than twelve inches!

Well, by the time I came along, roads for the most part were free of stumps this high. We did have stumps in the roads, however. Most of the country roads had many stumps and many exposed roots, and if you've never tried to sleep on a pallet in a wagon with the horses trotting over a road like that, you haven't lived. About the most likely thing I can compare this experience to is having someone pound you on the head with a base-ball bat.

And during the rainy season, East Texas has as much mud as any place I've ever seen, and it was not uncommon for big chuckholes to appear in the road. I remember one occasion in Center. We'd had a terrible rain for a long time, maybe a week or more. It had rained every day. I remember seeing a big mud hole that was dug out so deep that one man who was coming along, in order to pass, had to get his team over in the hole. Well, one little mule fell in the water and went completely out of sight right there in the street.

Roads usually were very narrow, and if you met someone in another wagon or by accident a car, you had a problem figuring out who was going to pull off into a ditch, how to negotiate passing. I remember the road that came closest to our house was a little country road. And there was a law at that time requiring residents of each county to give a certain number of days per year in roadwork. I know my father was obligated and was usually a foreman of the crew. It was his job to delegate the different types of work for the men to do. They would meet at a given place in the community, and he would designate so many people with axes to chop roots out of the road. Or in some cases, where the water had washed away a little bit, maybe other men would be told to shovel, fill up potholes. And if a stump seemed to be giving an unusual amount of trouble, if the water had washed away so that it was getting a little bit taller because the dirt was getting lower, the stump might be dug out of the road.

Most of the heavy traffic on this road was log wagons, pulled by mule teams consisting of six mules. One of the wheeler mules, the one on the right rear next to the wagon, would be the mule that the log man, the mule skinner, would ride. He had a big long whip that would reach all the way up to the front team.

Now, like I said, in that country we got a lot of rain, and certain times the roads, which didn't have too much clay base, would rut out so deep that you couldn't pull all the wagons through there with mules. Their hooves are rather sharp and would cut through the mud, so they don't have much trac-tion. Instead of mules in wet weather, they moved the logs out with oxen. It took a few more oxen than it did mules to pull the wagon. I have seen teams that consisted of six yokes, meaning twelve oxen pulling one load of logs. They could pull through the mud better than mules because they have cloven feet, which divide and spread out, giving them much more of a base and better traction through the mud.

The fellow who crowded the oxen forward didn't ride one of them like the man did with the mules. He walked along the side, and in addition to a long whip, he carried a prod pole, which he used to gouge up an ox every now and then if he seemed to be sloughing off.

And then around 1921 something happened. There were getting to be quite a few automobiles in the country. Of course none of us could see that we, in our life time, would own an automobile, but I'd say at least a third of the families in the area did have cars. And then by some means or another it was decided to create a shorter road from Houston to Shreveport, and it passed right through our county. This road became known as "the Airline from Houston to Shreveport." It no longer serves that purpose, but today this road generally is called Texas Number Seven. Some parts of this road were over new roadbeds, and some parts followed existing roads. So lucky for us it came through at our north property line.

And because of this, in 1921 we began building a new house on this new road, something like a half a mile from where we were living prior to this. I remember that there were lots of men working, perhaps a dozen teams with big plows. It took three mules to pull the plow, with one man to drive the team and one man to handle the plow. Also, they had this scraper that moved dirt, called a Fresno, which had a long dump handle with a rope trailing on it. And this was what they moved the dirt to build up this road-bed. It took more than a year to prepare the roadbed and build the bridges.

It was on this road that I took my first ride, going as fast as forty miles an hour! I'd never ridden in an automobile but once or twice, and this particular time I was riding in an open car that had a speedometer on it. I'd never seen a speedometer before. We got up to forty miles an hour going down a hill, and I was so scared that I was hardly able to get my breath.

So paved roads made a big difference in the life-style of most people. Our grandfather was a Baptist preacher who was a very careful and friendly person who everybody in the country knew. He said it was "all bosh that an old man couldn't learn to drive." So, without much instruction he got in behind the wheel of his new car and started off. He wasn't very cautious, however, many times running over a bush or into a tree. There were trees all around his house. One time he was going to town and going up one of those long red hills, and there was a man meeting him on a wagon. This man called out to him, "Hello, Brother Crocker." Well, grandpa could hear him all right, but couldn't see who it was. So he turned around to see better and in so doing pulled the steering wheel and turned right over into the ditch. This ditch was about thirty feet deep but narrowed toward the bottom so that the sides caught him, not really hurting him much. The motor was killed in the fall, so there really wasn't much damage. The man with the wagon came back and got some more people, who came along, also on wagons. They tied on to his car and pulled it back on the road.

But this didn't cure his desire to see anybody who called to him and recognize who they were so he could speak to them. About a week or two later he was down in the eastern part of town, near a sawmill and a cotton gin. They always had a tank or pond to get water for steam to power these operations. In this case the water came up to maybe twenty feet from the road. A man had brought a load of lumber and was pulling out from the sawmill when he called to my grandfather. Grandpa turned around to see who it was, and by turning he pulled the steering wheel and just drove right off into the water. Well, that just about did it for him.

He decided he had to be more cautious. The next week I rode with him to town, and as we were chugging up the road we met someone on a wagon. And he called out, "Hello, Brother Crocker." Brother Crocker, my grandfather, didn't even turn his head. He just sat like a statue humped over that steering wheel, staring straight ahead. He did raise one finger, however. He couldn't bear not to speak somehow. And out of the corner of his mouth, he asked, "Who was that?" But he didn't dare move that steering wheel or turn his eyes from the road ahead.

One time we were going down somewhere close to the Sabine River, way in the lower part of the county. We had a gathering they called a fifth Sunday meeting, or an annual meeting of some kind, in the church group that he served. I was sixteen years old and had been driving for a couple of years. We'd had an automobile since 1924. I had been driving for a couple of years, so he got me to drive for him, since we were going over some pretty rough roads. It was back in the country where pine timber of long slender pine poles were thick as the hair on a dog's back. Nobody would miss them, so they cut trees along the road for a mile. There must have been as many as three hundred of these poles lying side by side—they just floored the road with them. This worked pretty good so long as a big truck or perhaps a log wagon hauling logs didn't come through. These would separate the poles, creating a monumental series of chuckholes. And this had happened so much that most of the poles were buried down in the dirt by the time we got there. We started down this long hill way too fast for some reason or another—I guess I'd never driven over a thing like this before.

Grandpa's car had the first what we called oversize, or balloon, tires, giving a lot more bounce than our T-Model, on which the first tires were such little things, not much bigger than a bicycle tire. Now these oversize tires looked like they were four times that size, and the coiled springs also had a lot of bounce to them. I remember that as we started down this long hill it became like a roller coaster, with all these big chuckholes made during the rainy season acting like catapults, vaulting us many feet into the air and slinging us far down the slope to crash into another hole and then repeat the process again and again!

When we hit the first two or three chuckholes my feet were bounced off the brakes, and I had no way in the world of stopping the car. All I could do was hang on and just hope and pray that we wouldn't turn over. When we bounced it seemed we went six to eight feet in the air, and when we would come down we'd hit another bump and up again like a yo-yo. I don't imagine a kangaroo could have done any better than we did for at least a half a mile down that hill. My grandfather always wore a great big black Stetson hat, and the picture I had of him hammering himself against the top of that car (a cloth top with wooden braces that held it in place with one strut located just over his head) was pathetically funny. And by the time we got to the bottom of the hill, he was hanging on to the side of the car for dear life but couldn't keep from beating his head against the car top. His hat was knocked almost down to his shoulders, with none of his face showing. He was a terrible sight but nonetheless the calmest person I've ever seen. He wouldn't even talk much, for there wasn't much to say. When we got down to the bottom of the hill we just stopped the car, sat there, and got ourselves put back together. Grandpa asked, "Did you get scared?"

"No," I lied, still out of breath.

"Me neither," he said.

Another thing that was very important to rural East Texas was the putting in of the telephone. By a little bit after the turn of the century, quite a few communities had telephone lines down most of the county roads. These lines were made of an inferior wire, and pretty soon they started rusting, so communication quality got less as this happened. The lines did have insulators, glass insulators, that they put on a kind of stick made for that purpose and tagged to the pole. All these early poles were nondescript things that usually were only about fifteen or eighteen feet high. None of them were treated, so they didn't last for very long. But usually the reason a phone line came out all the way from town, six or eight miles or even further out into the woods, was that somebody down the way, a pretty big important landholder, could carry the main cost of the expense of the thing, especially the wire. I have no idea how much it cost to buy that much wire, but money, scarce as it was, made it not easy to do. So there would be as many as ten or twelve telephones hooked up on a party line.

Back in those days, the phone was a big box hanging up on the wall with a handle, or a crank, as they called it. You twisted that thing real hard, and the impression people had was that the harder you twisted it, the farther it would ring. I've seen people get on there and just really go at that thing with a vigor like they were going to ring it off the wall. "Twist it long and hard," they thought, that way they would get somebody's attention. You would determine whether or not it was your call by the way it rang. Our number was two longs and three shorts, and there were all variations going up as high as four longs.

An energetic person might ring for two minutes and wear himself out in a frenzy before he got the four longs run. And there seemed to be no inhibition about listening in. In fact, this was one of the things that kept the women from going stir-crazy. They listened in on the party line for entertainment as well as communication. I've seen my mother stand and listen for an hour laughing, just bowling over about something she had heard. In another way listening in was a social event. Today, AT&T is talking about having an office call with about as many as four or five people involved in it. But that's nothing. Sixty-five years ago in East Texas on a party line, we had eight women or more all on the same line talking to each other at no extra cost or trouble.

I remember one time my mother was listening in for entertainment and heard something so funny she had to hang up the phone and come tell us about it.

There were two sisters. One lived up close to town and the other one down below us. Both of them, let's say, were more than pleasantly plump. They were just about like walking bales of fresh-ginned cotton, if you can imagine that! That's about the size they were, and they had been talking for about thirty minutes, visiting about all they had done. Then one of them said to the other one, says, "Guess what I done today?"

"I don't know. What did you do?"

"Well, I went down and bought myself a pair of tennis shoes."

"Tennis shoes? What are you gonna do with them?"

"Well, I'm gonna wear 'em. I'm even gonna wear 'em to church tomorrow."

"You mean you are gonna wear them tennis shoes to church?"

"Of course, I'm not gonna wear nothin' else!"

And somehow, this struck my mother slightly humorous. She saw this big fat, roly-poly woman going to church with nothing but her tennis shoes on, so she had to come back in the other side of the house and share it with us! You see the party line was a great invention.

One event pretty popular with the teenage boys happened around Christmastime. I'm not real sure what we called it, but in folklore they are spoken of as being shivarees or serenading. The idea was that the boys in the communities would gather at any given place, usually at the school-house or some church house, and each person would bring some type of noisemaker. Usually three or four of the older boys would bring shotguns. Now these shotguns were dangerous things to have in a group like that, except the older boys were always careful enough. The ones who used the shotguns were very sure to shoot in the air or in the ground, away from anybody, when they made the noise with them.

The idea was to slip up unnoticed to someone's house, and all at once, on a given signal, everyone would break out their noisemaker and start charging around the yard and around the house. Then after running around the house a couple of times, we would go stand outside the door and yell, "Cake! Cake! Cake!" hoping that the people inside would bring out a big frosted cake so everybody could help himself to a big piece of it. This happened quite often. People were good-natured and were glad to have any kind of company. Also, if word got around that you were generous with your cake, no mischief would happen to your house. Usually some type of mischief would happen in any case, and the favorite was pushing over the outhouse. In rare cases it would be removed from the premises, loading it up on a wagon and hauling it two or three miles and setting it on a storefront—in one case or two, even lifting it on top of another house and setting it over the chimney. Many times, items like buggies were pulled away, with one or two boys pulling in front and one or two boys in back pushing. They might take a buggy three or four miles before they conveniently left it astride a fence or, as I said, atop somebody's house.

Another item of mischief was to take wheels from wagons. Now, wheels were held on wagons by the use of a big hub, and there was a wrench to hold the wagon tongue to what they call the fifth wheel. This wrench was both a pin and a wrench. It was pretty easy to take a wheel off by getting two or three guys to hold up the wagon bed while another removed the wheel. If one wanted to be real mean, as in a few cases I knew about, he'd cut down a tree, trim the stump down to a point, and set the wagon wheel down over it, and then brad this down with the ax so it was very difficult to get the wheel off. This type of mean activity was not the normal thing. Most of the group I remember participating in were never involved in things of this nature. We might do something in the manner of running a wagon off down the road or into a creek bed, but this really didn't hurt anything. It was just a bother for the owner to have to hook up a team and pull it back to the house.

Sometimes there might be different groups of serenaders, coming from other communities that would kind of invade homes located on the border of the two communities. They were subject to maybe two or three groups of these frolicking serenaders. This I realize is the type of activities that today happen around Halloween or New Year's Eve. However, for some reason we never observed Halloween. I didn't even know about Halloween, and New Year's Eve had no meaning either. All this stuff that people do today was usually done at Christmastime—even firecrackers were shot at Christmastime. This was the time that most people in the area showed a frivolous nature, making Christmas the main gala time of the year.

I remember some boys coming over to visit our house. My older brother, being up in the teenage years, thought he was a man of the world. I remember them talking about how much drinking whiskey they were going to accumulate. Mostly this was more talk than anything. But that was the type of preparation usually made for Christmas. Now, when we ran around a house making noise with a dinner bell or cow bell or shooting a gun or whatever, we had to be careful if the people had a bad dog, though it often tucked its tail and left because of all this noise. But there could be some other things that we needed to watch for, notably stretched wires. I happened to be one who did that sort of thing at our house. If I knew some boys from another community were coming to serenade our house, I'd usually rig up a few booby traps to make it a little more interesting. It was a lot of fun for me to think of these big double-jointed old boys running around my house tripping over my wire. Likewise, when we chased around a house, we usually were very careful. I was always in front because I could run so fast I led the pack. So, it was my job to look out for booby traps. On rare occasions some old sorehead would not see any fun to this sort of thing at all, and he'd come out front with his shotgun and threaten to blow us out of the yard. On one or two occasions two or three shots were actually fired. Well, you can imagine how fast we got away from there! Once a man had fired at a group his reputation was settled, making any serenading done around his house after that of the covert type. Volunteers might slip in and do something on the meaner side without letting him know about it. He might wake up tomorrow wondering where his privy was or maybe where his wagon was or something like that. But usually they didn't go around his house after he had shot at them.

We had all sort of strange types of medicine, mostly because people in the early days didn't have access to drugstores. Even if we had, it costs money to get medicine. I was born without use of anything but a midwife. My aunt Mary was the one who brought me into the world, and there wasn't a birth certificate or anything. There were many things that we used for medicine. One of the patent medicines I remember best was used because everybody had chills and fever because of the unsanitary conditions we had—mosquitoes and the water we drank. This was a tonic that had a sweet, syrupy taste with some bitter-tasting granules in it. This was about the most commonly used as any medicine we had and was called Groves' Chill Tonic.

People were always having a deep chest cold, a bruise, a boil, or something that called for a clay mix with iodine in it. We called it anitphlogestine. It came in a little, round metal box about two inches high and two or three inches in diameter with a nice smell to it. You'd smear this soft clay out on a piece of cloth, hold it in front of the fire to get it hot, then hold it on your chest, and it seemed to relieve congestion in the chest.

The same sort of treatment could be had if we'd just go out and get some clay off the side of the road, mix a little vinegar with it, heat it up in a skillet on the stove, then smear some on a piece of cloth and put it on the chest. That was pretty effective too. The heat probably had as much to do with it as anything, of course, but the clay had a drawing effect. One of the things we used if we had a wound or something that appeared to have blood poisoning was half of a young chicken while it was still warm. We put the raw side of the chicken over the wound and it would draw the poison out.

We had two different types of buckeye, and I still carry a big buckeye in my pocket. We were poorly informed in many circles, and we had never heard of arthritis. I doubt if it had even been invented over in East Texas, at that time at least. And surely we'd never heard of cortisone. But we did know that if we carried one of these buckeyes, we would not be bothered by rheumatism. I'm seventy-five years old, and I don't have rheumatism; maybe this Ohio buckeye that I carry in my pocket is the reason. Who knows?

Another thing we used in the early days that might have been effective—though it might not; it might have been pure superstition—was a bag of the foulest-smelling stuff in the world called asafetida. You'd make a bag of that and tie it on a string around your neck and wear it. We were wearing it to keep from catching whooping cough. We were having a scourge of whooping cough coming through the country. Later on we caught it anyway. It slipped up on us. I wore that asafetida many, many long months, mostly during the wintertime. Just imagine, if you've got it on a string and got your collar buttoned, you don't smell it too much. However, you'd accidentally unbutton your collar, get a whiff of that, and boy, it'll nearly raise your scalp. I could guarantee you, no self-respecting germ would come near a bag of asafetida.

Now, there's one thing that I'm reluctant to get into. I know some people might be embarrassed by this, but one of the most memorable things to happen to me when I was a youngster was the time I caught the seven-year itch. My brother brought it, but since I slept with him, I caught it. I'm not too sure when this was. I think it was something that was brought back by the soldiers from World War One. Anyway, it was pretty widespread in Texas. People all over our area and others, too, contracted this dreadful skin disease, and it was pretty contagious.

When you scratched this stuff with your fingers and nails it seemed to get more infected. We heard that you should get a soft corncob and scratch yourself with that corncob and it'd be a lot better. It sounds rather ludicrous, but this is what we did, and it worked. We'd carry around a cob in our pocket to scratch with.

After you'd had it a long time, it was called the seven-year itch, and it seemed like it was going to last that long. I could recognize a person who had the itch as far as I could see him or smell him. There was a tendency to have clear blisters form between the fingers and on the back of your neck. If I saw some kid running around with blisters on his neck, I knew he had the itch. Of course, those of us who had it didn't shy away from other sufferers too much, because theirs was probably no worse than ours. My brother got it first, and I thought it was kind of funny all the antidotes he was trying. See, this itch got all over the cheeks of his seat, and scratching would tend to create more sores.

Well, he'd heard that if you took some salt and rubbed it on there the sores would heal. We went down to a well about three quarters of a mile down the road from the house we were living in then. He took his overalls off and backed up to the well because he wanted to be sure that when he rubbed the salt on there, if it was as bad as he thought it might be, I would be able to pour a bucket of water on him real fast to get it off. So all he had on was his shirt, and he took a handful of regular old meat-curing salt and rubbed it on that raw seat, and he let out a squall that sounded like two panthers fighting. I thought he was going to jump in the well. He started screaming for me to throw that bucket of water on him, so I threw one bucket on him. Then he said draw up another one! And another! I threw three or four buckets on him. And he was standing there jumping up and down in the mud and sitting down in the mud and everything else. It was a hysterical sight to me. I was so tickled that I could hardly draw the water.

My laughing didn't last too long, though, because I came down with it too. We tried everything. It seemed we'd start scratching it and just go mad. We couldn't keep from scratching it. We slept in the same bed, and we'd go to sleep, it seemed, to a rhythm of scratching, both of us clawing that itch. Then my brother heard that you could dig up some poke roots and boil them and rub yourself real good with that. We had a fireplace in the room where our bed was, so he got over there by the fireplace with his pan of poke juice and took a rag and soaked it real good. He started patting himself with it. It was more subtle than the salt was, but within about thirty seconds it started taking effect, and I thought he was going to jump through the window! He started hollering and jumping up and down. There wasn't a thing in the world I could do, no water I could throw on him or anything. All I could do was just hold my sides and almost die laughing. It was highly comical to me.

Everyday at school, boys and girls would compare notes. What in the world can you do? What have you learned? Somebody came up with the idea to get some cold cream, that facial cream girls used. We were just beginning to have knowledge of that sort of thing. We could buy a box of it for about a dollar, maybe a little more. Then there was some stuff that had carbolic acid in it. You put a few drops of that in there and they said that would do the trick. We didn't have a dollar to buy any of that stuff, so we never got to try it. Finally, my cousin had heard that the surefire thing to do was to get some powdered sulfur and mix it with any kind of grease and swab yourself down with it real good, and keep the same clothes on for two weeks. That we did. We all ganged up together and went over to Grandpa's house, which was about three quarters of a mile down the road. For two weeks we slept on the back porch on some old quilts, and for two weeks we didn't take a bath. We didn't change clothes or anything. We slept on these same quilts that we were going to throw away anyway. At the end of two weeks all of our scales had healed up, so we all took a good bath, put on clean fresh clothes, then took our old clothes and quilts we had slept on out in the back yard and made a big bonfire. And all during this two weeks we had our beds and bedclothes out in the sun. I suppose there's nothing better as a disinfectant than sunlight anyway. We never had any recurrence of it after that. No more seven-year itch. Thank the Lord!

In the early days there was more trouble in having something to eat every day than anything else. One of the things that seemed to be up to nature was honey from the woods bees. We always managed to have eight or ten hives that our bees stayed in. We'd make these hives by taking boxing plank, that is one-inch-by-twenty-inch board, nailing them into a kind of square box, maybe a little longer than it was broad. There was a flat board across the top, and down at the bottom we'd put a V-shaped notch in each side. We put these stands, or hives, on a couple of timbers or poles to keep them up off the ground. We normally put all these in the same area because many times bees will sting people and not everybody knows how to handle bees. Anyone who'd been stung half a dozen times in a flurry of bee activity wouldn't likely forget it. It's very painful.

About twice a year we removed the excess honey from the hives. This served as a pretty good source of food because we understood that there wasn't any type of food any less free of harmful bacteria than honey. I don't know if it's true or not, but I've always heard this, so we considered it to be both a food and a medicine. It was supposed to be highly nutritious, and we used it as a base for cough syrup and other medicines. With six or eight hives of bees we'd usually wind up each year with several gallons of honey.

There was a special way we removed the honey from the hives. My father was the only one with nerve enough to rob them. We took a tightly rolled up piece of an old quilt and tied a string around one end of it for a handhold, set it on fire on the flared end, and had as good a smoke tool as we were able to get. I understand that regular bee people had a little container filled with some kind of material that smoked a lot with a flare on it that directed smoke a little better than we could with a cotton torch.

My father always took a little dishpan or small tub and a butcher knife and a big long fork. He had directed the smoke all the way around the hive, to drive the bees up into it to conceal themselves from the smoke. For some reason this contained them; they didn't want to get out. I guess they were stifled by the smoke up in that area. Then he would take a hammer and bump the lid a little to get the nails loose, then pull it off. The layer of honeycomb up near the top would be the new stuff, where the new honey would be. Then my father reached down in there with his knife and cut off the little crossbar stuck to the frame of the box. Then he'd take his fork and lift the honey out. He might have as much as three or four pounds of honey in one big comb, maybe a foot long and six inches wide. He put this in his tub or dishpan until he'd gotten most of it out. He never took all of it because there needed to be some in there to feed the bees, in case something happened. Then he put the lid back on and went to the next hive.

Most of us stood off at a safe distance and watched. On some occasions I had nerve enough to come up and hold the tub or just stand there. Maybe I'd hold the smoke while he used the knife and fork. I always felt a little bit nervous doing this because I never really considered myself a bee man. It would usually take about thirty minutes to rob all the hives if we had as many as six or eight.

It seemed to be the practice of bees that in the spring of the year when they hatched a new crop, there was always a new queen in each hive. Maybe the new queen decided she should leave the hive or maybe the old queen chased her off. I don't know. I do know that it was the common thing that if we had six or eight hives we had two or three departure groups of bees. This new queen would crawl outside and a lot of her followers would come with her and they'd take off. Many times we'd be out in the field working and hear a swarm of bees coming overhead. It was just a loud droning sound. About April of every year we would be prepared for this. We'd have an extra hive or two ready and a wagon sheet handy. When a swarm came over—say a hundred feet in the air—we could hear them before we could see them, because they circled around a little looking for a place to settle. We had to be alert enough and start making some kind of sound to attract them. We used a cow bell or a plow point struck with a hammer to attract them. If we made enough noise, we could herd them to the new hive. Many times the swarm would settle on the limb of a tree, usually a pretty good-size branch, tending to form a big blob. They might be just hanging to each other, forming a mass as much as eight or ten inches in diameter—just a big wad of bees. We spread our wagon sheet down on the ground and put the beehive beside it. It was a pretty good idea to let them stay on the tree until about dark. When it got just dusky dark we took a pole and raked them off the limb. They'd fall on the wagon sheet and start crawling in the hive because it had dark holes in it. Before we knew it, we had all the bees in a new home, and when it got good and dark we'd just pick the hive up and carry it home and set it beside the others. The bees always seemed fully content with this.

In a wooded area, it's not uncommon at all to have several hives of bees nest in hollow trees, especially during the time when there's not a lot of rainfall and they might be having trouble finding water. It's easy to locate a bee tree. They fly in a straight direction, not doing a lot of zigzagging around, wasting time, giving a lead on which direction it is. It's easy to follow them until you find a sizable tree that might have a hollow in it. By sitting and watching a little while, you can see the bees coming and going.

Now, it wasn't unusual at all for early settlers to cut a tree just to get the honey out of it, without any thought of what might happen to the bees or even trying to capture them or anything. There are certain animals like coons, bears, foxes, and wolves who eat both honey and the bees. Most animals are very fond of honey.

Most boys in East Texas grew up looking for one excitement or another. One of the major sources of excitement for boys any age was a wasp nest, or a bumblebee or yellow jacket nest. For some reason we thought it was about as much fun as anything in the world to see how many wasp nests we could knock out of trees or barns. We had a ready-made weapon to fight them with, too. We'd break off a pine top, and all those needles are just perfect. We'd slap a wasp with all those stickers, and if we had a proper-size pine top we could stand and ward off a dozen wasps coming down at once. Of course, if one got through and popped you real good, this made you pay the price for all the fun you were having. This was something we did every weekend. We'd go out and look for wasps, yellow jackets, or bumblebee nests. Now, bumblebees have their nests in the ground. They weren't too common, but if we looked around long enough we could usually find a bumblebee hole in the ground, up next to a tree or a bush. This hole would be at least an inch in diameter. It would go down for a little, and then it would run parallel to the top of the ground and then down again. We had a little trick in capturing bumblebees. They tend to go into a dark hole, so we'd get an earthen jug, not one that's clear but one made of earthenware, half fill it with water, then, with a long pole we'd beat on the ground and then run off about a hundred feet and get behind a bush where they couldn't see us. They'd come boiling out of there. There might be as many as fifteen or twenty of them. There's always been an expression, somebody was "as mad as a hornet." Boy, if you've never seen a bumblebee coming out of his nest when someone has been beating on the ground over it, you've never seen anything mad!

These bees made a pretty good circle around for a few minutes, then they quieted down and got ready to go back in the nest. Well, they saw this jug sitting there with its dark hole, so they just flew down into it. The secret to it was when they hit the water at the bottom they got their wings wet and couldn't fly. It only took about ten minutes and we had all the bees trapped in the jug. Then you get you a clear glass bottle, a whiskey bottle or something like that, and put about two dozen bumblebees in it, and after their wings get dry, they're all right. Their wings being wet just enabled us to capture them. This is the way the trick worked: You'd get the bees with the wet wings in the whiskey bottle plugged with a cork with a hole in it with a string up the middle. This string would have a big knot in the end of it so that you could pull the cork out with it. You'd need a little bit of a hole around this string in the cork so the bees could get some air in the bottle. Then we were loaded for anybody who needed the bee treatment.

My dad used to tell me there were often five or six itinerant preachers, brimstone-type people, frequenting their home since his father was a circuit-riding Methodist preacher. These fellows seemed to prey on his generosity. They'd land there and stay a week or two, and if nothing was said, they might even stay longer, just freeloaders. This wasn't easy on people who had to put up with them because there were quite a number of children, so there wouldn't be beds enough to go around. My father's two older brothers, Uncle Dick and Uncle John, slept together in a bed. And this old gentleman had to sleep with them. Now, you can imagine some old codger coming in when there were already two in a bed and then add another. If he stayed around two or three weeks, mooching food and chewing tobacco and everything, you'd get pretty fed up with it. Well, they did too, so they decided to give him the bee trick. They caught about two dozen bees, loaded up the whiskey bottle, and put it in the bed. This old gentleman usually was the first one to retire because in those days there was nothing to read and nothing else for anybody to do. So he'd just crawl in the bed. Also, that way he managed to get plenty of room, and the others could just take whatever was left. On this occasion he crawled in the bed and his foot struck the bottle and he wondered what in the world it was. He reached down and pulled on the bottle, but the string in the cork was tied to the bedpost at the foot. So it pulled the cork out. And all the shaking around and pulling on the bottle had disturbed the bees, and they come swarming out of there, all up under the quilt. This old boy pretty near tore the roof off. He came running through the house with the quilt flying behind his tail, yelling at the top of his lungs. He was calling to my grandfather, "The bumblejackets are after me! The bumblejackets are after me!" Of course, Uncle Dick and Uncle John were barely able to control themselves. They couldn't afford to let on that they knew anything about it because there was no telling what their dad might do. Needless to say, bright and early the next morning, this old gentleman was ready to hit the road. Sometimes they had to use extreme measures to get things accomplished, and putting bumblebees in the bed, I should imagine, would be very effective.

Old Blue

C. L. Embrey was born in 1902 near Mount Pleasant in East Texas. He grew up there in Titus County as a farm boy with a keen eye and memory. He answered the call of God and has served as a preacher for many years. He now lives in Laird Hill, Texas.

Mr. Embrey has written and published his own book called *Our Good Old Days*, an account of rural life in East Texas. With realistic description, he recreates what life was like in a time of cotton picking and coon dogs, hog killing and corn shucking, and neighbors helping and kinfolks visiting. It is a story ranging from the humorous to the heart-touching.

Among the subjects covered is a review of country schools in East Texas. Then, as now, certain students had trouble getting to school on time. C. L. Embrey describes one such situation with humor and understanding.

Because of kids who played on the way to school, and played hooky and didn't get there at all, the teachers began demanding that parents send a note with the child when they were late, or when they had to stay home. Some parents cooperated in this and some just didn't care that much about it.

This boy came in around noon and the teacher asked him for his note from his parents. He said, "I ain't got no note, but I can tell you why I was late. Pa sleeps naked." The teacher said, "Bill, we don't want to hear one thing about how your Pa sleeps." Bill said, "Well, you want to know why I'm late, its like this. Pa sleeps naked, and something got in our chickens last night, and Pa took the double barrel shotgun out to kill whatever was in the chicken house. We got an old hound we call Blue. As Pa was slipping up on the hen house old Blue cold-nosed him, and we picked chickens till ten o'clock." Since all farm kids know how cold a dog's nose is, and how the sudden touch of his nose under those conditions would feel, this was enough said. Just a question of how many chickens were left after emptying both barrels in the hen roost. These were the good old days.